Building Adaptive Organisations

Building Adaptive Organisations is a practical guide to thriving in an era of volatility, complexity, and rapid technological change. The book argues that the 300-year-old organisational model, designed for stability and control, is no longer fit for the demands of Industry 4.0 and the changing workplace. The outdated pyramidal enterprise has bred disengaged workforces, out-of-touch leaders, and cultures that collapse under constant disruption.

The book presents a compelling alternative that transforms organisations into self-organising, emergent ecosystems. Drawing on industrial-revolution history, organisational theory, original models, and case studies, it demonstrates how to ingrain adaptability into the heart of systems and culture. *Building Adaptive Organisations* argues that enduring adaptability will never come from top-down leadership, isolated agile initiatives, complicated nested circles, mindset shifts, or cultural makeovers. Instead, the study focuses on five critical system levers that drive adaptability: culture, design, technology, people, and process. It provides practical guidance on how to build an adaptive culture across the organisation's architecture; designing modular structures with self-organising governance and flexible workflows; integrating digital transformation into the organisation's core operations; enabling people strategies that support adaptive workforces; and implementing transformational change as a shared, emergent, enterprise-wide endeavour.

Offering clear concepts, tools, and pathways, this book equips system leaders and organisational designers to build adaptive, responsive organisations capable of navigating the turbulence of Industry 4.0 and an increasingly unpredictable world.

Richard Kelly, PhD, is an author and organisational culture and leadership specialist with over 30 years of experience in the private and public sectors. Based in the UK, Richard has spent the past 15 years working as an independent organisational development and leadership consultant for companies across Europe and South America, focusing on system-wide cultural and behavioural transformation. He is the author of *Constructing Leadership 4.0* and *The Nature of Business Transformation.*

Building Adaptive Organisations

A Systems and Culture Approach for Thriving in a Changing Workplace

Richard Kelly

Routledge
Taylor & Francis Group
LONDON AND NEW YORK

Designed cover image: Getty Images - NeoLeo

First published 2027
by Routledge
4 Park Square, Milton Park, Abingdon, Oxon OX14 4RN

and by Routledge
605 Third Avenue, New York, NY 10158

Routledge is an imprint of the Taylor & Francis Group, an informa business

British Library Cataloguing-in-Publication Data
A catalogue record for this book is available from the British Library

ISBN: 978-1-041-15613-0 (hbk)
ISBN: 978-1-041-15611-6 (pbk)
ISBN: 978-1-003-68034-5 (ebk)

DOI: 10.4324/9781003680345

Typeset in Adobe Garamond Pro
by Deanta Global Publishing Services, Chennai, India

To my family

Contents

Contents

Figures

Tables

Preface

Twelve years ago, I started a blog to share ideas on organisational development and leadership. Informed by my PhD in organisational and behavioural science and decades of working in the field of organisational and people development, I thought I had a lot to say.

Truth be told, I had grown increasingly weary of off-the-shelf OD and leadership models built around status leadership and the leader-as-influencer, and I needed to get a few things off my chest. I have always been drawn to collective thinking and collective decision-making; it is a theme that threads through my personal and working life, my politics, and my published work.

I became absorbed by ideas about the organisation as a beehive, a collective intelligence where everyone contributes through "waggle-dancing", and swarm leaders harvest the collective decision-making like gathering honey. These ideas eventually evolved into my first book, *Constructing Leadership 4.0: Swarm Leadership and the Fourth Industrial Revolution*.

My research and professional background left me uneasy about a book that championed collective swarm leadership, without offering a supporting organisational framework or process. Thus, I began work on The Nature of Business Transformation: A Swarm Intelligent Approach to *Reinventing Organisations*, exploring how business processes need to be upgraded to support this new way of working as a business superorganism.

During the Covid-19 lockdown, I took on a research side-project on organisational culture to boost my income. Suddenly, I was looking at everything through the lens of system culture. It became apparent to me that you can never truly achieve an enduring organisational change without a system-level cultural transformation, and I began sketching some ideas which, four years on, became *Building Adaptive Organisations: A Systems and Culture Approach for Thriving in a Changing Workplace*. This book is not another "future of work" treatise; it is a practical guide to building an organisational system and culture at the business architecture level.

Two reflections come to mind. The first is that I seem to have done everything back to front; the sequence of my publications should perhaps have been culture–process–leadership rather than the other way around. The second thought, and perhaps a justification for the sequencing, is that the world has changed exponentially since researching for my first book. In 2015, the Brexit referendum hadn't happened, nor had any of the unstable geopolitics that followed it. In an era of relative stability, undertaking an ambitious cultural transformation to create a new adaptive organisation would have been a big ask. In 2025, as this book hopes to show, it is essential .

Writing a professional book, for me, is like completing a complex jigsaw puzzle. I imagined the big picture almost four years ago and have worked most days on the puzzle (picking out pieces and making connections). At times, I worked on one corner only to realise it belonged somewhere else in the puzzle. Now, as the book clicks into place, I am thrilled that others will get the chance to explore these ideas and make their own connections.

I have enjoyed puzzling it all out and have never been tempted to hand the task over to an intelligent machine. Amid the rise of tools such as ChatGPT, calls grow among author-representative bodies to label books as organic or human-authored. I fully support this initiative and declare that this book springs entirely from human intellect.

I hope it sparks insight and value to those who read it.

Richard Kelly
London 2026

Acknowledgements

I am deeply grateful to all the people who have shaped and encouraged this book, including former professors, students, colleagues, clients, family, and friends, including my BBC Proms friends.

A special thanks to Dr Mario Chiasson for our weekly conversations on every aspect of organisational development, leadership, and transformation, and for your invaluable insights into future technologies. Your wisdom, coaching, and guidance have been truly inspiring. Warm thanks also to Dr Arvid Kingl for our rich and stimulating discussions on AI and quantum computing, Nicole Ruduss for sharing your expertise on bicycle mechanics, which helped shape Chapter 8, and Kate Hobbs for helping with the cover design. I am grateful to the Society of Authors (SoA) for their steadfast support and guidance. Special recognition goes to the outstanding Senior Management Team of District Francophone Sud in Dieppe, NB, Canada, who are undertaking a pioneering systems transformation.

Finally, I would like to acknowledge, in alphabetical order, the many remarkable people who have directly influenced this book. Your contributions, encouragement, and inspiration are deeply appreciated: Mireille Bertin Post, Monique Boudreau, Rejean Boudreau, Dr Jennifer Charteris, Sylvie Dallaire, Dr Bernadette Doerr, Mireille Fontaine-Vautour, and Dr Viktor Freiman.

Chapter 1

Introducing the Adaptive Organisation

211 Revere Avenue in Bend (Oregon) is the address of the last Blockbuster store. Christopher Harress (2013) reminds us that the firm was once a leading, iconic global brand that, at its peak, operated 9,000 rental video stores and generated revenues of $5.9 billion. It declared bankruptcy in 2010 and is now a tourist destination and a footnote in MBA case studies. The road to Blockbuster's downfall includes a missed opportunity in 2000 to acquire a small, loss-making DVD-by-mail and subscription-based startup. The $50 million deal fell through because Blockbuster assessed the startup as a niche offering. It rejected and ridiculed the subscription-based business model and sent the young founders packing. The startup was Netflix. Co-founder Mark Randolph recalls how, in 2000, senior Blockbuster executives "laughed us out of the room" (cited in Mollman 2023). Fast forward to 2010, while Blockbuster was filing for bankruptcy, Netflix's market capitalisation was $9.27 billion. Today, Netflix has a market capitalisation (net worth) exceeding $350 billion.

When reviewing Blockbuster's demise, many commentators focus on a company that lacked innovation and failed to embrace the digital era. This is all true, but there is a deeper story. Alan Payne (2021) believes the company was "built to fail". According to Payne, underlying cultural factors led to Blockbuster's dramatic downfall; it simply wasn't an adaptive organisation. While the entertainment sector was transitioning to digital (Apple iPods were already transforming the music industry), Blockbuster was stuck in an analogue world of VCRs and VHS tapes. Structure and leadership issues held the company back, but fundamentally, it was a cultural issue that led to Blockbuster's downfall. It was an extremely insular and closed organisational culture that was unable to adapt to a changing world and workplace.

DOI: 10.4324/9781003680345-1

Cameron and Quinn explored the distinction between closed (controlled) and open (adaptive) organisations in 2011 with their "Competing Values Framework" (CVF). This well-researched and highly influential model, shown in Figure 1.1, has been used for decades to understand organisational culture.

The framework is organised along two axes: internal versus external and controlled versus adaptive. It highlights four major cultural values based on Cameron and Quinn's research.[1] These cultural values are hierarchy (insular and focused on organisational control), market (outward-looking and focused on maintaining stability and control), clan (inward-looking and focused on teamwork), and adhocracy (from ad hoc, meaning outward-looking and flexible).

Blockbuster was dominant in the hierarchy quadrant, signifying its structured and controlled culture blinded it to progress. It was severely lacking in the other three quadrants, which diminished its adaptive capability and led to many of its problems. A CVF reading of Blockbuster quickly raises red flags.

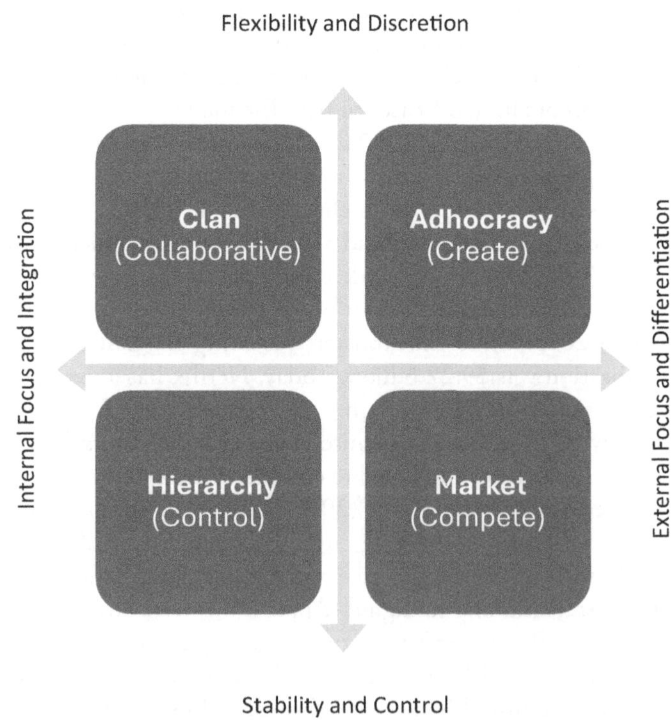

Figure 1.1 Cameron and Quinn's *The Competing Values Framework* (Cameron and Quinn, 2011, 39).

(i) *Blockbuster was fixed in its ways and not adaptive.*
The leadership was fixed on a single acquisition growth strategy. CEO Wayne Huizenga took over from founder David Cook in 1987. Huizenga, co-founder of Waste Management, aggressively bought businesses and rapidly scaled them as part of his strategic plan (a blitzscaling strategy that certainly worked for McDonald's). Once he acquired Blockbuster, he adopted a "build baby build" approach (Payne 2021, 63). But as Alan Payne (2021) points out, Huizenga enjoyed the thrill of acquisition, but lacked the skills to develop businesses and didn't have the right team around him. Future Blockbuster CEO, Sumner Redstone, called the former Blockbuster leadership "deal guys" who were "great builders but far from excellent operators" (Redstone and Knobler 2001, 27). The business lacked focus and innovation. Moreover, as Jordan Williams (2021) observed, the company's leadership and governance were highly conservative, with investors demanding the censorship of movies that conveyed anti-Christian messages, contained sexual content, or included LGBTQ+ themes.

(ii) *Blockbuster had little sense of clan or community.*
There was a lot of elite decision-making at Blockbuster. Only a handful of "friends of Wayne" (Payne 2021, 35) were part of the decision-making club. David Kahn, a Blockbuster franchisee who joined the company in 1988 as a district manager, remarked, "A lot of franchisees were known as 'friends of Wayne', and you didn't see mom-and-pop operators getting involved; it was driven by corporations on the franchising side of things" (cited in McLoone 2021). According to Alan Payne (2021), employees who had daily contact with customers and could see the problems and challenges arising on the ground were ignored and silenced. For example, Blockbuster had a late fee model relating to overdue returns. This significantly contributed to the company's revenue, accounting for 16 per cent of Blockbuster's income at its peak, but it infuriated customers. The "friends of Wayne", lacking in empathy, were oblivious to the highly controversial issue of late fees.

(iii) *Blockbuster lacked a market-competitiveness perspective, ignoring key competitors.*
Blockbuster was an inward-looking and insular company that made some odd miscalculations about its competitors and the broader rental ecosystem. At the height of its success in 2002, Ben Unglebee (2019) reports that Blockbuster listed Walmart, Target, and Best Buy as its major competitors. Staggeringly, it ignored its direct competitor, Hollywood Video/Video Central, and the rise of streaming services such as Netflix. Despite its aggressive "build baby build" acquisition culture, Blockbuster turned down the chance to acquire Netflix for $50 million. This indicates an

out-of-touch and alpha leadership that lacked basic business acumen, intuitive sensemaking, and awareness of the business ecosystem.

A brief comparison with Netflix reveals a dynamic online subscription startup that had organisational capabilities and skills which allowed it to operate effectively across all four CVF quadrants. Netflix was a highly efficient startup that was supremely collaborative and had an intuitive sense of the commercial value of the emerging digital and platform economy and the broader digital ecosystem. This made them a highly responsive and adaptive organisation.[2]

This opening case study contains two contrasting models. First is the tale of an innovative startup (Netflix) that had an inherent adaptive culture, was highly attuned to the market zeitgeist and ecosystem, was value-driven rather than rule-driven, and anticipated and embraced future system trends such as online subscription, the platform economy, online streaming, and the rise of the digital consumer. The second is a traditional high-street bricks-and-mortar retail brand (Blockbuster) that was a deeply bureaucratic, hierarchical monoculture, where the CEO, "friends of Wayne", and conservative backers called the shots, ignoring their employees and competitors. The executives at Blockbuster lacked an innovative, adaptive mindset and failed to anticipate emerging trends and view their business through the lens of systems.

Like Netflix, Blockbuster began its life as a young startup, but (unlike Netflix) it had a closed, controlled culture that couldn't adapt to the changing events impacting its business. Alan Payne (2021) suggested that this closed culture was locked into Blockbuster's business architecture. Netflix belongs to a group of adaptive organisations, including DuPont, LG, Nokia, Nintendo, Western Union, American Express, and Apple, that have survived and flourished by anticipating trends and continuously reinventing and adapting their business models.

Blockbuster, on the other hand, belongs to a group of well-known modern brands, including Eastman Kodak, Pan Am, Woolworths, and Toys "R" Us that failed to adapt to evolving trends and went under. As Clayton Christensen remarks in *The Innovator's Dilemma,* "the list of leading companies that failed when confronted with disruptive changes in technology and market structure is a long one" (Christensen 1977, xvi).

This introductory chapter explores the three core themes that appear in the book's title: adaptive organisations, systems and culture, and changing workplaces. It concludes with a chapter-by-chapter overview of the book.

Defining the Adaptive Organisation

No authoritative definition of the adaptive organisation currently exists. Similar concepts are widely used, such as adaptable, adaptability (Staber and Sydow 2002), ambidexterity (Birkinshaw and Gibson 2004), organisational agility

(Felipe, Roldán, and Leal-Rodríguez 2017), and adaptive enterprises (Gownder 2019). Since the Covid-19 pandemic, a few major consulting firms, including KPMG, Deloitte, and McKinsey, have started to adopt the term "adaptable organisation" in strategy papers, and it feels like it is a current issue. Denison, Haaland, and Goelzer provide a helpful perspective:

> Adaptable organizations are driven by their customers, take risks and learn from their mistakes, and have capability and experience at creating change. They are continuously changing the system so that they are improving the organizations' collective abilities to provide value for their customers.
>
> (Denison, Haaland, and Goelzer 2003, 100)

Robert Ployhart and Scott Turner argue that organisational adaptability is "the extent to which a firm creates or responds to changing demands or opportunities in the environment" (Ployhart and Turner 2014, 75). Julia Cline and Amelia Goodwin (2024) echo this by describing organisational adaptiveness as the "ability to change or evolve over time in response to changing circumstances". The authors draw a useful distinction between adapting to oncoming change and consistently responding to continuous change. In a chapter entitled "Adapt" in *The Lean Startup*, bestselling author Eric Ries pithily describes an adaptive organisation as "one that automatically adjusts its process and performance to current conditions" (Ries 2011, 227).

To summarise, an adaptive organisation is an open ecosystem that sustains its competitive advantage by remaining responsive to change, achieved through cultivating an adaptive business architecture and maintaining strong strategic alignment.

Martin Reeves and his coauthors (2010) outline several defining characteristics of an adaptive organisation. They describe it as having a modular structure, a free flow of knowledge and power, a reliance on guiding principles rather than strict rules, a set of adaptive values, and leadership that operates primarily through context-setting. These characteristics, among others, are explored throughout this book.

Thriving in Uncertainty: The Case for Adaptive Organisations in a Work 4.0 Context

The idea of the adaptive organisation, of course, is far from new. Modern organisations have adapted through pandemics, trade wars, and financial crises over three centuries.

The concern over the rise of machines during the first industrial revolution, for example, reflects the debate we are having today about the rise of artificial intelligence and automation. A key context for building adaptive organisations throughout the modern industrialisation period is the emergence of a "complex, ambiguous, and uncertain environment" (Bennis and Nanus 1985, 85),[3] which disrupts business landscapes and radically impacts business processes, workflows, and culture. Jonathan Brill makes a similar point in his recent book, *Rogue Waves*:

> Our world is becoming more volatile. Phenomena like pandemics and financial crises, artificial intelligence and automation, social unrest and trade wars are colliding to unleash massive, unexpected waves of change. The companies that understand how these changes will impact them can profit from the chaos.
>
> (Brill, 2021, 1)

Recent *Innosight* research shows that the average company lifespan is diminishing (Viguerie, Calder, and Hindo 2021). As Mark Perry (2019) observes, many of the 1955 Fortune 500 companies are now extinct. This is also the case for the S&P 500 index and the UK FTSE 100. Digital Darwinism and disruption are increasingly playing a role in this. DXC Technology (2017) reports that from the year 2000, 52 per cent of listed companies in the Fortune 500 have "gone bankrupt, been acquired, or ceased to exist as a result of digital disruption". Elizabeth MacBride (2015) reminds us that businesses crave certainty, and Scott Wich (2025) reflects on how companies have used risk matrices and planning tools to manage such uncertainty. Charles Handy (1996), on the other hand, believes we are "beyond certainty". We are finally beginning to understand that companies that develop an "adaptive advantage" (Reeves et al. 2010), such as Netflix, flourish; and companies that maintain a closed mindset, such as Blockbuster, fold.

A Changing Workplace

Workplace culture has gone through three distinct cycles over the last 300 years and is now entering a fourth stage, in which organisations will need to be more adaptive than at any time in their history. In partnership with the EU, the German Ministry of Labour and Social Affairs has produced green and white papers that use a helpful organising timeline labelled Work 1.0 to 4.0 (Federal Ministry of Labour and Social Affairs 2015, 2017), which broadly align with the four industrial revolutions that occurred during this time frame. Figure 1.2

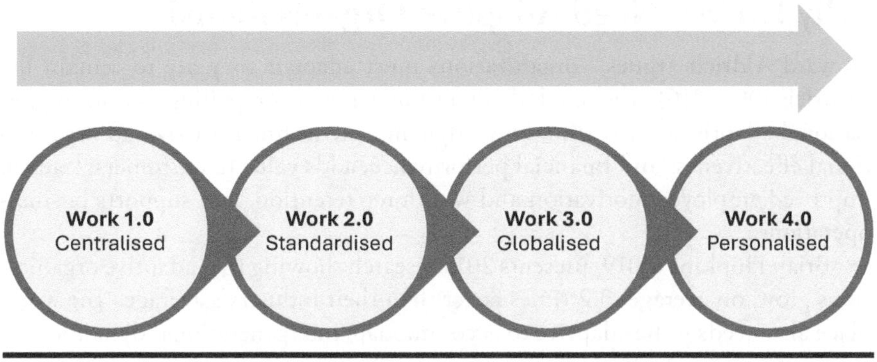

Figure 1.2 Four workplace systems and the corresponding cultural norms (Work 1.0 to 4.0).

shows Work 1.0 to Work 4.0 in a timeline, with each era being characterised by a cultural norm.

Work 1.0 corresponds to the first industrial centre of production. The new steam-based machinery led to more centralised ways of organising work. Work 2.0 was an era of standardisation in which labour was organised according to the emerging principles of mass production and classical management theory.[4] Work 3.0 covers the period of globalisation and the rise of digital technology, knowledge-based industries, and the social market economy.

According to the white paper *Re-Imagining Work*, Work 4.0 will be "more interconnected, digital and flexible" (Federal Ministry of Labour and Social Affairs 2017, 203). It is a period dominated by new AI-enabled and green-based technology, mass consumer personalisation, an on-demand ecosystem economy, and "rightsized" organisations. These trends will drive a transition as seismic as the first industrial revolution and, as William E. Fulmer (2000) argues, are reinforcing the need for adaptive organisations. The fourth industrial revolution is a highly volatile and uncertain period held together by networks, customisation and personalisation.[5] It is already having a profound impact on the workplace.

Organisations need to navigate uncertainty and customise goods and services, which requires them to be highly responsive and adaptive to ensure survival. As Azeem Azhar (2021) comments, traditional businesses cannot rely on past models that "succeeded yesterday". Heifetz, Grashow, and Linsky make a similar point when they say, "Many organizations get trapped by their current ways of doing things, simply because these ways worked in the past" (Heifetz, Grashow, and Linsky 2009, 51). A more systemic solution and framework for creating truly adaptive and enduring enterprises is urgently needed. This book addresses this need. It explores how to build a sustainable adaptive organisation that flexes with complexity and uncertainty. It posits that to build enduring adaptability, we must rewire the business architecture and develop robust strategies for people, digital, and change transformation to support the new organisational culture.

Why Do We Need Adaptive Organisations?

Howard Aldrich argues, "organizations must adapt if they are to remain fit" (Aldrich 1999, 216). The scholarly literature makes a compelling case for organisational adaptiveness. It shows how dynamic environments drive up organisational effectiveness and financial performance, adds value to customers, leads to improved employee motivation and workforce retention, and supports business operations.[6]

Brian Hopkins (2019) presents 2019 research showing that adaptive organisations grow, on average, 3.2 times faster than their industry's average. The workplace also needs to be adaptive to accommodate intergenerational dynamics.[7]

Systems and Culture: How Open Systems Drive Work 4.0 Adaptive Cultures

The opening case study showed that adaptive organisations are open systems and that, to cultivate adaptability, organisations need to transform their cultures from closed to open systems. Closed systems are highly structured, inflexible, mechanical monocultures that lead to top-down governance and a workforce that is controlled and disengaged. Open systems, on the other hand, are organic, adaptive, self-organising, emergent, decentralised ecosystems that result in collective working and a more efficient flow of business intelligence.

Richard Daft provides a classic distinction between open and closed systems. "A closed system", he writes, "does not depend on its environment; it is autonomous, enclosed, and sealed off from the outside world". Whereas "[a]n open system must interact with the environment to survive... It must continuously change and adapt to the environment" (Daft 1986, 10).

Nic Kramer and Jacob de Smit (1977) observe that closed systems are internally focused, block the flow of business intelligence, and have little or no interaction with the environment.[8] Kathy Allen (2018) succinctly expresses this when she says, "Closed systems have firm boundaries between the organization and the outside environment". Open cultural systems enable a more transparent, more effortless flow of business intelligence than closed cultures because they have fewer barriers, bottlenecks, and roadblocks to navigate. Bob Waisfisz (2015) includes open and closed cultures in his Multi Focus Model. His research indicates that employees favour open systems, which have a transparent, supportive feel, where newcomers and outsiders are made to feel welcome. This contrasts with closed systems where everything is secretive, and newcomers and outsiders must fit in to "prove themselves".

Traditional organisations tend to be closed (pyramidal) systems in which business intelligence snakes through layered hierarchies of alpha decision-makers, management structures, and bureaucratic organisational policies and compliance. In a closed system, business intelligence stems from central governance and executive decision makers. It is pushed down and through the organisation via hierarchies and flows back up to the apex (C-Suite). This creates organisational status, stasis, fear, conditioning, groupthink, subserviency, and conformity. Endless meetings take place to clarify and justify decisions to the command chain. The general workforce, steeped in presenteeist culture and rarely permitted to make decisions, is paradoxically criticised by senior leadership for not showing enough initiative or speaking out. This reduces employees to supervised data gatherers at the feet of tribal chiefs in the C-suite. These chiefs make all the decisions, hold high status, and receive major perks such as shares, bonuses, and private executive parking. This model is deeply flawed and needs to be urgently abandoned in Work 4.0.

Figure 1.3 visualises the flow of business information through open and closed systems.

Historically, large traditional firms control decision-making through hierarchy, conditioning, and chain-of-command directives, which reinforce a controlled, closed culture. The failure to embrace complexity and navigate organisations in a more inclusive, self-organising way (open culture) has directly resulted in a disengaged, toxic culture in which the organisation rarely evolves. As we move into a more complex and uncertain environment, this kind of outdated organisation will struggle to remain relevant and competitive unless it cultivates a more open and adaptive culture and ecosystem.

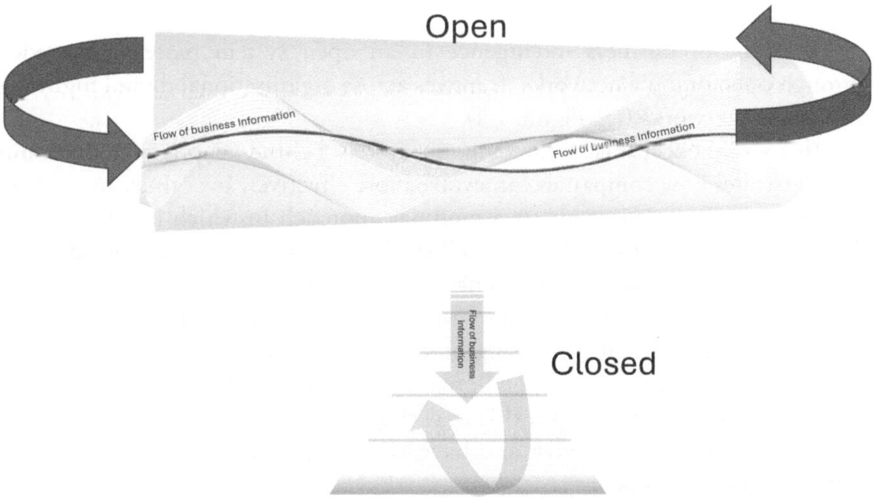

Figure 1.3 The flow of business information through open and closed systems.

Figure 1.4 An open organisation in which business intelligence flows through a self-organising ecosystem.

The flow of business intelligence in an open system passes unimpeded through open organic networks. It moves across organisational digital highways and people networks (see Figure 1.4).

This visual encapsulates the dynamic system behind adaptive organisations and illustrates how companies can evolve more effectively over time. In terms of adaptive structure, it introduces a modular approach in which innovation and decision-making occur at the local cell level. These adaptive units spread across the organisation, gradually reshaping its cultural DNA, while also connecting with external organisations to form a broader ecosystem. In terms of adaptive governance, this is a self-organising process in which collective innovation and decision-making replace traditional, managed, and programmatic intervention. In terms of adaptive workflow, this is a "rightsized" organisation where human and machine resources coexist and have an emergent and coevolving relationship with the workflow.

All system leaders should have this visual permanently in front of them. Rather than micromanaging or getting caught up in day-to-day operations, system leaders should operate at a higher level, focusing on organisational ecosystems rather than individual tasks. Their perspective is big-picture, akin to viewing a neon-lit cityscape from 30,000 feet.

Open systems are self-organising, decentralised ecosystems with emergent business processes, enabling the improved flow of business intelligence. The three dimensions of ecosystem, self-organising, and emergent systems are part of the business architecture and organisational design that need to be reimagined. Let's investigate this now.

The Architecture of Adaptive Organisations

As we shift into what Schwab (2016) and others term the "exponential age" of the fourth industrial revolution, the ongoing challenge for business organisations is to build a "permanent state of adaptability" (Joerg Esser 2021). This book argues that this transformation will occur across systems and culture through changes to "business architecture" (Kuehn 2024) at the level of structure, governance, and workflow, supported by digital, people, and hybrid transformational change strategies.

Figure 1.5 is an important visual that shows at a glance all the key dimensions and drivers behind building an adaptive organisation. This book dedicates a chapter to each of these drivers.

At the centre of this visual is the business architecture or organisational design. This is the organisation's interconnected structure, governance, and workflow (also known as business process). If the structure is hierarchical, governance is top-down, and the workflow is programmatic, then the organisation tends to have a closed and rigid culture. If, on the other hand, the structure is an ecosystem, the governance is self-organising, and the workflow is emergent, then the organisation is more likely to have an open and adaptive culture.

Three interlinking transformational strategies support building an adaptive organisation: digital, people, and the change process. To effectively enable the transition to an adaptive organisation, these strategies must align with the culture and organisational design. This Forrester research beautifully illustrates this alignment:

> To become an adaptive enterprise requires significant investments in technology transformation, in culture building, and in setting up structures and processes. For example, an adaptive enterprise must be able to alter its business concept based on insights that improve the company's odds of fulfilling future customer demand.
>
> (Gownder 2019)

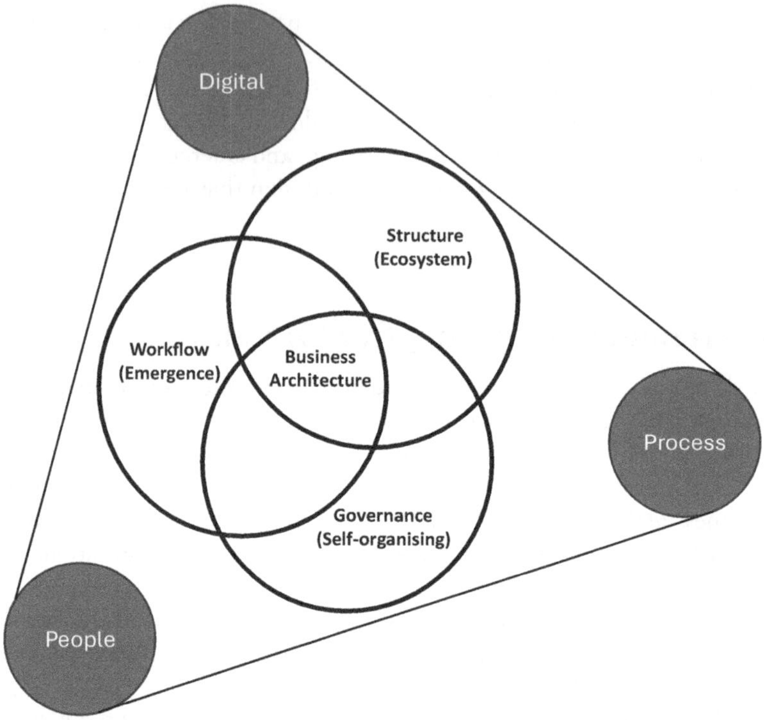

Figure 1.5 Building an adaptive organisation at the systems and culture level.

Numerous historical themes and drivers also promote organisational adaptiveness, including leadership, adaptiveness through structural design (Bock et al. 2012), and adaptiveness through personal effectiveness and trust (Esser 2021; Brassey et al. 2021). Organisational adaptability has additionally been channelled through select process interventions such as Agile Scrum (Sutherland 2014), Holacracy (Robertson 2016), and Swarmocracy (Kelly 2022).

While these themes are well-researched and valid, this book focuses on building adaptive organisations through system and cultural transformation to benefit the entire enterprise. To create a truly holistic adaptive culture, organisations cannot rely exclusively on transformational leadership, structural tweaks, personal effectiveness, or off-the-shelf frameworks; adaptability needs to be a systemic part of organisational design and strategy, one that shifts the culture from a closed to an open system.

Only by creating adaptive structures, adaptive governance, adaptive workflow, and mobilising strategies can organisations hope to achieve the kind of adaptive culture that begins to address the challenges of the exponential age.

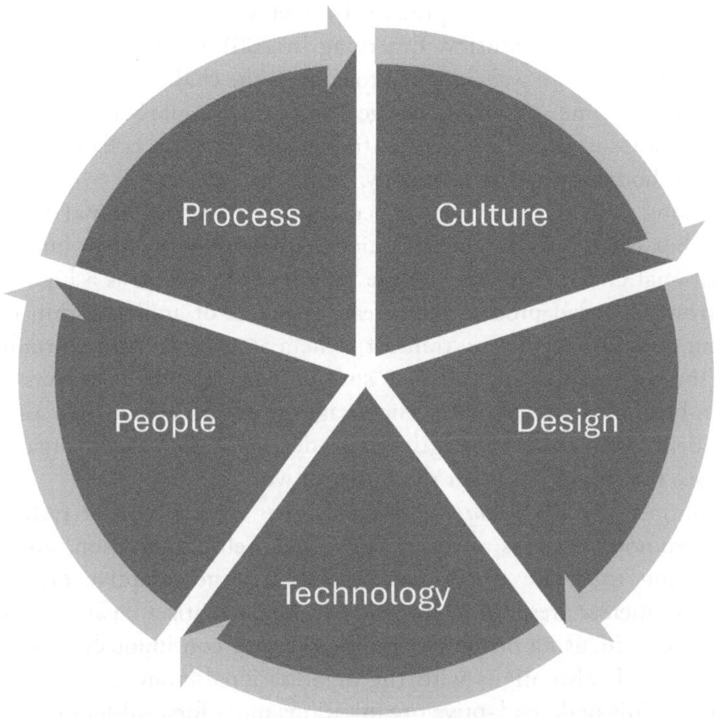

Figure 1.6 The five system levers that drive adaptive organisations.

This book will explore building an adaptive organisation through five system levers. These system levers are culture (Chapter 3), design (structures, governance, and workflow; covered in Chapters 4–6), technology (Chapter 7), people (Chapter 8), and the change process (Chapter 9). The last chapter is dedicated to the change process, but change transformation is integrated throughout the book with each chapter contributing to the transformational story. Figure 1.6 illustrates these five system levers, which all promote and propel organisational adaptability.

A Comparison of the Adaptive Organisation with Holacracy and Agile Scrum[9]

Building Adaptive Organisations involves an organisation-wide system reconfiguration of business processes and architecture to create a self-sustaining and enduring Work 4.0 culture that is ready to meet the disruptive challenges of Industry 4.0. Although it shares some common ground with Holacracy and Agile Scrum (particularly its decentralising and collective nature), there are some fundamental differences.

Agile Scrum is a team-led, prescriptive methodology that originated in the software development industry. Emerging in 2001 from a group of software practitioners in Utah, it was designed to address the challenge of delivering software projects on time and within budget. Since then, Agile Scrum has expanded beyond software to become a general framework for team collaboration with a distinct methodology and terminology.

For a long time, Agile Scrum has been a popular organisational development concept, but there is a growing disquiet that it is now a "silver bullet" in the organisational change toolbox.[10] Agile Scrum is often seen as a highly technical, narrowly-focused process that creates pockets of agility within organisations, but does not necessarily transform them as a whole. Agile is traditionally used in short, contained cycles called "sprints". Jonathon Brill observes that such "modern business practices" can "encourage an inward rather than an outward focus" (Brill 2021, 6). Its strength lies in dealing with isolated organisational challenges, not in preparing for the future of work.

In contrast, *Building Adaptive Organisations* takes a broader systems-based view. It promotes systems analysis, emergence, self-organisation, and cultural normalisation to create truly cross-functional[11] and adaptive organisations. Rather than merely prescribing processes, it re-systematises business models and infrastructure, focusing on how organisations can continuously adapt to their environments. It also aligns with the organisational strategies for people and technology. This makes adaptive organisations more forward-looking, anticipatory, and sustainably adaptive.

Holacracy is a governance model created by Brian Robertson and famously embraced by Tony Hsieh, CEO of Zappos. At its core, it replaces traditional management with overlapping circles of peer-to-peer teams, all bound by a complex constitution of rules. Robertson describes it as "a fundamental shift in the way power works and the way a company is organised" (Robertson 2015, 59), but in practice, it functions as a decentralised hierarchy. The model's complexity has proved to be its downfall. Medium abandoned Holacracy for "getting in the way of the work" (Doyle 2016), and Zappos quietly scaled it back after Hsieh's tragic death, reintroducing managerial hierarchy to regain control and customer focus (Groth 2022).

While Holacracy decentralises authority and introduces democratic elements, it doesn't escape its rule-heavy, process-driven tendency. Former employees, known as Zapponians, were scathing in the media about Holacracy, calling the concept "half-baked" and a "buzzword" (Bernstein et al. 2016), complaining that they were subject to a rigid and complex system of rules and workplace constitutions. Critics such as Steve Denning (2014) argue that Holacracy fragments workflows, is too internally focused, complicates basic management practices such as discipline and compensation, and, according to Ethan Bernstein and coauthors (2016), leads to confusion over roles and responsibilities. In effect, it's less of a cultural revolution than yet another "internal management system" (Weirauch, Galliker, and Elfering 2023, 1).

Building Adaptive Organisations presents a systemic rethinking of adaptive culture at the level of organisational design and strategy. To establish an enduring, normalised adaptive culture that is future-ready for Industry 4.0 challenges and a Work 4.0 environment, a new understanding of adaptability and adaptive organisations is urgently needed. This is the book's central purpose.

Building Adaptive Organisations: Overview, Structure, and Flow of the Book

Building Adaptive Organisations is a practical guide for thriving in an era defined by volatility, complexity, and rapidly changing technology. It argues that the 300-year-old closed system, designed for stability and control, is not fit for purpose for the demands of Industry 4.0 and the changing workplace. The outdated pyramidal organisation has produced disengaged workforces, out-of-touch leaders, and cultures that collapse under constant disruption.

The book presents a compelling alternative that transforms organisations into self-organising, emergent ecosystems. Blending industrial-revolution history, organisational theory, original models, and case studies, it demonstrates how to embed adaptability at the core of both systems and culture within organisations.

Building Adaptive Organisations argues that enduring adaptability will never come from top-down leadership, isolated agile initiatives, complicated circles, mindset shifts, or superficial cultural reinventions. Instead, it requires resystematising the five system levers that drive adaptability: culture, design, technology, people, and process.

In practice, this involves building an inherent adaptive culture that reinforces system-wide transformation; designing modular structures with self-organising governance and fluid workflows; integrating digital capabilities into the core business architecture; enabling people strategies that support adaptive workforces; and implementing a transformational change that is an emergent, enterprise-wide, shared endeavour.

Offering clear concepts, tools, and guiding principles, this book equips system leaders and organisational designers to systemically build externally-focused cultures capable of navigating the turbulence of Industry 4.0. It is an essential guide for organisations determined not only to survive but to thrive in an increasingly unpredictable world.

The book is not structurally partitioned into formal parts or sections. This is to preserve the organic flow and natural interrelatedness of the book. It is not a prescriptive study but an organic one where ideas naturally interlink and flow

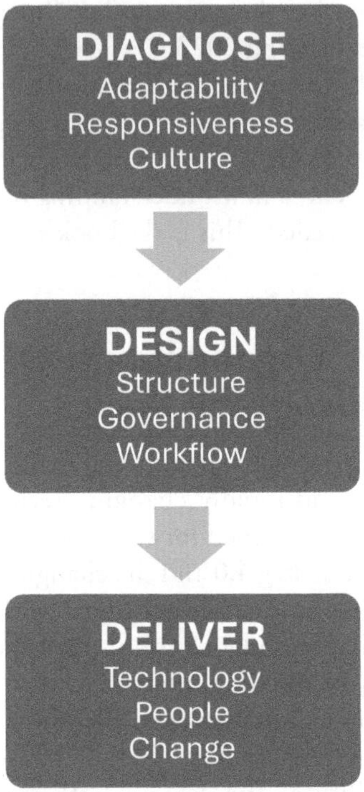

Figure 1.7 The natural structure and flow of *Building Adaptive Organisations* based on the 3D consulting model.

across boundaries. The book is both about complex adaptive systems and is also a complex adaptive system.

That said, the book naturally self-organises into three dimensions based on the 3D consulting model (diagnose, design, and deliver), shown in Figure 1.7, a widely used business consultancy model that helps structure problem-solving and transformational change.

Chapters 1–3 (the diagnose phase) provide a conceptual foundation for the book, exploring adaptive organisations, responsive systems, and open cultures. It helps the reader understand the difference between reactive and responsive organisations. Jonathon Brill (2021) calls this form of diagnosis "the undercurrent" in his book *Rogue Waves*. Chapters 4–6 (the design phase) look at three organisational designs of structure, governance, and workflow, which are cultural pillars of the business architecture. These chapters explore how each of these pillars will need to be recast to create a more enduring adaptive organisational culture. Chapters 7–9 (the delivery phase) investigate how digital, people, and change strategies can be aligned with the organisational design to further promote adaptability.

At the end of each chapter, there will be some guiding principles rather than a set of concluding remarks. One of the characteristics of an adaptive organisation, according to Martin Reeves and his coauthors (2010), is that it has "A limited number of guiding principles [that] replace detailed standard operating procedures, which are impractical for managing unpredictable change". Every organisation is different, and readers are advised to personalise their own approach.

Chapter-By-Chapter Flow of the Book

This chapter (Chapter 1) introduced the concept of the adaptive organisation and explained why adaptability is business-critical. It opened with a cautionary story of Blockbuster, which began as an innovative startup in 1985 but collapsed 25 years later due to rigid leadership, cultural insularity, and a failure to recognise shifting markets. In contrast, Blockbuster's adversary, Netflix, illustrated how cultural openness supports ongoing adaptability. This comparison set up the chapter's key question: how can organisations stay adaptive in an increasingly complex and uncertain environment? The chapter introduced the five system levers essential for building adaptive organisations: culture, organisational design, technology, people, and change processes. The core argument of the chapter (and the book) is that thriving in the exponential age and changing workplace (Work 4.0) requires continuous, system-level and cultural adaptation, not top-down leadership or rigid processes.

Chapter 2, part of the diagnose cluster, examines organisations through a systems lens, structured around three organising principles of perspective, patterns, and proactivity (collectively known as the 3Ps System Model). Drawing on examples and case studies, including LEGO's use of systems thinking to rebuild its market position in the early 2000s, the chapter demonstrates how systems theory can help organisations navigate complexity and evolve from closed entities into interconnected, self-organising ecosystems. It introduces the STEP-WIDE wheel, a practical systems tool that identifies eight external forces shaping organisational environments. By applying this systems tool, organisations can better understand their collective impact, identify emerging patterns, and develop a proactive rather than reactive outlook. The chapter provides a holistic framework on the underlying system levers outlined in Chapter 1 that shape organisational adaptability

Chapter 3 examines culture as a core system lever and a foundational force in creating truly adaptive organisations capable of thriving in complex environments. Drawing on a Starbucks case study, it illustrates that enduring adaptability cannot be achieved through structural change alone; to be lasting, adaptability must be ingrained and normalised within the culture itself. The chapter contrasts imposed, top-down cultural interventions with more sustainable, systems-based approaches grounded in socialisation, organisational design, and strategic alignment, demonstrating that adaptive cultures are most effective when they develop organically rather than being externally imposed.

Chapter 4 introduces the central role of structural design within the business architecture. A Pixar case study shows how structure reinforces purpose, enables innovation, and enhances organisational adaptability and responsiveness. The chapter traces the evolution of organisational forms from pre-industrial models to contemporary Work 4.0 structures, highlighting the increasing importance of modular and ecosystem-based approaches. It explains why adaptive structures are essential for navigating complexity and sustaining organisational performance in rapidly changing environments. It outlines the principles that guide effective structural design, strategic alignment, and continuous evolution.

Chapter 5 explores why adaptive governance has become essential for organisations operating in volatile and rapidly evolving environments. As intelligent machines become an increasing reality in organisational life, traditional twentieth-century governance models are struggling to keep pace and urgently require a new digital governance. Drawing on Cisco's experience as an early pioneer of adaptive governance, the chapter shows how organisations can balance innovation with compliance by cultivating collective governance, mobilising employees as system leaders, and embedding adaptability into their core decision-making cultures.

Chapter 6 examines how organisational workflows contribute to building adaptive organisations. It traces their evolution across the industrial revolutions, showing how closely they connect with organisational structure, governance, and wider digital, people, and transformational change strategies. The chapter shows how adaptive workflows operate in complex environments, why small design decisions can have system-wide effects, and how personalised, context-specific workflow design (exemplified by the "Spotify Model") enhances organisational responsiveness. The chapter presents some key design principles for developing adaptive workflows.

Chapter 7 explores how digital transformation can strengthen an organisation's ability to adapt and evolve. It posits that true digital transformation goes beyond isolated technological upgrades. It requires a system-wide strategic approach that aligns technology with the organisation's business architecture (structure, governance, and workflows) and supports human-machine interactions and organisational change initiatives. Using the example of Eastman Kodak, the chapter illustrates the pitfalls of developing new technologies without integrating them into a broader strategic vision. To support organisations in this shift, the chapter introduces the DT DRAW model (Diagnose, Resource, Adopt, Weigh Up), a practical framework for developing integrated, adaptive digital transformation strategies.

Chapter 8 introduces a system-and-skills people strategy for building enduring adaptive organisations. It presents a dual approach: system-led initiatives that shape adaptive behaviours through organisational socialisation and interaction with the environment, and skills-led initiatives that strengthen individual capabilities through targeted personal development. Drawing on case studies from Adobe and Zappos, the chapter presents the people strategy steering wheel, which brings together eight system initiatives for building an adaptive workforce alongside eight skills-based interventions that develop adaptive mindsets. Together, these elements show how organisations can shape the environment and equip people to thrive in continually changing workplaces.

Chapter 9 brings together the book's core themes by presenting a transformational change approach for building more open and adaptive organisations. It contrasts the consequences of a failed transformation, illustrated through a Boeing case study, with a successful transformation using a fictionalised case study. The chapter assesses programmatic, hybrid, and emergent change models, emphasising that system and culture transformation is best achieved through a hybrid approach. The chapter distils key concepts through the 3D consulting model (diagnose, design, deliver) and presents some guiding principles on the role of formal leadership in enabling adaptive transformational change.

Notes

1. This is from original research by Quinn and Rohrbaugh (Quinn and Rohrbaugh 1983).
2. Cameron and Quinn reflect on the nature of adaptability: "It is not that all four types of cultures must be emphasized equally. Rather, it is that the organization must develop the capability to shift emphases when the demands of the competitive environment require it". This is precisely what Netflix managed to achieve and the reason why it was and is a successful adaptive organisation. (Cameron and Quinn 2011, 68).
3. The US Army War College used the now popular acronym VUCA (which stands for Volatile, Uncertain, Complex, and Ambiguous) in their strategic leadership programme. Herbert Barber talks of the etymology of the term in a 1992 Journal of Management Development paper (Barber 1992) where he credits Warren Bennis and Burton Nanus for inspiring the acronym when they talked about a "complex, ambiguous, and uncertain environment" (Bennis and Nanus 1985, 85).
4. Some authors who write about adaptive organisations, such as Allen and Sawhney (2015) and Sarta, Durand, and Vergne (2020), link closed and controlled organisations back to early twentieth-century classical management theories, including Taylor's scientific management (1911/1998), Fayol's administrative theory (1916/1949), and Weber's bureaucracy model (1922/1979).
5. Research related to this includes: Pech and Vrchota (2022); Devarajan and George (2016); Aheleroff et al. (2021); Wolniak and Grebski (2023); Wang and Ahmed (2007); Torn and Vaneker (2019); and Barata, Cardoso, and Cunha (2023).

6. Research into adaptability improving financial performance includes: Alpay, Büyükbalcı, and Dülger (2018); Chatman et al. (2014); Franczak and Weinzimmer (2022); Denison, Haaland, and Goelzer (2003); Evans (2023). Research into adaptability aligning with customers' needs and adding value to customers include Stalk and Hout 1990; and Denison, Haaland, and Goelzer 2003). Research into adaptability increasing workforce motivation includes Diamantidis and Chatzoglou (2018); Sunarsih and Mashithohv (2016). Research showing how adaptability supports business operations includes organisational crisis management (Deverell and Olsson 2010), organisational change (McGreevy, 2008), organisational innovation (Ruiz-Moreno et al. 2016; Tuominen, Rajala, and Möller 2004; Yang and Hsu 2010; Akgün, Keskin, and Byrne 2012), and strategic execution and decision making (Klein 2011; Murunga and Karugu 2019).
7. Researchers on intergenerational dynamics include: Huyler et al. (2024); Magagula (2024); Wang and Ahmed (2007); Djabi and Shimada (2013).
8. A counter view comes from Stephen Robbins, who argues that closed systems have "little applicability to the study of organizations" (Robbins 1990, 13).
9. Several authors have explored the concept of the "quantum organisation". For example, Ralph H. Kilmann (2011) contrasts "Newtonian" (mechanistic) organisations with "quantum" ones, using principles from quantum mechanics metaphorically to describe the shift from rigid to adaptive systems. Danah Zohar (2022) similarly characterises organisations as complex adaptive systems modelled on quantum-inspired ideas of interconnection, emergence, and uncertainty. These "quantum organisations" share many characteristics with adaptive organisations, such as self-organising teams, emergent structures, and decentralised decision-making. However, many scientists warn that applying quantum metaphors in social systems can be misleading, since the terminology is borrowed from physics and loses its precise scientific meaning when applied metaphorically. Sabine Hossenfelder (2018), for example, critiques the popular misuse of quantum mechanics in non-scientific contexts as bordering on pseudoscience. Given this controversy, the notion of the quantum organisation is acknowledged here but not further developed.
10. Authors who express this view include Abishara (2023); Bryar and Carr (2021); and Hopkins (2019).
11. Mary Pratt defines cross-functional teams as "a workgroup made up of employees from different functional areas within an organization who collaborate to reach a stated objective". (Pratt 2023).

Bibliography

Abishara, Susan. 2023. *Is This the End of Agility? Who Wants to Be Fast and Adaptive Anyway*. Publish Central.

Aheleroff, Shohin, Naser Mostashiri, Xun Xu, and Ray Y. Zhong. 2021. 'Mass Personalisation as a Service in Industry 4.0: A Resilient Response Case Study'. *Advanced Engineering Informatics* 50 (October): 101438. https://doi.org/10.1016/j.aei.2021.101438.

Akgün, Ali E., Halit Keskin, and John Byrne. 2012. 'Antecedents and Contingent Effects of Organizational Adaptive Capability on Firm Product Innovativeness: Organizational Adaptive Capability'. *Journal of Product Innovation Management* 29: 171–89. https://doi.org/10.1111/j.1540–5885.2012.00949.x.

Aldrich, Howard. 1999. *Organizations Evolving.* Sage.

Allen, Jennifer M., and Rajeev Sawhney. 2015. *Administration and Management in Criminal Justice: A Service Quality Approach.* 2nd edition. SAGE.

Allen, Kathy. 2018. 'Closed and Open Systems: The Importance of Worldviews to Leadership'. Insights. Katheen Allen: Unique By Design, August 9. https://kathleenallen.net/insights/closed-and-open-systems-the-importance-of-worldviews-to-leadership/.

Alpay, Güven, Pınar Büyükbalcı, and Meral Dülger. 2018. 'How Are Strategy and Organizational Culture Related? A Conceptual Discussion'. In *Consumer Behavior, Organizational Strategy and Financial Economics*, edited by Mehmet Huseyin Bilgin, Hakan Danis, Ender Demir, and Ugur Can, vol. 9. Eurasian Studies in Business and Economics. Springer International Publishing. https://doi.org/10.1007/978-3-319-76288-3_7.

Azhar, Azeem. 2021. 'The Exponential Age Will Transform Economics Forever'. Wired, September 6. https://www.wired.com/story/exponential-age-azeem-azhar/.

Barata, João, Jorge C. S. Cardoso, and Paulo Rupino Cunha. 2023. 'Mass Customization and Mass Personalization Meet at the Crossroads of Industry 4.0: A Case of Augmented Digital Engineering'. *Systems Engineering* 26 (6): 715–27. https://doi.org/10.1002/sys.21682.

Barber, Herbert F. 1992. 'Developing Strategic Leadership: The US Army War College Experience'. *Journal of Management Development* 11 (6): 4–12. https://doi.org/10.1108/02621719210018208.

Bennis, Warren G., and Burt Nanus. 1985. *Leaders: The Strategies for Taking Charge.* Nachdr. Harper and Row.

Bernstein, Ethan, John Bunch, Niko Canner, and Michael Y. Lee. 2016. 'Beyond the Holacracy Hype'. https://hbr.org/2016/07/beyond-the-holacracy-hype.

Birkinshaw, J., and C Gibson. 2004. 'Building an Ambidextrous Organisation'. Sloan Management Review, July 15. https://sloanreview.mit.edu/article/building-ambidexterity-into-an-organization/.

Bock, Adam J., Tore Opsahl, Gerard George, and David M. Gann. 2012. 'The Effects of Culture and Structure on Strategic Flexibility During Business Model Innovation'. *Journal of Management Studies* 49 (2): 279–305. https://doi.org/10.1111/j.1467–6486.2011.01030.x.

Brassey, Jacqueline, Aaron De Smet, Ashish Kothari, Johanne Lavoie, Marino Mugayar-Baldocchi, and Sasha Zolley. 2021. 'Future Proof: Solving the "Adaptability Paradox" for the Long Term'. Business Management. McKinsey & Company, August 2. https://www.mckinsey.com/capabilities/people-and-organizational-performance/our-insights/future-proof-solving-the-adaptability-paradox-for-the-long-term.

Brill, Jonathan. 2021. *Rogue Waves: Future-Proof Your Business to Survive & Profit Radical Change.* McGraw Hill.

Bryar, Colin, and Bill Carr. 2021. *Have We Taken Agile Too Far?* Business. Harvard Business Review. https://hbr.org/2021/04/have-we-taken-agile-too-far.

Cameron, Kim S., and Robert E. Quinn. 2011. *Diagnosing and Changing Organizational Culture: Based on the Competing Values Framework*. 3rd edition. The Jossey-Bass Business & Management Series. Jossey-Bass.

Chatman, Jennifer A., David F. Caldwell, Charles A. O'Reilly, and Bernadette Doerr. 2014. 'Parsing Organizational Culture: How the Norm for Adaptability Influences the Relationship Between Culture Consensus and Financial Performance in High-Technology Firms: Parsing Organizational Culture'. *Journal of Organizational Behavior* 35 (6): 785–808. https://doi.org/10.1002/job.1928.

Christensen, Clayton M. 1997. *The Innovator's Dilemma: When New Technologies Cause Great Firms to Fail. The Management of Innovation and Change Series*. Harvard Business School Press.

Cline, Julia, and Amelia Goodwin. 2024. 'Building an Adaptive Organization'. Slalom, June 28. https://www.slalom.com/us/en/insights/building-adaptive-organizations-with-ai.

Daft, Richard L. 1986. *Organization Theory and Design*. 2nd edition. West Pub. Co.

Denison, Daniel R., Stephanie Haaland, and Paulo Goelzer. 2003. 'Corporate Culture and Organizational Effectiveness: Is There a Similar Pattern Aournd the World?' *Organizational Dynamics* 33 (1): 98–109. https://doi.org/10.1016/j.orgdyn.2003.11.008.

Denning, Steve. 2014. 'Making Sense of Zappos and Holacracy'. Leadership Strategy. Forbes, January 15. https://www.forbes.com/sites/stevedenning/2014/01/15/making-sense-of-zappos-and-holacracy/#602fee253207.

Devarajan, Vittal, and Bejoy Joseph George. 2016. *Industry 4.0: Business in the Age of Personalisation*. World Economic Forum, June 27. https://www.weforum.org/stories/2016/06/industry-4-0-business-in-the-age-of-personalisation/.

Deverell, Edward, and Eva-Karin Olsson. 2010. 'Organizational Culture Effects on Strategy and Adaptability in Crisis Management'. *Risk Management* 12 (2): 116–34. https://doi.org/10.1057/rm.2009.18.

Diamantidis, Anastasios D., and Prodromos Chatzoglou. 2018. 'Factors Affecting Employee Performance: An Empirical Approach'. *International Journal of Productivity and Performance Management* 68 (1): 171–93. https://doi.org/10.1108/IJPPM-01-2018-0012%2520Article%2520history%2520Share%2520Icon%2520Share.

Djabi, Mélia, and Sakura Shimada, S. 2013. 'How Does Generational Diversity Contribute to the Organizational Dynamic? An Empirical View.' Paper presented at European Group for Organizational Studies (EGOS), Montréal. 29th EGOS Colloquium, Montréal, July.

Doyle, Andy. 2016. 'Management and Organization at Medium'. The Medium Blog, August 12. https://medium.com/blog/management-and-organization-at-medium-2228cc9d93e9.

DXC Technology. 2017. *Digital Transformation Is Racing Ahead and No Industry Is Immune*. Business. Harvard Business Review, July 19. https://hbr.org/sponsored/2017/07/digital-transformation-is-racing-ahead-and-no-industry-is-immune-2.

Esser, Joerg. 2021. *The Secret of Adaptable Organizations Is Trust*. Business Management. Harvard Business Review, March 15. https://hbr.org/2021/03/the-secret-of-adaptable-organizations-is-trust.

Evans, Nicholas D. 2023. 'Why Adaptability Is the New Digital Transformation | CIO'. Business. CIO, October 30. https://www.cio.com/article/657149/why-adaptability-is-the-new-digital-transformation.html.

Fayol, Henri. 1916. *General and Industrial Management*. Translated by Constance Storrs. Pitman.

Federal Ministry of Labour and Social Affairs. 2015. *Green Paper Work 4.0: Re-Imagining Work*. Green Paper. German Federal Ministry of Labour and Social Affairs. https://www.bmas.de/EN/Services/Publications/arbeiten-4-0-greenpaper-work-4-0.html.

Federal Ministry of Labour and Social Affairs. 2017. *White Paper Work 4.0: Re-Imagining Work*. White Paper. German Federal Ministry of Labour and Social Affairs. https://www.bmas.de/EN/Services/Publications/a883-white-paper.html.

Felipe, Carmen, José Roldán, and Antonio Leal-Rodríguez. 2017. 'Impact of Organizational Culture Values on Organizational Agility'. *Sustainability* 9 (12): 2354. https://doi.org/10.3390/su9122354.

Franczak, Jennifer, and Laurence Weinzimmer. 2022. 'How SMEs Leverage Adaptability, Risk-Taking, and Action Into Positive Performance: A Moderated Mediation Model'. *Journal of Small Business Strategy* 32 (4): 16–29. https://doi.org/10.53703/001c.40318.

Fulmer, William E. 2000. *Shaping the Adaptive Organization*. AMACOM.

Gownder, J. P. 2019. 'The Future of Work Is an Adaptive Workforce'. Innovation and Tech. Forbes, August 1. https://www.forbes.com/sites/forrester/2019/08/01/the-future-of-work-is-an-adaptive-workforce/.

Groth, Aimee. 2022. 'Zappos Has Quietly Backed Away from Holacracy'. Leadership. Quartz, July 20. https://qz.com/work/1776841/zappos-has-quietly-backed-away-from-holacracy.

Handy, Charles B. 1996. *Beyond Certainty: The Changing Worlds of Organisations*. Arrow.

Harress, Christopher. 2013. *The Sad End of Blockbuster Video: The Onetime $5 Billion Company Is Being Liquidated As Competition From Online Giants Netflix And Hulu Prove All Too Much For The Iconic Brand*. International Business Times (IBT), May 12. https://www.ibtimes.com/sad-end-blockbuster-video-onetime-5-billion-company-being-liquidated-competition-online-giants.

Heifetz, Ronald A., Alexander Grashow, and Martin Linsky. 2009. *The Practice of Adaptive Leadership: Tools and Tactics for Changing Your Organization and the World*. Harvard Business Press.

Hopkins, Brian. 2019. *Adaptive Enterprises Are Growing Three Times Faster Than Their Competitors*. Forrester, May 28. https://www.forrester.com/blogs/adaptive-enterprises-are-growing-at-3x-faster-than-competitors/.

Hossenfelder, Sabine. 2018. *Lost in Math: How Beauty Leads Physics Astray*. First edition. Basic Books.

Huyler, Debaro, Lourdes Gomez, Tonette S. Rocco, and Maria S. Plakhotnik. 2024. 'Leading Different Generational Cohorts in the Workplace: Focus on Situational and Inclusive Leadership'. *New Horizons in Adult Education and Human Resource Development* 37 (1): 6–19. https://doi.org/10.1177/19394225241297230.

Kelly, Richard. 2022. *The Nature of Business Transformation: A Swarm Intelligent Approach to Reinventing Organisations*. Routledge.

Kilmann, Ralph H. 2011. *Quantum Organizations: A New Paradigm for Achieving Organizational Success and Personal Meaning*. Paperback ed., 1. print. Kilmann Diagnostics.

Klein, Andrew. 2011. 'Corporate Culture: Its Value as a Resource for Competitive Advantage'. *Journal of Business Strategy* 32 (2): 21–28. https://doi.org/10.1108/02756661111109743.

Kramer, Nic J. T. A., and Jacob de Smit. 1977. *Systems Thinking : Concepts and Notions*. Martinus Nijhoff. http://archive.org/details/systemsthinkingc0000kram.

Kuehn, Whynde. 2024. 'Designing for Change: Building an Adaptive Organization Through Business Architecture'. *Designing for Change: Building an Adaptive Organization Through Business Architecture. Architecture & Governance Magazine*, October 23. https://www.architectureandgovernance.com/elevating-ea/designing-for-change-building-an-adaptive-organization-through-business-architecture/.

MacBride, Elizabeth. 2015. 'Zakary Tormala: Why Certainty Matters in Business'. Insights. Stanford Graduate School of Business. https://www.gsb.stanford.edu/insights/zakary-tormala-why-certainty-matters-business.

Magagula, Nozibheva. 2024. 'Bridging the Generational Divide: Creating Adaptive Workplace Cultures for Gen Z and Millennials'. African International Advisors, April. https://www.africaia.com/insights/bridging-the-generational-divide-creating-adaptive-workplace-cultures-for-gen-z-and-millennials.

McGreevy, Malcolm. 2008. 'Adaptive Change in an Evolving World of Work'. *Industrial and Commercial Training* 40 (7): 355–63. https://doi.org/10.1108/00197850810912225.

McLoone, Kieran. 2021. 'Where Are They Now: Blockbuster'. Global Franchise, July 20. https://www.global-franchise.com/news/where-are-they-now-blockbuster.

Mollman, Steve. 2023. 'Blockbuster "Laughed Us Out of the Room," Recalls Netflix Cofounder on Trying to Sell Company Now Worth Over $150 billion for $50 Million'. Business. Fortune, April 14. https://fortune.com/2023/04/14/netflix-cofounder-marc-randolph-recalls-blockbuster-rejecting-chance-to-buy-it/.

Murunga, Edgar Sikuku, and Jane Esther Karugu. 2019. 'Organizational Culture and Strategy Execution at Commission for University Education, Kenya'. *International Journal of Current Aspects* 3 (V): 76–90. https://doi.org/10.35942/ijcab.v3iV.62.

Payne, Alan. 2021. *Built to Fail: The Inside Story of Blockbuster's Inevitable Bust*. Lioncrest Publishing.

Pech, Martin, and Jaroslav Vrchota. 2022. 'The Product Customization Process in Relation to Industry 4.0 and Digitalization'. *Processes* 10 (3): 539. https://doi.org/10.3390/pr10030539.

Perry, Mark J. 2019. 'Comparing 1955's Fortune 500 to 2019's Fortune 500'. Educational. Foundation for Economic Education FEE, May 24. https://fee.org/articles/comparing-1955s-fortune-500-to-2019s-fortune-500/.

Ployhart, Robert E, and Scott F Turner. 2014. 'Organizational Adaptability'. In *Individual Adaptability to Changes at Work: New Directions in Research*, edited by David Chan. Organization and Management Series. Routledge. 73–91. https://doi.org/10.4324/9780203465721.

Pratt, Mary K. 2023. 'Cross-Functional Team'. Tech Target, November 1. TechTarget. https://www.techtarget.com/searchcio/definition/crossfunctional.

Quinn, Robert E., and John Rohrbaugh. 1983. 'A Spatial Model of Effectiveness Criteria: Towards a Competing Values Approach to Organizational Analysis'. *Management Science* 29 (3): 363–77. https://doi.org/10.1287/mnsc.29.3.363.

Redstone, Sumner, and Peter Knobler. 2001. *A Passion to Win*. Simon & Schuster.

Reeves, Martin, Yves Morieux, Michael Deimler. 2010. 'People Advantage'. Culture. BCG Global, March 25. https://www.bcg.com/publications/2010/strategy-behavior-culture-people-advantage.

Ries, Eric. 2011. *The Lean Startup: How Today's Entrepreneurs Use Continuous Innovation to Create Radically Successful Businesses*. 1st edition. Crown Business.

Robbins, Stephen Paul. 1990. *Organization Theory: Structure, Design, and Applications*. 3rd edition. Prentice Hall.

Robertson, Brian J. 2015. *Holacracy: The New Management System for a Rapidly Changing World*. Henry Holt and Company.

Robertson, Brian J. 2016. *Holacracy: The Revolutionary Management System That Abolishes Hierarchy*. 1st ed. Portfolio Penguin.

Ruiz-Moreno, Antonia, Carmen Haro-Domínguez, Ignacio Tamayo-Torres, and Teresa Ortega-Egea. 2016. 'Quality Management and Administrative Innovation as Firms' Capacity to Adapt to Their Environment'. *Total Quality Management & Business Excellence* 27 (1–2): 48–63. https://doi.org/10.1080/14783363.2014.941718.

Sarta, Andrew, Rodolphe Durand, and Jean-Philippe Vergne. 2020. 'Organizational Adaptation'. *Journal of Management* 47 (1): 43–75. https://doi.org/10.1177/0149206320929088.

Schulze, Jonas Hermann, and Felix Pinkow. 2020. 'Leadership for Organisational Adaptability: How Enabling Leaders Create Adaptive Space'. *Administrative Sciences* 10 (3): 37. https://doi.org/10.3390/admsci10030037.

Schwab, Klaus. 2016. *The Fourth Industrial Revolution: What It Means and How to Respond*. World Economic Forum, January 14. https://www.weforum.org/stories/2016/01/the-fourth-industrial-revolution-what-it-means-and-how-to-respond/.

Staber, Udo, and Jörg Sydow. 2002. 'Organizational Adaptive Capacity: A Structuration Perspective'. *Journal of Management Inquiry* 11 (4): 408–24. https://doi.org/10.1177/1056492602238848.

Stalk, George, and Thomas M. Hout. 1990. *Competing Against Time: How Time-Based Competition Is Reshaping Global Markets*. Free Press.

Sunarsih, Nenah, and Heriyanni Mashithoh. 2016. 'The Influence of Organizational Culture Adaptability in Regard to the Organizational Commitment of the Staff of Universitas Terbuka.' *Review of Integrative Business and Economics Research* 5 (1): 199–209.

Sutherland, Jeffrey Victor. 2014. *Scrum: The Art of Doing Twice the Work in Half the Time*. 1st edition. Crown Business.

Taylor, Frederick Winslow. 1911. *The Principles of Scientific Management*. Dover Publications.

Torn, I.A.R., and T.H.J. Vaneker. 2019. 'Mass Personalization with Industry 4.0 by SMEs: A Concept for Collaborative Networks'. *Procedia Manufacturing* 28: 135–41. https://doi.org/10.1016/j.promfg.2018.12.022.

Tuominen, Matti, Arto Rajala, and Kristian Möller. 2004. 'How Does Adaptability Drive Firm Innovativeness?' *Journal of Business Research* 57 (5): 495–506. https://doi.org/10.1016/S0148-2963(02)00316-8.

Unglebee, Ben. 2019. 'A Timeline of Blockbuster's Ride from Megahit to Flop'. Retail Dive, October 7. https://www.retaildive.com/news/a-timeline-of-blockbusters-ride-from-megahit-to-flop/564305/.

Viguerie, S. Patrick, Ned Calder, and Brian Hindo. 2021. '2021 Corporate Longevity Forecast'. Innosight, May. https://www.innosight.com/insight/creative-destruction/.

Waisfisz, Bob. 2015. *Constructing the Best Culture to Perform*. Itim International.

Wang, Catherine L., and Pervaiz K. Ahmed. 2007. 'Dynamic Capabilities: A Review and Research Agenda'. *International Journal of Management Reviews* 9 (1): 31–51. https://doi.org/10.1111/j.1468–2370.2007.00201.x.

Weber, Max, Guenther Roth, and Claus Wittich. 1922. *Economy and Society: An Outline of Interpretive Sociology*. University of California Press.

Weirauch, Lena, Sibylle Galliker, and Achim Elfering. 2023. 'Holacracy, a Modern Form of Organizational Governance Predictors for Person-Organization-Fit and Job Satisfaction'. *Frontiers in Psychology* 13 (January): 1021545. 1–14. https://doi.org/10.3389/fpsyg.2022.1021545.

Wich, Scott. 2025. 'Recognizing Certainty in Uncomfortable Uncertainty'. *Management Report for Nonunion Organizations* 48 (5): 3–4. https://doi.org/10.1002/mare.31170.

Williams, Jordan. 2021. 'Why Was Blockbuster Bad? Censorship Controversy Explained'. Screen Rant, August 24. https://screenrant.com/blockbuster-video-store-censorship-problems-controversy-explained/.

Wolniak, Radosław, and Wies Grebski. 2023. 'The Customization and Personalization of Product in Industry 4.0'. *Scientific Papers of Silesian University of Technology Organization and Management Series* 2023 (180). https://doi.org/10.29119/1641-3466.2023.180.38.

Yang, Yi-Chun, and Jih-Ming Hsu. 2010. 'Organizational Process Alignment, Culture and Innovation'. *African Journal of Business Management* 4 (11): 2231–40. https://doi.org/10.5897/AJBM.9000446.

Zohar, Danah. 2022. 'What Makes a Quantum Organization?' In *Zero Distance*, edited by Danah Zohar. Springer Singapore. https://doi.org/10.1007/978-981-16-7849-3_15.

Chapter 2

Systems at Work

Seven LEGO sets are sold every second somewhere in the world, according to Barry Elad (2025). With more LEGO minifigs than real people on the planet (Cuff 2021), LEGO is one of the most iconic products and brands of our time. The company, however, has had its fair share of ups and downs. It was a highly adaptive startup that lost its way before rediscovering its adaptive and responsive essence later in its corporate life.

LEGO 1.0

Founded by Ole Kirk Christiansen in 1916, LEGO began life as a carpentry shop in Billund, Denmark. From the beginning, it was a highly responsive and adaptive company. Henry Wiencek (1987) describes how the main workshop burnt down in 1924, but Ole Kirk used the opportunity to expand. In the 1930s, the Great Depression hit rural Denmark, resulting in fewer customers and, therefore, a severe cash flow problem for the organisation. To minimise waste, Ole Kirk made miniature versions of his products as design aids. Henry Wiencek (1987) explains that this inspired Ole Kirk to make inexpensive wooden toys, many of which reflected modernity, such as buses, cars, trains, trucks, aeroplanes, and yo-yos.

LEGO is an abbreviation of the Danish words "leg godt", meaning to "play well".[1] The name of the company originated from an employee competition (an early form of crowdsourcing) where, according to Henry Wiencek (1987), the prize was a homemade bottle of wine. The startup phase coincided with the Nazi occupation of Denmark, yet LEGO continued operating. Charles Fishman (2001) described how the post-war "plastic age" was embraced by the company, and it bought an injection-moulding machine for producing plastic toys in 1947. In 1949, after many prototypes, the company created the "automatic binding

DOI: 10.4324/9781003680345-2

brick" which went on to become the iconic LEGO toy. The LEGO reputation and brand steadily grew through trade fair attendance. By the 1950s, the LEGO brick was being exported across Europe. The company achieved a major commercial breakthrough by forming strategic partnerships, especially with Lucasfilm Ltd. and the *Star Wars* brand.

This early phase illustrates a startup company that had an external system perspective that was acutely aware of the demographic, geopolitical, and economic challenges it faced. It embraced the plastic age and procured new technology despite being cash-strapped; it aligned itself with computers (Wiencek 1987); and, according to Johnny Davis (2017), it had its factories close to markets to take advantage of the new transport infrastructure to export its products across Europe. Henry Wiencek (1987) reminds us that education is at the heart of LEGO and its values, positioning the company as a global force for learning through a system of play (Roos and Victor 2018). It created LEGO Education and the LEGO Foundation in the 1980s and, according to Derek Newton (2020), became a leading classroom learning aid.

This external systems perspective depicts an early-stage startup characterised by innovation, collaboration, resilience, adaptability, and a growth mindset. It signals an open/responsive culture that embraces connectivity and business ecosystems.

LEGO 2.0

In the early 2000s, LEGO hit a brick wall. Johnny Davis (2017) reports that by 2003, the company was $800m in debt and sales were plummeting 30% year-on-year. There were multiple reasons for this downturn. Patent protection for the LEGO brick expired in 1988, and cheaper non-LEGO bricks saturated the market. Also, competition was coming from the electronic games industry.[2] But the collapse was more systemic than expiring patents and computer games. Oliver, Samakh, and Heckmann (2007) contend that the company also suffered from misaligned supply chain issues. A detailed investigation by David Robertson and Bill Breen (2013) reveals a business that was deeply siloed. The company had diversified from its core product with ambitious theme parks (Legoland), video games, and jewellery. This diversification almost destroyed them. They strayed too far from their core product and company values into areas in which they had little or no expertise. They didn't accurately estimate the additional materials needed for these new product lines, which led to supply chain issues and further damaged their reputation. Johnny Davis (2017) reflects that their core growth strategy of offering themed *Star Wars* and *Harry Potter* kits lasted only as long as the films' cinema runs. By 2003, it was clear that the company was in deep trouble and was approaching what David Robertson and Bill Breen (2013) call a "near-death experience" (Robertson and Breen 2013, 6) as it faced bankruptcy and a chronic "fragmentation of the brand"

(Schultz and Hatch 2003, 9). In a 2001 interview with *Fast Company*, the then-CEO, Kjeld Kirk Kristiansen, grandson of the original founder, acknowledged that this decline towards becoming a "slow company" had been a few years in the making (the company had posted its first-ever loss in 1998). Kristiansen acknowledges, "We became a heavy institution… We were losing our dynamism – and our fun also" (cited in Fishman 2001).

LEGO 3.0

By 2015 LEGO had rebuilt itself into the most profitable toy company in the world (Merrill 2022). Johnny Davis (2017) describes how LEGO had overtaken Ferrari as the top global brand and achieved the "greatest turnaround in corporate history".

The transformational journey began in 2004, when Jørgen Vig Knudstorp, a former McKinsey consultant in his thirties, took over from Kristiansen as the new CEO. A systems mindset had built the original firm, and a systems mindset was required to rescue it. Knudstorp reflected that the company had ceased being part of a system and had become a "monolith" (cited in Robertson and Breen 2013, 55). Thus began a slow period of reinvention for the company as it returned to its core principles and values:

- LEGO improved workflows by cutting complexity and streamlining production. The new CEO refocused the company on its core values.
- LEGO sidestepped potential production glitches by scheduling for the "enterprise as a whole" (Oliver, Samakh, and Heckmann 2007).
- LEGO aligned strategy and business goals with every project.
- According to David Robertson and Bill Breen (2013), LEGO increased collaboration through teaming and a shared vision and built key performance indicators (KPIs) into performance reviews, holding colleagues accountable for results.
- LEGO listened again to customers. Antorini, Muñiz, and Askildsen (2012) tell how the company established feedback loops by collaborating with customer communities, connecting with fans and inviting them to contribute to new designs as "citizen developers". Moreover, the firm solicited direct feedback from children via an "inner circle forum". LEGO even embraced hackers' ideas rather than pursuing lawsuits against them, establishing a constructive partnership between consumers and designers (Robertson and Breen 2013).
- Majken Schultz and Mary Jo Hatch (2003) explain how LEGO exploited and leveraged its high-profile global brand.

- David Robertson and Bill Breen (2013) note that the company encouraged business leaders to adopt a systems-wide, panoramic view and to learn from setbacks.
- LEGO continued to place education at the core of its activities.

These initiatives transformed LEGO from a reactive, internally focused organisation to a responsive, customer-centric company that embraced co-creativity, user insight, and external collaboration. This was accomplished through a systems approach involving sensemaking, feedback loops, integration, big-picture (holistic) thinking, with an emphasis on emergence. Robertson and Breen remark, "for Knudstorp, his eureka moment came when he realized the LEGO System is not just a play system, it's also a business system" (Robertson and Breen 2013, 110).

The key to LEGO's turnaround is that it rediscovered the power of a systems approach. Several researchers view organisations as systems.[3] Understanding workplace culture through the lens of systems theory enables organisations to uncover hidden connections and promote a culture of adaptability, collective responsibility, and improved performance.

This chapter (titled "Systems at Work" because it is both systems in the workplace and systems in operation) demonstrates how systems theory can be used to gain a broader organisational perspective, build on past patterns, and shift organisations into a proactive mindset. A simple tool introduced in this chapter, known as the STEP-WIDE wheel, helps organisations to discern perspectives, patterns, and proactivity (the 3Ps Systems Model). It enables organisations to transition from rigid, reactive organisations to responsive, adaptive ones that can thrive in a changing business landscape.

Unpacking Systems[4]

Each key concept of systems theory (holism, interconnectivity, feedback loops, emergence, and modularity) can be found in the humble LEGO brick:

- David Gauntlett (2014) identifies LEGO bricks as part of a whole system of construction known as a "system of play".
- LEGO is an "interlocking system of building blocks" (Schultz and Hatch 2003, 7) where "everything connects to everything else" (Gauntlett 2014, 190–191).
- LEGO embraced the idea of feedback loops via customer communities to improve its product.
- Emergence is at the heart of the LEGO story, a "complete discovery system from birth to school age" (Robertson and Breen 2013, 49).

- LEGO is a modular system in which each brick follows standardised dimensions (a stud-and-tube coupling system), allowing users with limited sets of components to build sets or merge sets to create "infinite possibilities" (Gauntlett 2014, 191).

Systems theory is a framework for understanding complex systems or sets of interrelated components working together as a whole. Alexander Bogdanov explores the origins of systems in social, biological, and physical sciences (Bogdanov 1989). More recently, systems is widely used across management, education, computer science, and design. Ludwig von Bertalanffy defines systems as "complexes of elements standing in interaction" (Bertalanffy 1969, 33). As a science, systems theory has its roots in the last century.[5] It has close relations with cybernetics, game theory, and complexity theory,[6] to name a few.

Systems theory doesn't have to be complicated. There is a great example of systems and chewing gum sales. In 2007, a puzzling phenomenon occurred in the retail industry, leaving marketing experts perplexed. Global chewing gum sales plummeted by 15 per cent. The reason for this sharp decline is rooted in systems theory. The drop in gum sales coincided with the rise in smartphone popularity in 2007. *The Economic Times Magazine* (2017) reports that consumers who once purchased strategically positioned gum at the checkout were now engrossed in their smartphones, leading to a decline in impulse purchases, such as chewing gum. This illustrates that exploring the interrelated systems and settings behind a problem can help us gain a fresh perspective.

Richard Daft characterises systems as "a set of interrelated elements that acquires inputs from the environment, transforms them, and discharges outputs to the external environment" (Daft 1986, 10). More recently, Herbert Nold and Lukas Michel (2021) have defined systems in terms of complex interactions and environmental forces:

> Rather than a system being the sum of the parts, the functions of a system are characterized by the complex interactions among all of its components and external forces. General systems theory assumes that components of the system and the system itself is open to environmental forces that shape and influence both the components and the system in its entirety.

Jennifer Allen and Rajeev Sawhney provide an excellent definition in a chapter entitled "open and closed systems":

> A systems view considers an organization as a set of interacting functions that acquire inputs from the environment,

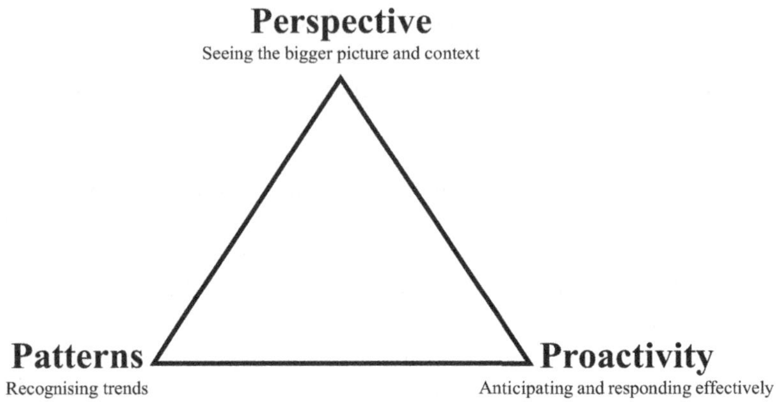

Figure 2.1 The 3Ps Systems Model.

> processes them, and then release the outputs back to the external environment.
>
> (Allen and Sawhney 2015, 27)

Systems theory acknowledges that systems are everywhere, including in the natural world.[7] It is a valuable workplace tool for navigating various systems and assisting organisations to move away from siloed (closed) structures towards interconnected (open) dynamic workplaces. In a systems context, organisational transformation is not about following step-by-step processes; it requires rethinking and reshaping the underlying culture. A systems approach provides organisational decision-makers with perspective, enables the visualisation of patterns, and inspires proactivity. This is shown as the 3Ps Systems Model (see Figure 2.1)

The system perspective refers to an awareness of the broader context of the system and its influences. System patterns involve sensemaking as a way of anticipating future scenarios and possibilities, while system proactivity means acting on data and supporting the organisation to transition from reactive to responsive (Wu and Parker 2011). The 3Ps Systems Model forms the organising principle of this chapter.

Let's explore this now.

Perspective: Eight Business Ecosystems and the STEP-WIDE Wheel

STEP-WIDE is an acronym that represents eight business ecosystems that impact the workplace. Viewing the organisation through this business ecosystem lens can help broaden perspective. STEP-WIDE stands for sources of energy

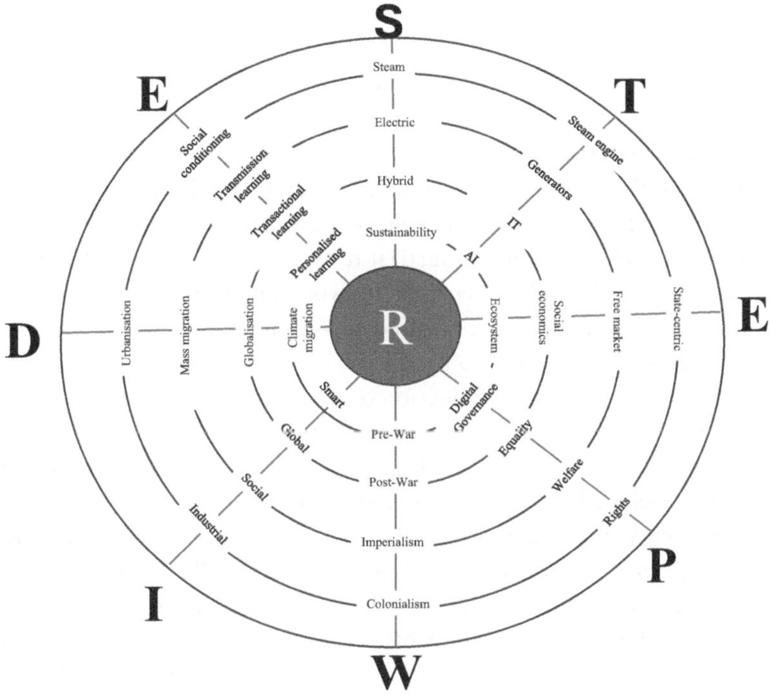

Figure 2.2 The STEP-WIDE Wheel.

(S), technology (T), economy (E), political reform (P), world order (W), infrastructure (I), demographics (D), and education (E). Figure 2.2 illustrates this as a system wheel divided into eight coactive sections representing external forces that have influenced the workplace for nearly 300 years (across four industrial cycles).

This system tool helps to demystify Work 4.0 and supports the organisation on its path towards becoming an ecosystem. The STEP-WIDE wheel illustrates how past culture and system trends form an intrinsic part of the future of the workplace. It further demonstrates the interconnected and evolutionary nature of systems at work and helps us process the broader environment that has shaped and continues to shape the workplace. At its core, it is a lens that supports organisations to step wider, broadening their perspective, and seeing themselves as part of an ecosystem. The wheel uses the well-applied typology of Industry 1.0 to 4.0, which is a standard typology used in both academic and policy literature.[8] Nick von Tunzelmann (2003) discusses how the epicentre across the four industrial revolutions changed over time: Britain in Industry 1.0, the United States in Industry 2.0, and East Asia in Industry 3.0. East Asia continues to be influential in Industry 4.0. The leading country focus in this chapter is Britain because the country has played a major role in each of the industrial revolutions. Other regions are discussed where relevant.

Let's look at each STEP-WIDE category on the wheel.

1. Source of energy
   Jianfeng Yang and coauthors (2021) and Hannah Ritchie (2021) both highlight the role of evolving energy sources in driving the industrial revolutions. Before the first industrial revolution, energy came from manual labour, animals, and biomass like firewood and charcoal. Industry 1.0 saw a shift to more efficient coal-fired steam engines. Industry 2.0 switched to electricity, with coal, oil, and gas continuing as key energy sources. Industry 3.0 saw the introduction of a hybrid fossil-renewable energy mix and nuclear power, alongside early investments in sustainable green energy such as wind, solar, and hydropower, although these remained largely underdeveloped during this period. Industry 4.0 is embracing sustainable energy, including alternative, green, renewable, and clean energies, aiming for net zero by 2050 (Bouckaert et al. 2021), with AI (Artifical Intelligence) optimising renewable infrastructure.[9] Future energy may include advanced nuclear, geothermal (Robbins 2022), biotechnology (Auta et al. 2024), locally generated energy systems (Rifkin 2012), and an advanced quantum-based solution.
2. Technology
   General-purpose technologies (GPTs), which Boyan Jovanovic and Peter Rousseau identify as technologies "that transform both household life and the ways in which firms conduct business" (Jovanovic and Rousseau 2005, 1184), have been central to each industrial revolution, driving innovation, and, as Normando Laudiceia Souza and coauthors (2020) mention, transforming systems. In Industry 1.0, the steam engine led to mechanised production and revolutionised transport. Industry 2.0 was shaped by the electrification of the assembly line, leading to mass production and enhanced workplace efficiency. Industry 3.0 marked the digital age, with information technology, personal computing, and the internet reshaping communication, commerce, and data processing, and paving the way for advancements in robotics, artificial narrow intelligence (ANI), and blockchain (Singh 2023; Souza et al. 2020). Now, Industry 4.0 is being shaped by AI-enabled technology (including generative and, in the future, cognitive and explainable artificial intelligence), machine collaboration, and quantum computing.[10] This is set to transform sectors such as transport, healthcare, and automation, all supported by growing processing power and the pursuit of sustainable energy solutions.

3. Econom
The economy has also played a role in each industrial revolution. Before Industry 1.0, many countries in Europe were agrarian economies, with rural trade regulated by guilds that provided social, economic, educational, and religious functions for employers and employees in skilled crafts.[11] Britain was a dominant economy in Industry 1.0 largely because of its state-centric protectionist model[12] where high import tariffs protected domestic manufacturing, while internal industries operated with minimal regulation. As Judit Kapás (2008) observes, Industry 2.0 marked a transition from factory-based to firm-based economies. Economic leadership shifted to the US. Britain moved towards free market capitalism, though debates over protectionism persisted in parliament. Theodore Saloutos (1962) argues that the US pursued protectionist policies throughout Industry 2.0. East Asia was the epicentre of Industry 3.0[13] and characterised by a hybrid economic model influenced by social economics (market capitalism with strategic government intervention) that served the digital and green economies.[14] Venkat Atluri and Miklós Dietz (2023) and Claus Otto Scharmer (2013) all believe that, in Industry 4.0, the focus is shifting towards an ecosystem economy in which interconnected regional networks prioritise sustainability and shared resources. There is a growing hostility towards fossil fuel dependency, signalling the potential for cooperative, tech-enabled economic ecosystems. Greg Satell (2013) argues that we are moving into a highly collaborative and connected economy called the semantic economy, "where information flows freely across once impermeable boundaries of firm and industry". Another important aspect of the future economy is sustainability and the development of economic models, including the green economy (Richard 2022), the circular economy, and doughnut economics (Raworth 2017). It should be noted here that the current rise in nationalism undermines this economic ecosystem.
4. Political reform
Political reform has played a cruical role in shaping employee rights and conditions worldwide, including in the UK. In Industry 1.0, unregulated factories exposed workers (including women and children) to dangerous machinery and exploitation (Nguyen 2021). This prompted early trade union movements, as well as landmark UK legislation between 1802 and 1878 aimed at improving worker safety and reducing child labour in factories and mines. Industry 2.0 introduced greater social consciousness, marked by reforms in welfare, health, and housing. The period saw the rise of socialism and the establishment of Britain's first pension and insurance schemes. That said, class, gender, and racial inequalities persisted. Industry 3.0 saw the expansion of employee protections alongside a more diverse

and knowledge-based workforce, including equal pay, anti-discrimination laws, and the emergence of the UK welfare state (Whiteside 2014). As Industry 4.0 unfolds, regulatory reforms are developing in response to automation and AI, such as the new EU AI Act (EY 2024; Clemmons 2024). Anil Shankar (2022) reports that the US Biden administration campaigned for a Bill of Rights for an AI-Powered world. The exponential age will bring other challenges that relate to worker rights, including technological unemployment. This could lead to robot taxes, universal basic income, and protections for gig and contingent workers, necessitating a redefinition of rights in an increasingly machine-dominated workplace.

5. World orde
   Changes in the world order have consistently shaped each industrial revolution, driven by the pursuit of natural resources, economic dominance, and the softening of global boundaries through technological advancement. In Industry 1.0, J.R. Ward (1994) tells how the five colonial powers (Britain, Portugal, Spain, the Dutch Republic, and France) shifted from feudalism to global colonisation, exploiting land, labour, and resources, and often sparking wars and independence movements. Wang Xiaonan (2019) explores how some of these conflicts were a direct consequence of tariffs and the protection of natural resources. Industry 2.0 saw the rise of neo-imperialist nations (Germany, Italy, Russia, Japan, and the US), which intensified local and global conflict. In Industry 3.0, Michael T. Klare (2014) observes that global tensions persisted under the Cold War and "energy wars", despite post-war treaties, unions, and global alliances. Now, in Industry 4.0, global connectivity presents both hope and danger. It offers the real posibility of post-globalisation ecosystems, but it is also triggering a resurgence in nationalism. Srdjan Korać (2018) notes that global resource-driven conflicts are increasingly adopting AI-driven warfare. Drones and AI warfare are being deployed in the Ukrainian/Russian conflict by both sides. Some argue we have gone from a post-war to a pre-war footing (Beale 2024; Channer 2024). A dystopian alternative to connected ecosystems and Marshall McLuhan's (1962) "global village" is the shift towards what Yanis Varoufakis (2023) and others term technofeudalism, where corporate power trumps national influence.
6. Infrastructur
   Each industrial revolution has contributed to the ongoing evolution of infrastructure in response to technological, social, and economic pressures. Before Industry 1.0, infrastructure in Britain was local and rural, but, as the 1844 *Report of the Royal Commission on the State of Large Towns and Populous Districts* (1844–1845) identified, industrialisation brought rapid urbanisation, necessitating the development of housing, transport,

and sanitation systems. Despite some tied cottages supplied by factory owners, there were limited housing schemes for the urban working classes. The infrastructure was developed to transport goods and raw materials (first by canal and later by railways, funded by "railway mania" stocks). Robert Wilde (2025) talks about how public health crises spurred government intervention, leading to foundational urban infrastructure reforms, privately financed by local businessmen and landowners (Smith 2020). Charitable foundations built hospitals in urban centres such as London. In Industry 2.0, infrastructure expanded significantly, especially in the US, through mass electrification, road building (to support the increase in automobiles), and the emergence of national grids and airports. This represented a decisive shift towards social planning. Industry 3.0 saw a post-war boom in social infrastructure in the UK and Europe, especially in healthcare and public housing. Towards the end of Industry 3.0, private investment dominated large global infrastructure projects. This era also saw a global investment in digital infrastructure, especially in the Asia-Pacific region. In Industry 4.0, infrastructure will be increasingly shaped by digital technologies such as smart and learning factories (Baena et al. 2017), IoT, and sustainable energy, which require transformative investment in data storage. Regions such as Asia-Pacific are leaders in smart, sustainable infrastructure suited to an AI-driven, interconnected world.

7. Demographics and population change
   Demographic changes across industrial revolutions (including shifts in birth rates, life expectancy, and migration) have been widely researched.[15] Some argue that industrial revolutions are as much of a demographic revolution as a technological one.[16] Demographic and population theory has long been shaped by Malthus's 1798 *Essay on the Principle of Population*, which argued that unchecked growth leads to poverty, famine, and disease. Yet the experience from Industry 1.0 to 4.0 suggests the opposite: industrialisation thrives on expanding populations. Before Industry 1.0, high birth rates were offset by high infant mortality and low life expectancy, keeping populations stable. However, with the rise of industrialisation, although diseases such as the bubonic plague struck, improved agriculture, reduced infant mortality, and urbanisation doubled the global population to 1 billion by 1805 (Roser and Ritchie 2023), with a rise in social mobility among the middle classes. Despite another global pandemic, namely the Spanish flu, Industry 2.0 saw continued urbanisation and an increase in migration, particularly in the US, where, according to Charles Hirschman and Elizabeth Mogford (2009), immigrants and their children accounted for one-third of the US population by 1920, equating to half of the manufacturing workers. This drove global population

growth to 2 billion by 1929. In Industry 3.0, the post-war baby boom increased life expectancy, pushing the global population to 4 billion by 1974. Globalisation encouraged international mobility and contributed to the rapid spread of COVID-19 (Jeanne et al. 2022). In Industry 4.0, the global population surpassed 8 billion in 2022 and is expected to reach 9.7 billion by 2050 (United Nations nd).

Population growth is slowing for the first time in world history. An ageing population and shrinking workforce may create labour shortages. According to Paul Morland (2024) the ratio of workers to retirees in the UK has fallen from four to one to three to one and is projected to reach two to one in the near future. Economic and climate-related migration (Vince 2022), alongside the rise of digital nomads (Bearne 2023), will alter global demographic patterns. Regarding future demographic movements, the International Monetary Fund (IMF) predicts that economic migration from Africa and the Middle East will continue to rise through 2050 and will be a source of growth for industrial nations (Engler et al. 2020). It is also predicted that by 2050 the world's population of people aged over 60 will double, exceeding 2 billion.[17] This will mean the global workforce will shrink by 2050. This could lead to a global talent shortage of millions of workers (Gaines 2021), although this may be offset by technological unemployment in heavily automated industries (Peters 2019).

8. Education

As industrial societies evolved from their agrarian roots through successive technological eras, Sasha O. Becker and Ludger Woessmann (2019) show how education became a crucial strategy for equipping each generation with the skills, knowledge, and work ethic needed for changing workplace demands. Before Industry 1.0, only the wealthy had access to structured institutional education. Children from poor families worked alongside family members in the fields or cottage industries. In the 17th century, only 15–20% of husbandmen (poor farmers and labourers) were literate compared with 60% of yeomen (wealthy farmers) and 100% of the gentry (Hailwood 2014). In 1776, Adam Smith argued in *The Wealth of Nations* that widespread education was needed to support new industrial skills and grow factory production. The only real schooling opportunities in Industry 1.0 for children outside of the elite public school system were privately funded schools. These included Charity Schools, which promoted religious doctrine (UK Parliamentary 2024), and Factory Schools, financed by wealthy industrialists such as Robert Owen for children of factory workers. Joel Mokyr (2001) argues that education for the poor served more to socially condition the labour force than to teach technical skills and knowledge.

The shift towards Industry 2.0 saw the introduction of compulsory, standardised, transmission-based education. This involved teacher-centric instruction, structured lessons, a formal classroom layout, and a standardised curriculum that included some vocational subjects. The school culture was rule-based and disciplinarian, reflecting the need for a more educated workforce capable of following instructions and operating sophisticated production-line machinery. In the US, Puritan settlers valued education because they wanted their children to read the Bible, so schoolrooms and home learning were a substantial part of US culture. Education was part of social mobility and the American dream. According to *The Atlantic* correspondent Jerome Davis (1927), Henry Ford had very strong views on education and pioneered the learn-by-doing approach.

With Industry 3.0 came social reform and the rise of the knowledge economy, resulting in a greater need for a technologically educated workforce. This led to greater access to higher education for the working classes. There was a rise in student-centric pedagogies emphasising inquiry and self-directed learning, particularly through the influence of personal computing. This was a transactional period of education, marked by many learner-centric theories.

Industry 4.0 is shifting towards what Loose, Ryan, and Jagielo-Manion (2023) and others term personalised learning. Immersive and simulation-based learning prepares students for a future of AI, automation, and lifelong upskilling, enhancing human proficiency in the 4Cs: critical thinking, collaboration, communication, and creativity (Amzat and Padilla-Valdez 2017). There are some early adopters of this type of personalised and immersive education in the UK (the Livingstone Academy), Canada (the New Brunswick school system), and the US (the Alpha school in Austin, Texas, which is a pioneer in AI-based teaching).[18] This paradigm shift demands a rethink of policy on access, funding, and the purpose of education itself. Education will need to prepare people for a world of machine dependency and the possibility of technological unemployment.

Patterns: Four Gears of the STEP-WIDE Wheel

Another component of the systems wheel is the four gears, which correspond to the four industrial revolutions (see Figure 2.3). Contemplating the workplace in this way helps us to identify patterns.

Figure 2.3 illustrates four shaded bands of the STEP-WIDE wheel, which can be mapped onto the main systems wheel. These bands, or "gears", correspond to the four industrial eras spanning three centuries (1750 to the present),

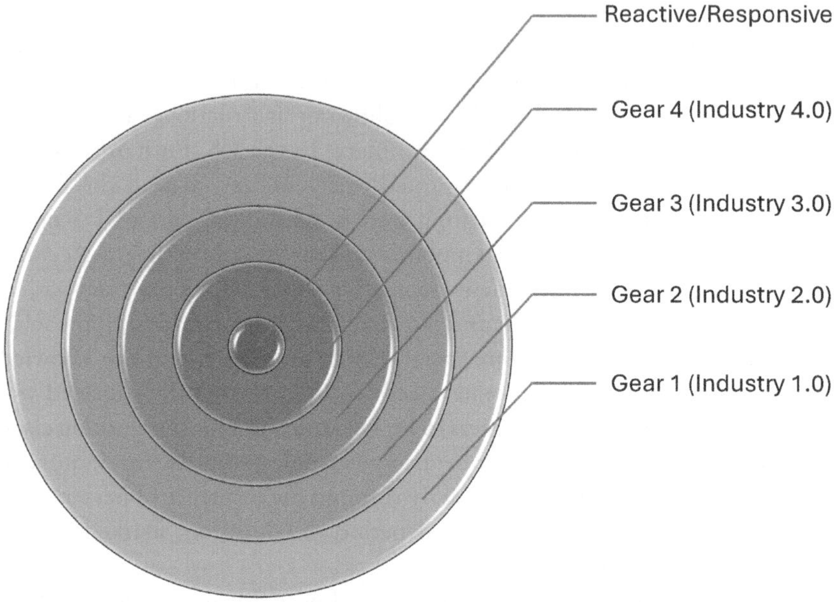

Figure 2.3 The four STEP-WIDE gears from Industry 1.0 (outer gear) to Industry 4.0 (inner gear).

from Industry 1.0 on the outer band to Industry 4.0 at the centre. The following section examines each of these gears in detail.

i. First Gear: Industry 1.0 and the Steam Age
Industry 1.0, driven by steam power, revolutionised production through large, centralised operations, boosting output, and fuelling a protectionist economy reliant on tariffs and expanding global trade. Political reform supported economic interests, restricted worker resistance, and began regulating child labour. Urban infrastructure supported industrial growth, while rural workers, displaced by a declining agrarian economy, migrated to urban centres. The demand for skilled labour led to factory-based education. Centralised labour and expanding imperial trade further accelerated production and consumerism, but led to conflict over trade and resources.
ii. Second Gear: Industry 2.0 and the Steel Age
Industry 2.0, powered by electricity and driven by innovations such as the motorised assembly line, ushered in mass production, consumerism, and a shift towards market economies. Britain and the United States adopted standardised, interventionist policies. Political reforms improved worker

rights and provided social welfare. Industrialised warfare and territorial competition intensified global conflict, while advances in steel, transport, and urban infrastructure supported economic growth. The demand for skilled labour led to a universal, standardised education. The era was producer-led, with protectionist tendencies, particularly from the US. Industry 2.0 was characterised by global conflict.

iii. Third Gear: Industry 3.0 and the Digital Age
Industry 3.0, marked by mixed energy sources and the rise of digital technology, especially computers, brought widespread automation and globalisation in the workplace. Economies became more mixed, blending free markets with state intervention, and political reforms promoted diversity, equality, and international investment. Digital infrastructure, including data storage and cryptocurrencies, expanded alongside global supply chains. Globalisation led to greater post-war collaboration among some nations (especially EU countries), but also raised concerns about borders, migration, and sovereignty, as evidenced by Brexit. Improved health and welfare systems contributed to ageing populations, impacting economies and welfare costs. Education, notably higher education and research in digital technologies, was prioritised in major economies as established manufacturing countries such as the UK shifted to a knowledge-based economy.

iv. Fourth Gear: Industry 4.0 and the Age of AI
Industry 4.0, the AI/Quantum Age, is shaped by sustainable energy, automation, AI, and the ongoing development of advanced quantum computing. Green technologies and infrastructure are developing as the world targets zero fossil fuel emissions by 2050.[19] The rise of machine autonomy is set to transform work, reducing human labour and raising ethical, legislative, and existential challenges arising from machine collaboration and the possibility of technological unemployment. It will also lead to AI-driven smart environments. Education will shift towards personalised learning that focuses on the 4Cs: critical thinking, collaboration, communication, and creativity. Traditional centralised workplaces are likely to decline, and the gig and remote working economy may finally come of age. A combination of technological unemployment, climate change, and an ageing population will create geopolitical tensions, making adaptability and responsiveness essential for future organisations in a volatile, uncertain world.

Establishing patterns in this way enables companies to anticipate future work trends and challenges and build adaptive and responsive organisations.

Table 2.1 Reactive Versus Responsive Organisations

STEP-WIDE (Reactive)	*STEP-WIDE (Responsive)*
Closed mechanical organisational culture	Open organic organisational culture
Reacts to situations/events	Proactively anticipates situations/ events
Addresses issues after they have occurred	Prevents issues from occurring
Short-termism	Long-termism
One-dimensional system	Complex adaptive system
Set routines	Continuous improvement
Views things from a standalone	Views things from an ecosystem

Proactivity: The Hub of the Issue

The central part of the wheel is called the hub. On a rear pushbike wheel, the hub has a bike cassette. The bike cassette establishes the chain reaction best suited to the terrain. In the STEP-WIDE wheel, the hub contains the letter R. The R stands for two possible chain reactions, depending on the organisation's cultural terrain. It can either represent "reactive", corresponding to a closed organisation that responds to events (it is being driven), or for "responsive", corresponding to an open organisation that adapts to events (it is a driver). Table 2.1 highlights the differences between the reactive and responsive organisations.

STEP-WIDE (Reactive)

Organisations that are STEP-WIDE (Reactive) retrospectively react to events. They have an inherently standalone and monocultural outlook. They are classic pyramidal organisations that are short-termist, internally focused, and closed. They often miss opportunities and fail to address issues on time. Reacting to events rather than actively shaping and influencing them has been a significant factor behind organisational failure to move and adapt with the times. In a letter to customers, shareholders, and employees as part of the 2000 Annual Report for General Electric, Jack Welch comments, "when the rate of change inside an institution becomes slower than the rate of change outside, the end is in sight" (Welch 2000, 5).

The following are some STEP-WIDE examples where companies have been reactive rather than responsive.

- New energy-based technologies (from steam pumps to electric belts) have been adopted rather than developed by the workplace.
- Economic conditions set by the central government have driven organisational change for centuries (Chartered Institute of Personnel and Development 2019).
- Organisations have tended to adopt legislation rather than shape it.
- Organisations have traditionally stayed away from geopolitics.
- Organisations tend to view infrastructure-based development as a governmental responsibility, even though they benefit enormously from good infrastructure.
- Organisations have also benefitted from demographic shifts but tend not to directly support the development of local housing and infrastructure.
- Organisations benefit from an educated workforce, but have historically not collaborated with educational institutions.

STEP-WIDE (Responsive)

STEP-WIDE (Responsive) organisations are inherently proactive, adaptive, and situational. They are emergent, open ecosystems that proactively anticipate external events and situations. They are highly adaptive, opportunistic, long-term-focused, proactive, and a vital part of the business ecosystem. They tend to approach organisational life organically, take a long-term perspective, seize opportunities, and proactively address issues. Response.org is a community that is committed to creating and growing responsive organisations, regularly holding global conferences. In their 2013 manifesto, they declare:

> Responsive Organizations are built to learn and respond rapidly through the open flow of information; encouraging experimentation and learning on rapid cycles; and organizing as a network of employees, customers, and partners motivated by shared purpose.
>
> (Responsive.org, 2025)

Organisations need to step wider, be more responsive, and begin to play a central role in shaping the ecosystem. They need to accelerate what Ben Hecht (2013) and others call their "collective impact" with outside parties, including competitors, suppliers, partners, and customers. Kramer (2016) argues that companies must sometimes team up with governments, NGOs, and even rivals to advance the economic benefits of social progress through the value of ecosystems. Table 2.2 highlights recent organisational examples of highly responsive companies that have been proactive across the eight STEP-WIDE business ecosystems.

Table 2.2 List of Responsive STEP-WIDE Companies

Category	*Company*	*Example*	*Source*
Source of Energy	Patagonia	An outdoor gear and clothing retailer that has built an entire employee value and business proposition around "saving the planet".	Patagonia 2025
Technology	Boston Dynamics	A robotics and AI company that is firmly committed to creating human-affirming robots that support *Homo sapiens* and actively legislate against weaponising robots.	Boston Dynamics 2025
Economy	Ben & Jerrys) (formerly part of Unilever, now under The Magnum Ice Cream Company)	A brand that even after being acquired continued to proactively encourage fair trade and sustainable livelihoods for local producers.	Fairtrade Foundation 2025
Political Reform	Salesforce	A cloud-based software company with over 75,000 global employees who proactively use their business platform to encourage political, social, and government reform. Notably, they oppose discriminatory legislation.	Salesforce 2025
World Order	Unilever PLC	Unilever PLC seeks to create a fairer and socially inclusive world where nations, institutions, and societies coexist peacefully and prosperously by shaping the economic, social, and environmental foundations that enable a cooperative, rules-based, fair framework.	Department of Foreign Affairs (Ireland) 2023

(*Continued*)

Table 2.2 (Continued) List of Responsive STEP-WIDE Companies

Category	*Company*	*Example*	*Source*
Infrastructure	Ørsted	A global leader in renewable energy that funds local infrastructure projects in the US.	Ørsted 2025
Demographics	GitLab	A fully remote software development company with nearly 3000 employees across 70+ countries. Its "all remote" policy promotes regional workforce distribution.	GitLab 2021
Education	IBM	Through its SkillsBuild programme, IBM has committed to training 30 million people worldwide by 2030 with a focus on IT and AI Skills. It does this through free online courses and tailored learning experiences in schools and colleges, and through strategic educational partnership with organisations such as UNESCO.	IBM 2025

Synthesis: Systems at Work

This chapter demonstrated how applying a systems lens can help organisations navigate complexity, shape performance, and enhance adaptability. The 3Ps System Model (perspective, patterns, and proactivity) was used as a practical framework for understanding and navigating organisational challenges. Through case studies such as LEGO, the chapter illustrated the value of applying systems theory to support organisational objectives and transformation. The introduction of the STEP-WIDE wheel highlighted how recognising external forces enables organisations to see collective impact, detect emerging patterns, and adopt a proactive rather than reactive approach. Treating the organisation as an interconnected and evolving ecosystem is key to building adaptability, as it encourages a holistic focus. The functional side of "systems at work" supports the underlying system levers outlined in Chapter 1 (culture, design, people, technology, and process). These five system levers drive organisational adaptability and shape the chapters that follow.

Notes

1. The story goes that Ole Kirk Kristiansen didn't realise until years after naming the company that "lego" means "I put together" in Latin.
2. See Anderson and Ross (2016) and Schultz and Hatch (2003) for an excellent perspective on this.
3. These include Katz and Kahn (1966); Glaser and Halliday (1980); and McNamara (2005).
4. From the outset, it should be noted that this isn't a technical book about systems theory. There are authors who write on systems, from Ludwig von Bertalanffy (1969) to Michael C. Jackson (2024).
5. Alexander Bogdanov published *Tektologii͡a: vseobshchai͡a organizat͡sionnai͡a nauka (Tektology: Universal Organization Science)* in Russian between 1912 and 1917 (Bogdanov, 1989). Tektolgy is the study of underlying organising principles in social, biological, and physical sciences. Bogdanov likely influenced Ludwig von Bertalanffy and his General System Theory (GST), who heavily influenced peers, including Ross Ashby and his research on cybernetics.
6. Complexity theory, developed through the Santa Fe Institute and the work of Lewin (1992), Waldrop (1993), and Goodwin (1994), sees organisations as evolving, non-linear systems (Sherman and Schultz 1998; Pascale, Millemann, and Gioja 2000; Rzevski and Skobelev 2014). Lorenz's "butterfly effect" linked complexity to chaos theory, highlighting unpredictable but patterned behaviour (Lorenz 1972). Complex adaptive systems are characterised by learning and adaption (Holland 2006), while Dynamic Systems Theory describes self-organising, multi-component systems (Perone and Simmering 2017).
7. Researchers on systems and the natural world include Crowther et al. (2015); Barlow and Fisahn (2013); Woolley-Barker (2017); Kelly (2019a); Kelly (2019b); Kelly (2022); Marshall (2019); Kellaway (2021); Field and Magkourilou (2023).
8. Researchers who adopt the Industry 1.0 to 4.0 labels include Lorenz et al. (2015); Schwab (2016); Gilchrist (2016); Kelly (2019a); Singh (2023). While some, drawing on Kuhn's *Structure of Scientific Revolutions* (1962), frame these as discrete paradigm shifts (Schwab, 2016), others interpret them as continuous, interlinked transitions (Gatzweiler 2023).
9. Research relating to this includes Milone (2022); Spieler (2023); The Renewable Energy Institute (2023); Rozite, Miller, and Oh (2023); and He and NI (2022).
10. Quantum computing amplifies AI capabilities (Nandi-Ray 2025) and will unlock new markets.
11. Much of this has come from the following reading: Rota and Spinesi (2024); Bosshardt and Lopus (2013); Epstein (1991); Farr (2000); and Edgell and Granter (2005/20).

12. The idea that post-1750 Britain fully embraced Adam Smith's laissez-faire capitalism is misleading (Brebner 1848; Chang 2007; Monbiot 2008). Early industrial growth owed as much to protectionist and interventionist policies such as tariffs, export bans, and monopolistic controls, as to market forces, with true laissez-faire practices only emerging in the mid-nineteenth century (Caradonna 2014/2022).
13. Supporting research includes Ericson (2000); Turner (2021); and Roy (2018).
14. Researchers that comment on this include Rifkin (2015); Pasimeni (2021); Burnes and Choi (2021); and Buchanan (2016). Industry 3.0 marked a turn toward global trade liberalisation, with GATT in 1947 and the WTO in 1995 cultivating interconnected markets, international agreements, and free trade. Innovations like just-in-time production further integrated economies, exemplified by Toyota's "kanban" system. Yet this era of cooperation has faced backlash, as rising nationalism and protectionism (from Brexit to Trump) reminds us that globalisation and open borders remains a contentious policy.
15. Authors who promote this view include Zhou (2019); Wilde (2025); and Whelpton (1928).
16. Those who argue for this include Bar and Leukhina (2010) and Khan (2008). Rosenman argues that the controversial enclosure acts in the eighteenth century led to the loss of rights and access to open land for many farmers, leading to evictions and the impoverishment of generations of small farmers and villagers. This resulted in mass migration from rural to urban centres (Rosenman 2012).
17. Sources for this include Officer et al. (2020); World Health Organisation (2024); Government Office for Science (2021).
18. Alpha School in Austin, Texas is a leading educational institution that is using AI tutors and is achieving outstanding results (Baehr 2025). This is the shift towards personalised and adaptive education (Longmire 2024).
19. Recent geopolitical developments, including energy security concerns and supply chain disruptions, have prompted some analysts to question whether governments and corporations will be able to fully commit to achieving net-zero fossil fuel emissions within the originally stated timelines.

Bibliography

Allen, Jennifer M., and Rajeev Sawhney. 2015. *Administration and Management in Criminal Justice: A Service Quality Approach*. 2nd edition. SAGE.

Amzat, Ismail Hussein, and Nena Padilla-Valdez, eds. 2017. *Teacher Professional Knowledge and Development for Reflective and Inclusive Practices*. 1st edition. Routledge. https://doi.org/10.4324/9781315397702.

Anderson, Peter, and Jeanne W. Ross. 2016. 'Transforming the LEGO Group for the Digital Economy'. Center of Information System Researdh (CISR) – MIT Sloan Management, Center of Information System Researdh (CISR), no. CISR Working Paper 407 (March). https://cisr.mit.edu/publication/MIT_CISRwp407_TheLEGOGroup_AndersenRoss.

Antorini, Yun Mi, Albert M. Jr. Muñiz, and Tormod Askildsen. 2012. *Collaborating With Customer Communities: Lessons From the Lego Group*. Business. MIT Sloan Management Review, March 20. https://sloanreview.mit.edu/article/collaborating-with-customer-communities-lessons-from-the-lego-group/.

Atluri, Venkat, and Miklós Dietz. 2023. *The Ecosystem Economy: How to Lead in the New Age of Sectors Without Borders*. John Wiley & Sons, Inc.

Auta, Helen Shnada, David Oyeyemi Aboyeji, Isiaka Adedayo Adelere, et al. 2024. 'Biotechnology for Bioenergy Production: Current Status, Challenges, and Prospects'. In *Microbial Biotechnology for Bioenergy*, edited by Naga Raju Maddela, Sesan Abiodun Aransiola, Chizoba I. Ezugwu, Lizziane Kretli Winkelstroter Eller, Laura Scalvenzi, and Fangang Meng. Elsevier. https://doi.org/10.1016/B978-0-443-14112-6.00014-6.

Baehr, Jasmine. 2025. 'AI Is Running the Classroom at This Texas School, and Students Say "It's Awesome"'. *Fox News*, May 1.

Baena, Felipe, Alvaro Guarin, Julian Mora, Joel Sauza, and Sebastian Retat. 2017. 'Learning Factory: The Path to Industry 4.0'. *Procedia Manufacturing* 9: 73–80. https://doi.org/10.1016/j.promfg.2017.04.022.

Bar, Michael, and Oksana Leukhina. 2010. 'Demographic Transition and Industrial Revolution: A Macroeconomic Investigation'. *Review of Economic Dynamics* 13 (2): 424–51. https://doi.org/10.1016/j.red.2009.03.002.

Barlow, Peter W., and Joachim Fisahn. 2013. 'Swarms, Swarming and Entanglements of Fungal Hyphae and of Plant Roots'. *Communicative & Integrative Biology* 6 (5): e25299. https://doi.org/10.4161/cib.25299.

Beale, Johnathan. 2024. 'UK Citizen Army: Preparing the "pre-War Generation" for Conflict'. *BBC News*, January 25. https://www.bbc.com/news/uk-68097048.

Bearne, Suzanne. 2023. 'Digital Nomads: Rising Number of People Choose to Work Remotely'. *Newspaper*, November 4. https://www.theguardian.com/money/2023/nov/04/digital-nomads-work-remotely-tech-visas.

Becker, Sascha O., and Ludger Woessmann. 2019. 'Education and Socioeconomic Development During the Industrialization'. In *Handbook of Cliometrics*, edited by Claude Diebolt and Michael Haupert. Springer International Publishing. https://doi.org/10.1007/978-3-030-00181-0_75.

Bertalanffy, Ludwig von. 1969. *General System Theory: Foundations, Development, Applications*. Revised edition. Braziller.

Bogdanov, A. 1989. *Tektologii͡a: Vseobshchai͡a Organizat͡sionnai͡a Nauka* (*Tektology: Universal Organization Science*). Russian edition. Ėkonomicheskoe Nasledie. Ėkonomika.

Bosshardt, William, and Jane S. Lopus. 2013. 'Business in the Middle Ages: What Was the Role of Guilds?' *Social Education, National Council for the Social Studies* 77 (2): 64–67.

Boston Dynamics. 2025. 'Boston Dynamics Etnical Principles'. Company Website. Boston Dynamics. https://bostondynamics.com/ethics/.

Bouckaert, Stéphanie, Araceli Fernandez Pales, Christophe McGlade, Remme Uwe, Brent Wanner, and Laszlo Varro,. 2021. *Net Zero by 2050 – A Roadmap for the Global Energy Sector*. International Energy Agency (IEA), October. https://iea.blob.core.windows.net/assets/deebef5d-0c34-4539-9d0c-10b13d840027/NetZeroby2050-ARoadmapfortheGlobalEnergySector_CORR.pdf.

Brebner, John Bartlett. 1848. 'Laissez Faire and State Intervention in Nineteenth-Century Britain'. *The Journal of Economic History* 8 (S1): 59–73.

Buchanan, Geoff. 2016. 'From Samoa to Caepr Via Mumeka: The Hybrid Economy Comes of Age'. In *Engaging Indigenous Economy*, edited by Will Sanders, vol. 35. Debating Diverse Approaches. ANU Press. https://www.jstor.org/stable/j.cttld10hpt.8.

Burnes, Bernard, and Hwanho Choi. 2021. 'Hybrid Economy in the Digital Age: The Case of the Independent Music Community in Korea'. *Technology in Society* 65 (May): 101582. https://doi.org/10.1016/j.techsoc.2021.101582.

Caradonna, Jeremy L. 2014. *Sustainability: A History*. Revised and Updated edition. Oxford University Press. https://doi.org/10.1093/oso/9780197625026.001.0001.

Chang, Ha-joon. 2007. *Kicking Away the Ladder: Development Strategy in Historical Perspective*. Reprinted. Anthem Studies in Development and Globalization. Anthem Press.

Channer, Mark. 2024. 'Defence Secretary Warns UK Has "Come Full Circle, Moving from a Post-War to Pre-War World"'. *London Loves Business*, January 16. https://londonlovesbusiness.com/defence-secretary-warns-uk-has-come-full-circle-moving-from-a-post-war-to-pre-war-world/.

Chartered Institute of Personnel and Development. 2019. *Economic Transformation Remains the Biggest Driver of Change in Organisations*. CIPD Thought Leadership. Chartered Institute of Personnel and Development. https://www.cipd.org/en/views-and-insights/thought-leadership/people-profession/economic-transformation-driver-change-organisations/.

Clemmons, Elizabeth. 2024. 'Understanding The Digital Regulation Landscape | IDC Blog'. Markets and Trends. IDC, November 8. https://blogs.idc.com/2024/11/08/understanding-the-digital-regulation-landscape/.

Crowther, T. W., H. B. Glick, K. R. Covey, et al. 2015. 'Mapping Tree Density at a Global Scale'. *Nature* 525 (7568): 201–5. https://doi.org/10.1038/nature14967.

Cuff, Madeleine. 2021. 'There Are More Lego People than Real Ones, and Other Strange and Fascinating Facts about Our Planet – The i Paper'. *The I Paper*, May 12. https://inews.co.uk/news/environment/there-are-more-lego-people-than-real-ones-and-other-strange-and-fascinating-facts-about-our-planet-997706.

Daft, Richard L. 1986. *Organization Theory and Design*. 2nd edition. West Pub. Co.

Davis, Jerome. 1927. 'Henry Ford, Educator – The Atlantic'. *The Atlantic*, June. https://www.theatlantic.com/magazine/archive/1927/06/henry-ford-educator/649476/.

Davis, Johnny. 2017. 'How Lego Clicked: The Super Brand That Reinvented Itself'. Life and Style. *The Guardian*, June 4. https://www.theguardian.com/lifeandstyle/2017/jun/04/how-lego-clicked-the-super-brand-that-reinvented-itself.

Department of Foreign Affairs (Ireland). 2023. Case Study: Unilever PLC. Department of Foreign Affairs (Ireland). https://www.gov.ie/en/department-of-foreign-affairs/publications/case-study-unilever-plc/.

Edgell, Stephen, and Edward Granter. 2005. *The Sociology of Work*. 3rd edition. SAGE.

Elad, Barry. 2025. 'LEGO Statistics By Revenue, Net Sales, Gross Profit, Demographics And Notable Releases'. *Coolest Gadgets*, March 18. https://coolest-gadgets.com/lego-statistics/.

Engler, Philipp, Margaux MacDonald, Roberto Piazza, and Galen Sher. 2020. 'Migration to Advanced Economies Can Raise Growth'. IMF Blog, June 19. https://www.imf.org/en/blogs/articles/2020/06/19/blog-weo-chapter4-migration-to-advanced-economies-can-raise-growth.

Epstein, Steven. 1991. *Wage Labor & Guilds in Medieval Europe*. University of North Carolina Press.

Ericson, S. J. 2000. 'The Industrial Revolution in the Twentieth Century, with a Focus on Japan and the East Asian Followers'. *OAH Magazine of History* 15 (1): 24–29. https://doi.org/10.1093/maghis/15.1.24.

EY. 2024. 'Why Companies Must Prepare Now for the New EU AI Act.' Legal. EY Insights, July 17. https://www.ey.com/en_gl/insights/public-policy/why-companies-must-prepare-now-for-the-new-eu-ai-act.

Fairtrade Foundation. 2025. 'Helping Ben & Jerry's Provide Living Incomes'. https://www.fairtrade.net/us-en/for-business/benefits-of-being-certified/business-success-stories/helping-ben---jerry-s-provide-living-incomes.html.

Farr, James Richard. 2000. *Artisans in Europe, 1300–1914*. New Approaches to European History 19. Cambridge University Press.

Field, Katie, and Emily Magkourilou. 2023. 'Do Trees Really Stay in Touch via a "Wood-Wide Web"? Here's What the Evidence Says'. *The Conversation*, February 13. https://theconversation.com/do-trees-really-stay-in-touch-via-a-wood-wide-web-heres-what-the-evidence-says-199806.

Fishman, Charles. 2001. *Why Can't Lego Click?* Fast Company, August 31.https://www.fastcompany.com/43497/why-cant-lego-click.

Gaines, Jeremy. 2021. 'Europe To Be Short 44 Million Workers by 2050 Without Increased Immigration, New Study Finds'. Press Release. Center For Global Development. https://www.cgdev.org/article/europe-be-short-44-million-workers-2050-without-increased-immigration-new-study-finds.

Gatzweiler, Franz. 2023. *IR 4.0 Is Not a Scientific Revolution: A Paradigm Shift in the Making*. United Nations University, March 28. https://unu.edu/macau/blog-post/ir-40-not-scientific-revolution-paradigm-shift-making.

Gauntlett, David. 2014. 'The Lego System as a Tool for Thinking, Creativity, and Changing the World'. In *LEGO Studies: Examining the Building Blocks of a Transmedial Phenomenon*, edited by Mark Wolf. Routledge. https://doi.org/10.4324/9781315858012.

Gilchrist, Alasdair. 2016. Industry 4.0. Apress. https://doi.org/10.1007/978-1-4842-2047-4.

GitLab, Inc. 2021. The Remote Work Report 2021. https://about.gitlab.com/resources/downloads/remote-work-report-2021.pdf.

Glaser, S., and M. I. Halliday. 1980. 'Organizations as Systems'. *Human Relations* 33 (12): 917–28. https://doi.org/10.1177/001872678003301203.

Goodwin, Brian C. 1994. *How the Leopard Changed Its Spots: The Evolution of Complexity*. C. Scribner's Sons.

Government Office for Science. 2021. 'Demographic Trends'. Trend Deck 2021 / Foresight. https://www.gov.uk/government/publications/trend-deck-2021-demographics.

Hailwood, Mark. 2014. *"The Rabble That Cannot Read"? Ordinary People's Literacy in Seventeenth-Century England*. The Many-Headed Monster. https://manyheaded-monster.com/2014/10/13/the-rabble-that-cannot-read-ordinary-peoples-literacy-in-seventeenth-century-england/.

He, Ping, and Xiaoting Ni. 2022. 'Renewable Energy Sources in the Era of the Fourth Industrial Revolution: A Perspective of Civilization Development'. *Journal of Physics: Conference Series* 2301 (1): 012030. https://doi.org/10.1088/1742-6596/2301/1/012030.

Hecht, Ben. 2013. *Collaboration Is the New Competition*. Business. Harvard Business Review, July 10. https://hbr.org/2013/01/collaboration-is-the-new-compe?

Hirschman, Charles, and Elizabeth Mogford. 2009. 'Immigration and the American Industrial Revolution from 1880 to 1920'. *Social Science Research* 38 (4): 897–920. https://doi.org/10.1016/j.ssresearch.2009.04.001.

Holland, John H. 2006. 'Studying Complex Adaptive Systems'. *Journal of Systems Science and Complexity* 19 (1): 1–8. https://doi.org/10.1007/s11424-006-0001-z.

IBMSkillsBuild.2025.'Learners'.CompanyWebsite.IBM.https://skillsbuild.org/learners.

Jackson, Michael C. 2024. *Critical Systems Thinking: A Practitioner's Guide*. Wiley.

Jeanne, Ludovic, Sébastien Bourdin, Fabien Nadou, and Gabriel Noiret. 2022. 'Economic Globalization and the COVID-19 Pandemic: Global Spread and Inequalities'. *Geo Journal* 88 (1): 1181–88. https://doi.org/10.1007/s10708-022-10607–6.

Jovanovic, Boyan, and Peter L. Rousseau. 2005. 'General Purpose Technologies'. In *Handbook of Economic Growth*, edited by Philippe Aghion and Steven N. Durlauf, vol. 1. Elsevier. https://doi.org/10.1016/S1574-0684(05)01018-X.

Kapás, Judit. 2008. 'Industrial Revolutions and the Evolution of the Firm's Organization: An Historical Perspective'. *Journal of Innovation Economics & Management* 2 (2): 15–33. https://doi.org/10.3917/jie.002.0015.

Katz, Daniel, and Robert L. Kahn. 1966. *The Social Psychology of Organizations*. Wiley International edition. Wiley.

Kellaway, Kate. 2021. 'Secrets of a Tree Whisperer: "They Get Along, They Listen – They'Re Attuned"'. *The Guardian*, April 24. https://www.theguardian.com/environment/2021/apr/24/suzanne-simard-finding-the-mother-tree-woodwide-web-book-interview.

Kelly, Richard. 2019a. *Constructing Leadership 4.0: Swarm Leadership and the Fourth Industrial Revolution*. 2019th edition. Springer International Publishing : Imprint: Palgrave Macmillan. https://doi.org/10.1007/978-3-319-98062–1.

Kelly, Richard. 2019b. 'Teaching Your Company to Swarm'. *Management. Ivey Business Journal*. https://iveybusinessjournal.com/teaching-your-company-to-swarm/.

Kelly, Richard. 2022. *The Nature of Business Transformation: A Swarm Intelligent Approach to Reinventing Organisations*. Routledge.

Khan, Aubhik. 2008. *The Industrial Revolution and the Demographic Transition*. Business Review.

Klare, Michael T. 2014. 'Energy Wars: How Oil and Gas Are Fuelling Global Conflicts'. *Energy Post*, July 15. https://energypost.eu/twenty-first-century-energy-wars-oil-gas-fuelling-global-conflicts/.

Korać, Srdjan. 2018. 'Depersonalisation of Killing: Towards a 21st Century Use of Force "Beyond Good and Evil?"' *Filozofija i Drustvo* 29 (1): 49–64. https://doi.org/10.2298/FID1801049K.

Kramer, Mark R., and Marc W. Pfitzer. 2016. 'The Ecosystem of Shared Value'. *Harvard Business Review* 94 (10): 80–89.

Kuhn, Thomas S. 1962. *The Structure of Scientific Revolutions*. University of Chicago Press.

Lewin, Roger. 1992. *Complexity: Life at the Edge of Chaos*. Macmillan Pub. Co.; Maxwell Macmillan Canada ; Maxwell Macmillan International.

Longmire, Phillip. 2024. 'Beyond One-Size-Fits-All: The Shift to Adaptive Education'. Business. Medium, February 11. https://medium.com/@plongmire2023/beyond-one-size-fits-all-the-shift-to-adaptive-education-5ec90a63a2a7.

Loose, Crystal, Michael Ryan, and Rose Jagielo-Manion. 2023. 'Creating a Learning Environment for the Fifth Industrial Revolution'. In *Innovative Approaches to Technology-Enhanced Learning for the Workplace and Higher Education*, edited by David Guralnick, Michael E. Auer, and Antonella Poce, vol. 581. Lecture Notes in Networks and Systems. Springer International Publishing. https://doi.org/10.1007/978-3-031-21569-8_21.

Lorenz, Edward N. 1972. 'Predictability: Does the Flap of a Butterfly's Wings in Brazil Set Off a Tornado in Texas?' American Association for the Advancement of Sciences (139th meeting)., Massachusetts Institute of Technology (MIT). https://web.archive.org/web/20130612164541/http://eaps4.mit.edu/research/Lorenz/Butterfly_1972.pdf.

Lorenz, Markus, Michael Rüßmann, Rainer Strack, Knud Lueth, and Moritz Bolle. 2015. *How Will Technology Transform the Industrial Workforce Through 2025?* Corporate. Man and Machine in Industry 4.: 0, September 28. https://www.bcg.com/publications/2015/technology-business-transformation-engineered-products-infrastructure-man-machine-industry-4.

Malthus, Thomas Robert. 1798. *An Essay on the Principle of Population, as It Affects the Future Improvement of Society*. J. Johnson.

Marshall, Claire. 2019. 'Wood Wide Web: Trees' Social Networks Are Mapped'. *BBC*, May 15. https://www.bbc.com/news/science-environment-48257315.

McLuhan, Marshall. 1962. *The Gutenberg Galaxy: The Making of Typographic Man*. University of Toronto Press.

McNamara, C. 2005. *Field Guide to Consulting and Organizational Development with Nonprofits: A Collaborative and Systems Approach to Performance, Change, and Learning*. 1st edition. Authenticity Consulting.

Merrill, Paul. 2022. 'The Cautionary and Inspirational Story of How Lego Rebuilt Itself'. *The CEO Magazine*, June 15. https://www.theceomagazine.com/business/company-profile/rebuilding-lego/.

Milone, Carlo. 2022. 'Future of Renewable Energy: AI'. Quanta Part of QCS Staffing, September 15. http://www.quanta-cs.com/blogs/2022-9/is-artificial-intelligence-the-future-of-renewable-energy.

Mokyr, Joel. 2001. 'The Rise and Fall of the Factory System: Technology, Firms, and Households since the Industrial Revolution'. *Carnegie-Rochester Conference Series on Public Policy* 55 (1): 1–45. https://doi.org/10.1016/S0167-2231(01)00050–1.

Monbiot, George. 2008. 'One Thing Is Clear from the History of Trade: Protectionism Makes You Rich'. Opinion. *The Guardian*, September 8. https://www.theguardian.com/commentisfree/2008/sep/09/eu.globaleconomy.

Morland, Paul. 2024. 'Britain's Birth Dearth Is Holding Our Economy Back'. CapX, July 4. https://capx.co/britains-birth-dearth-is-holding-our-economy-back.

Nandi-Ray, Anita. 2025. *Quantum Governance : Why Boards Must Lead the Next Technological Revolution*. Business. Institute of Directors, India, May 8. https://www.iodglobal.com/blog/details/quantum-governance-why-boards-must-lead-the-next-technological-revolution.

Newton, Derek. 2020. 'LEGO Is Probably The Biggest Education Company On Earth'. Forbes, February 8. https://www.forbes.com/sites/dereknewton/2020/02/08/lego-is-probably-the-biggest-education-company-on-earth/.

Nguyen, Therese. 2021. 'What It Was Really Like As A Worker In The Industrial Revolution'. Grunge, January 28. https://www.grunge.com/321858/what-it-was-really-like-as-a-worker-in-the-industrial-revolution/.

Nold, Herbert, and Lukas Michel. 2021. 'Organizational Culture: A Systems Approach'. In *Accounting and Finance Innovations*, edited by Nizar M. Alsharari. IntechOpen. https://doi.org/10.5772/intechopen.97466.

Officer, Alana, Jotheeswaran Amuthavalli Thiyagarajan, Mira Leonie Schneiders, Paul Nash, and Vânia De La Fuente-Núñez. 2020. 'Ageism, Healthy Life Expectancy and Population Ageing: How Are They Related?' *International Journal of Environmental Research and Public Health* 17 (9): 3159. https://doi.org/10.3390/ijerph17093159.

Oliver, Keith, Edouard Samakh, and Peter Heckmann. 2007. 'Rebuilding Lego, Brick by Brick'. Strategy+Business, August 29. https://www.strategy-business.com/article/07306.

Ørsted. 2025. *Local Community Partnerships: Investing in Your Community, for Today and Tomorrow. Ørsted Our Impact.* Ørsted. https://us.orsted.com/our-impact/local-community-partnerships.

Pascale, Richard T., Mark Millemann, and Linda Gioja. 2000. *Surfing the Edge of Chaos: The Laws of Nature and the New Laws of Business.* Texere.

Pasimeni, Francesco. 2021. 'The Origin of the Sharing Economy Meets the Legacy of Fractional Ownership'. *Journal of Cleaner Production* 319 (October): 128614. https://doi.org/10.1016/j.jclepro.2021.128614.

Patagonia. 2025. 'Patagonia's Mission Statement'. Company Website. Patagonia. https://www.patagonia.com.hk/pages/our-mission?srsltid=AfmBOoqlbMhc_3wW2dUwi9eDlT5qAwSsk1IZMSqPa1mTfSSrg7CR6_9&utm.

Perone, S., and V.R. Simmering. 2017. 'Applications of Dynamic Systems Theory to Cognition and Development'. In *Advances in Child Development and Behavior*, edited by Janette Benson B, vol. 52. Elsevier. https://doi.org/10.1016/bs.acdb.2016.10.002.

Peters, Michael A. 2019. 'Beyond Technological Unemployment: The Future of Work'. *Educational Philosophy and Theory* 52 (5): 485–91. https://doi.org/10.1080/00131857.2019.1608625.

Raworth, Kate. 2017. *Doughnut Economics: Seven Ways to Think like a 21st-Century Economist.* Random House Business Books.

Responsive.org. 2025. 'Responsive Manifesto'. Business. Responsive.Org. https://www.responsive.org/.

Richard, Brice. 2022. 'A New Understanding of the Green Economy'. Sustainability. ARUP, November. https://www.arup.com/insights/a-new-understanding-of-the-green-economy/.

Rifkin, Jeremy. 2012. 'A New Economic Narrative: Industrial Revolution 3.0'. https://ourworld.unu.edu/en/a-new-economic-narrative-industrial-revolution-3–0.

Rifkin, Jeremy. 2015. 'Welcome to the Third Industrial Revolution'. *Wharton Magazine.* https://magazine.wharton.upenn.edu/issues/summer-2015/welcome-to-the-third-industrial-revolution/.

Ritchie, Hannah. 2021. 'How Have the World's Energy Sources Changed Over the Last Two Centuries?' Our World in Data, December 1. https://ourworldindata.org/global-energy-200-years.

Robbins, Jim. 2022. 'Can Geothermal Power Play a Key Role in the Energy Transition?' Yale E360, December 22. https://e360.yale.edu/features/can-geothermal-power-play-a-key-role-in-the-energy-transition.

Robertson, David, and Bill Breen. 2013. *Brick by Brick: How Lego Rewrote the Rules of Innovation and Conquered the Global Toy Industry*. 1st edition. Crown Business.

Roos, Johan, and Bart Victor. 2018. 'How It All Began: The Origins Of LEGO® Serious Play®'. *International Journal of Management and Applied Research*, December 21, 326–43. https://doi.org/10.18646/2056.54.18-025.

Rosenman, Ellen. 2012. 'On Enclosure Acts and the Commons'. History. Branch, December. https://branchcollective.org/?ps_articles=ellen-rosenman-on-enclosure-acts-and-the-commons.

Roser, Max, and Hannah Ritchie. 2023. 'How Has World Population Growth Changed over Time?' Our World in Data, December 28. https://ourworldindata.org/population-growth-over-time.

Rota, Mauro, and Luca Spinesi. 2024. 'Economic Growth Before the Industrial Revolution: Rural Production and Guilds in the European Little Divergence'. *Economic Modelling* 130 (January): 106590. https://doi.org/10.1016/j.econmod.2023.106590.

Roy, Mousumi. 2018. 'Asia's Role in the Four Industrial Revolutions'. *Education About Asia* 23 (1). https://www.asianstudies.org/publications/eaa/archives/asias-role-in-the-four-industrial-revolutions/.

Rozite, Vida, Jack Miller, and Sungjin Oh. 2023. 'Why Ai and Energy Are the New Power Couple'. IEA, November 2. https://www.iea.org/commentaries/why-ai-and-energy-are-the-new-power-couple.

Rzevski, G., and P. Skobelev. 2014. *Managing Complexity*. WIT Press.

Salesforce. 2025. 'Our Impact'. Company Website. Salesforce. https://www.salesforce.com/company/impact/.

Saloutos, Theodore. 1962. 'Protection and Industry: 1866–1919'. *Current History* 42 (250): 339–64.

Satell, Greg. 2013. 'The New Age Of Disruption'. Business. Forbes, September 21. https://www.forbes.com/sites/gregsatell/2013/09/21/the-new-age-of-disruption/?sh=6afbc9e379e1.

Scharmer, Claus Otto. 2013. *Leading from the Emerging Future: From Ego-System to Eco-System Economies*. 1st edition. With Katrin Käufer. BK Currents. Berrett-Koehler Publishers, Incorporated.

Schultz, Majken, and Mary Jo Hatch. 2003. 'The Cycles of Corporate Branding: The Case of the LEGO Company'. *California Management Review* 46 (1): 6–26. https://doi.org/10.2307/41166229.

Schwab, Klaus. 2016. *The Fourth Industrial Revolution*. 1st U.S. edition. Crown Business.

Shankar, Anil. 2022. 'Automated Governance and Trustworthy AI'. Company Website. IBM Think, June 7. https://www.ibm.com/think/insights/automated-ai-governance.

Sherman, Howard J., and Ron Schultz. 1998. *Open Boundaries: Creating Business Innovation Through Complexity*. Perseus Books.

Singh, Jahanvi. 2023. 'Inventions during the Industrial Revolutions (Industry 1.0–4.0)'. Medium, January 15. https://bootcamp.uxdesign.cc/inventions-during-the-industrial-revolutions-industry-1-0-4-0-73a0cb148a0f.

Smith, Tyler. 2020. 'The Road to the Industrial Revolution'. History. American Economic Association, April 15. https://www.aeaweb.org/research/transportation-industrial-revolution-spatial-uk.

Souza, Normando Laudiceia, Teresinha Fonseca, Jandira Reis Vasconcelos, Cleide Ane Barbosa Da Cruz, and Ana Eleonora Almeida Paixão. 2020. 'Pillars of Technological Advancement and Indicators of Scientific Production of Industry 4.0'. *International Journal for Innovation Education and Research* 8 (4): 245–57. https://doi.org/10.31686/ijier.vol8.iss4.2286.

Spieler, Marc. 2023. 'How AI Is Powering the Future of Clean Energy'. NVIDIA Blog, July 27. https://blogs.nvidia.com/blog/i-am-ai-clean-energy/.

The Economic Times Magazine. 2017. 'No Time to Kill: How Smartphone Is Pushing Chewing Gum Out of Fashion'. *The India Times*, July 5. https://economictimes.indiatimes.com/magazines/panache/no-time-to-kill-how-smartphone-is-pushing-chewing-gum-out-of-fashion/articleshow/59458784.cms.

The Renewable Energy Institute. 2023. *AI: The Secret to Unlocking the Potential of Renewable Energy?* The Renewable Energy Institute, June 14. https://www.renewableinstitute.org/ai-the-secret-to-unlocking-the-potential-of-renewable-energy/.

Turner, Paul. 2021. 'Management During the Third Industrial Revolution: Asian Tigers and Global Players'. In *The Making of the Modern Manager: Mapping Management Competencies from the First to the Fourth Industrial Revolution*, edited by Paul Turner. Springer International Publishing. https://doi.org/10.1007/978-3-030-81062-7_4.

UK Parliamentary. 2024. *Schooling Before the 19th Century*. UK Parliament. https://www.parliament.uk/about/living-heritage/transformingsociety/livinglearning/school/overview/before19thcentury/.

United Nations. n.d. *Population*. United Nations. https://www.un.org/en/global-issues/population.

Varoufakis, Yanis. 2023. *Technofeudalism: What Killed Capitalism*. The Bodley Head.

Vince, Gaia. 2022. 'The Century of Climate Migration: Why We Need to Plan for the Great Upheaval'. *The Guardian*, August 18. https://www.theguardian.com/news/2022/aug/18/century-climate-crisis-migration-why-we-need-plan-great-upheaval.

Von Tunzelmann, Nick. 2003. 'Historical Coevolution of Governance and Technology in the Industrial Revolutions'. *Structural Change and Economic Dynamics* 14 (4): 365–84. https://doi.org/10.1016/S0954-349X(03)00029-8.

Waldrop, M. Mitchell. 1993. *Complexity: The Emerging Science at the Edge of Order and Chaos*. 1st edition. A Touchstone Book. Touchstone.

Ward, J. R. 1994. 'The Industrial Revolution and British Imperialism, 1750-1850'. *The Economic History Review* 47 (1): 44–65. https://doi.org/10.2307/2598220.

Welch, Jack. 2000. *To Our Customers, Share Owners and Employees*. Annual Report. General Electric Company.

Whelpton, P. K. 1928. 'Industrial Development and Population Growth'. *Social Forces* 6 (4): 629–638. https://doi.org/10.2307/3004356.

Whiteside, Noel. 2014. 'The Beveridge Report and Its Implementation: A Revolutionary Project?' *Histoire@Politique* 24 (3): 24–37. https://doi.org/10.3917/hp.024.0024.

Wiencek, Henry. 1987. *The World of LEGO Toys*. Harry N. Abrams.

Wilde, Robert. 2025. *Population Growth and Movement in the Industrial Revolution*. ThoughtCo, May 5. https://www.thoughtco.com/population-growth-and-movement-industrial-revolution-1221640.

Woolley-Barker, Tamsin. 2017. *Teeming: How Superorganisms Work to Build: Infinite Wealth in a Finite World* (and Your Company Can Too). White Cloud Press.

World Health Organisation. 2024. 'Ageing and Health'. https://www.who.int/news-room/fact-sheets/detail/ageing-and-health.

Wu, Chiahuei, and Sharon K. Parker. 2011. *Proactivity in the Workplace*. Oxford University Press. https://doi.org/10.1093/oxfordhb/9780199734610.013.0007.

Xiaonan, Wang. 2019. 'A Brief History of Tariffs and War'. May 24. https://news.cgtn.com/news/3d3d514e3459444f34457a6333566d54/index.html.

Yang, Jianfeng, Yun Yu, Teng Ma, Cuiguang Zhang, and Quan Wang. 2021. 'Evolution of Energy and Metal Demand Driven by Industrial Revolutions and Its Trend Analysis'. *Chinese Journal of Population, Resources and Environment* 19 (3): 256–64. https://doi.org/10.1016/j.cjpre.2021.12.028.

Zhou, Haiwen. 2019. 'Population Growth and Industrialization'. *Economic Inquiry* 47 (2): 249–65. https://doi.org/10.1111/j.1465-7295.2008.00151.x.

Chapter 3

Developing Adaptive Workplace Cultures

It all started over a cup of coffee. In 1981, Howard Schultz, then working for a US subsidiary of Hammarplast, a Swedish kitchenware manufacturer, noticed that a small coffeehouse called Starbucks Coffee Company in Seattle was ordering an unusually large quantity of plastic cone filters for drip coffee makers. He grew curious and flew from New York to see them. From the moment Schultz entered the coffeehouse and took his first sip of Starbucks' coffee, he fell in love with what he describes in his book with coauthor Dori Jones Yang (1997) as the "romance" of carefully sourced, whole-bean Arabica coffee served in porcelain cups. Schultz was so impressed by the company that he left his executive position in 1982 to work for Starbucks as Director of Retail Operations and Marketing. By 1985, he was chairman. The company went public in 1992 and has since become a global brand. Today, it has a market cap that exceeds $100 billion and ranks among the top 200 most valuable global companies.

The point of interest here is not the firm's spreadsheets or financial performance, but how Schultz carefully preserved and nurtured its organisational culture.[1] At Starbucks, culture is not an afterthought; it is the driving force behind its strategy, growth, brand, and people.[2] Starbucks' mission (Our Starbucks Mission 2025) connects the coffee experience with the human experience, not through corporate charters and mandates, but through culture and values. As Schultz says, "it's the story of a team of people who built a successful enterprise based on values and guiding principles" (Schultz and Yang 1997, 8). For Schultz, organisational culture is key:

> Whatever your culture, your values, your guiding principles, you have to take steps to inculcate them in the organization early in its

DOI: 10.4324/9781003680345-3

> life so that they can guide every decision, every hire, every strategic objective you set… Establishing the right tone at the inception of an enterprise, whatever its size, is vital to its long-term success.
>
> (Schultz and Yang 1997, 81)

Davidson and Leinwand (2016) reflect on how these cultures, values, and general principles drive organisational purpose:

> The feel of Starbucks stores isn't created merely by the layout and the décor – it exists because the people behind the counter understand how their work fits into a common purpose, and recognize how to accomplish great things together without needing to follow a script.

In an open letter, Brian Niccol, who took over as Starbucks chairman and CEO, acknowledged that, in some stores, the company had lost its purpose and become transactional. In an initiative called *Back to Starbucks*, he pledged to reengage with Starbucks' core culture by empowering local baristas and reviving the "community coffeehouse" (Niccol 2024).

Building culture from the ground up in a young startup is challenging, but repairing a failing culture in a mature global company when the "water's already in the well" takes tremendous effort and deep soul searching (Schultz and Yang 1997, 80).

This opening Starbucks' case study sets up three key considerations central to this chapter on adaptive organisational culture:

- Adaptive culture forms the keystone of adaptive organisations.
- Culture lies at the heart of organisational strategy.
- Culture isn't decreed from the top; it permeates through the organisation. Hans Magnus Enzensberger is reported to have said, "Culture is a little like dropping an Alka-Seltzer into a glass – you don't see it, but somehow it does something" (cited in Brons 2005, 15).

Organisational Culture: Context, Definitions, and Models

Balthazard, Cooke, and Potter (2006) describe organisational culture as the glue that holds organisations together. A World Economic Forum (WEF) white paper identifies organisational culture as the "backbone" of the organisation:

> Culture is the backbone of any organization and is a powerful mechanism to align a diverse pool of talent with the needs of the business. It acts as a way to unite the workforce and establish a cohesive way of doing things through common behaviors and attitudes.
>
> (Spagnoletto et al. 2019, 12)

Organisational culture, which is a sensemaking process according to Watkins (2023), is widely recognised as a key driver of organisational success.[3] Dave Coates and Philip Atkinson argue, "It is the infrastructure, the glue that binds together people and processes to generate results." (Coates and Atkinson 1993, 525). Organisational culture can boost employee morale (Asiedu 2015; Serinkan and Kiziloglu 2021), organisational effectiveness, and overall people performance, which, in turn, as Ayme Zemke (2025) observes, attracts top talent. Jim Hemerling and coauthors (2018) argue that a strong culture drives up financial performance. Dysfunctional and misaligned cultures can cause catastrophic organisational failures (Hald, Gillespie, and Reader 2021).

Herbert Nold and Lukas Michel (2021) remind us that historically, organisational culture was not a priority. Interest in the subject only began in the US in the nineteenth century (Ertosun and Zafer 2018). There was renewed interest in the topic with the Hawthorne Studies of the 1920s and 1930s, which, among other things, highlighted how social norms and values in the workplace impacted workforce behaviour.

Over the last fifty years organisational culture has become a key priority (Giorgi, Lockwood, and Glynn 2015; Bersin 2015) and a source of sustained competitive advantage (Barney 1991). Theories concerning why organisational culture has become more critical in recent years include the United States' loss of its competitive advantage to Japan in the mid-twentieth century (Nneji, Asikhia, and Akpa 2021), the rise of digital transformation (Yuko et al. 2023), the Covid-19 pandemic (Müller et al. 2023; Brown et al. 2024), and shifting generational values (Väänänen 2023). In a recent survey, 67 per cent of respondents believed that culture is more critical to an organisation than strategy or operations (Carpenter et al. 2021).

Defining organisational culture is challenging. Oznur Ertosun and Zafer Adiguzel (2018) call it a broad, complex, and "difficult" term. The concept originated from Andrew Pettigrew's 1979 article, "On Studying Organizational Cultures".[4] Over the decades, numerous definitions and models of organisational culture have emerged. A common view of organisational culture is that it is "the way things are done around here" (Lundy and Cowling 1996, 168).[5] However, organisational culture is more nuanced than this. S.M. Davis defined it as "the pattern of shared beliefs and values that give the members of an institution meaning, and provide them with the rules for behavior in their organization" (Davis 1984, n1). Others characterise it in terms of shared attitudes, values, and behaviours (Adler 1986; Hollister et al. 2021).[6] Edgar Schein notably emphasised its tacit quality, arguing that culture is the "learned, shared, tacit assumptions on which people base their daily behavior" (Schein, 1999 24). More recently, Nebojsa Janicijevic viewed organisational culture as a body of "collective cognitive structures" encompassing assumptions, values, norms, and attitudes (Janicijevic, 2012 128). A common theme in the scientific literature for organisational culture is identified by Gail Latta :

> Culture is fundamentally about meaning making. Common to all definitions of *culture* in organizations is the assertion that culture is a socially constructed reality rooted in cognitive processes of meaning making.
>
> (Latta 2009, 42)

A concise description that forms a working definition for *Building Adaptive Organisations* is from Andrew Brown's *Organisational Culture*:

> Organisational culture refers to the pattern of beliefs, values and learned ways of coping with experience that have developed during the course of an organisation's history, and which tend to be manifested in its material arrangements and in the behaviours of its members.
>
> (Brown 1995, 8)

This encapsulates the idea of organisational culture as socially constructed and part of a "social climate" (Mohelska and Sokolova 2015, 1012).

Chapter 1 introduced Cameron and Quinn's (2011) *Competing Values Framework*; however, numerous other cultural models and frameworks have been developed over the years to measure and understand organisational culture (see Figure 3.1).

In addition to these cultural models and frameworks, several commercial instruments and surveys are available to assess organisational culture.[7]

While these models and frameworks can help identify cultural blind spots and raise awareness of organisational culture, they often conceptualise culture as a "standalone organizational attribute" (Herbert Nold and Lukas Michel 2021), rather than a complex adaptive system. Models such as the *Competing Values Framework* were developed over fifty years ago, at the height of Industry 3.0, when knowledge-based industries were structured in a pyramidal manner and

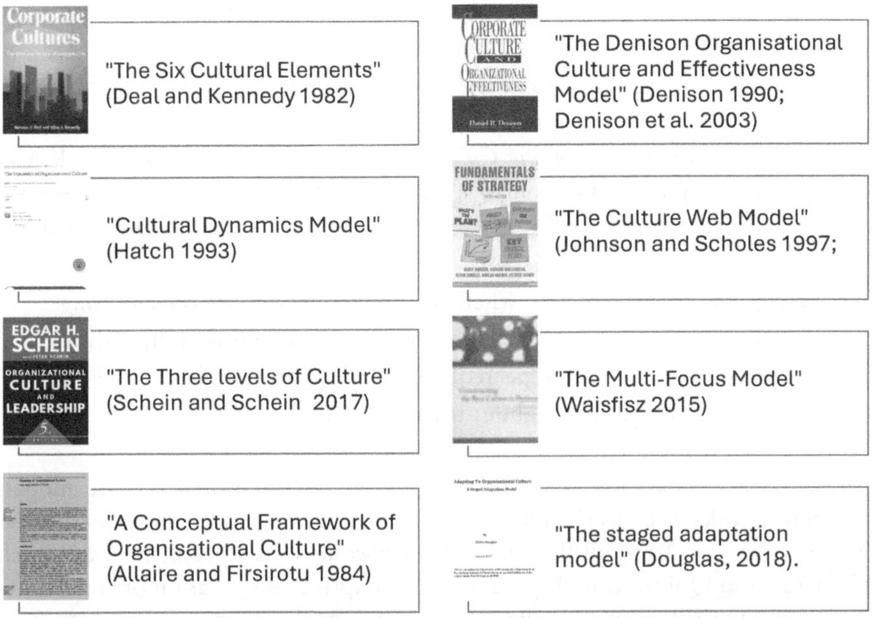

Figure 3.1 A selection of popular cultural models and frameworks.

managed through hierarchical systems, fixed employee models, status-based leadership, and presenteeism. As Tsui, Nifadkar, and Yi Ou (2007) argue, they are no longer relevant to today's challenges.

Adaptive Culture

Adaptive culture is widely recognised as a critical factor in the long-term success of organisations (Patel 2024; Kriegel 2023). Paul Fein (2019) reflects on how organisational culture can adapt to changing environments by being future-focused and responsive. Kilmann, Saxton, and Serpa provide a comprehensive definition of adaptive culture:

> An adaptive culture entails a risk-taking, trusting, and proactive approach to organizational as well as individual life. Members actively support one another's efforts to identify all problems and implement workable solutions. There is a shared feeling of confidence: the members believe, without a doubt, that they can effectively manage whatever new problems and opportunities will come their way. There is widespread enthusiasm, a spirit of doing

> whatever it takes to achieve organizational success. The members are receptive to change and innovation.
>
> (Kilmann et al. 1985, 356)

In their seminal work *Corporate Culture and Performance* (1992), John Kotter and James Heskett usefully compare adaptive cultures with "unadaptive" cultures.[8] Richard Claydon and Geoff Marlow (2022) link it to people performance:

> Adaptive cultures occur where the *sense-making, decision-making and action-taking* inherent to high performing teams become tightly coupled, rapidly and repeatedly iterated, deeply embedded, and widely distributed throughout the organisation.

Organisational adaptability features in several organisational culture models and frameworks, such as the Denison Organisational Culture and Effectiveness Model (Denison 1990, 2003) and the *Competing Values Framework* in which Cameron and Quinn formally characterise adaptive culture as an organisation's "capability to shift emphases when the demands of the competitive environment require it" (Cameron and Quinn 2011, 68).

Chapter 1 showed how adaptive organisations, such as Netflix, are more likely to survive in volatile, complex times when they grasp new opportunities and proactively adjust to changing conditions.[9] An adaptive culture offers several key advantages: it encourages diversification, enhances financial performance, improves customer services, strengthens overall business performance, drives innovation, and boosts employee motivation, satisfaction, and productivity. More recently, adaptability has been instrumental in ensuring that organisations are better prepared to undergo digital transformation.[10]

Building a Resilient and Adaptive Organisational Culture

Dave Coates and Philip Atkinson argue that "Eighty per cent of organisational cultures exist by accident or default, rather than design" (Coates and Atkinson 1993, 526). The challenge for organisations is to design and sustain a resilient, adaptive organisational culture that can thrive in volatile and uncertain environments.[11] There are numerous theories on shaping organisational culture, which can be broadly grouped into direct and indirect interventions.[12]

Shaping Organisational Culture through Direct Intervention

Direct intervention represents the traditional approach to shaping organisational culture and includes directive leadership, mergers and acquisitions, and top-down mandates and decrees.

1. Directive leadership
   Implementing culture through directive leadership is well-researched.[13] Top-down command, used for centuries in military contexts, can be an effective way to create stability; however, as Cameron and Quinn (2011) remind us, it stifles adaptability and innovation and can negatively impact organisational culture. Chapter 1 illustrated how Wayne Huizenga's directive and status-driven leadership style as Blockbuster's CEO was a significant contributor to the company's dysfunctional culture and organisational decline. Kotter, Akhtar, and Gupta (2021) argue that "relying on leaders to define the culture and cascade it throughout the organization, or fully outsourcing the responsibility of shaping and building culture to an HR group – rarely produce real results". A key risk of fashioning the organisation in the leader's image is that it reinforces monoculturalism, leaving the organisation vulnerable and directionless once the leader has quit the company. In extreme cases, toxic leaders can destroy organisational culture. WeWork's Adam Neumann is a notable example of an irresponsible leader whose "reckless spending, hard-partying lifestyle, and questionable business decisions ultimately led to his downfall" (Carlin 2022). The organisational culture had a direct impact on WeWork's valuation, which, according to Emanuele Midolo (2020), plummeted to less than a third of its value by the time Neumann resigned in 2019.
2. Mergers and acquisitions
   Another form of imposed culture is mergers and acquisitions. Organisational culture is seen as a critical factor in determining the success or failure of mergers and acquisitions.[14] Günter Stahl and Andreas Voigt (2008) believe mergers and acquisitions can create both obstacles and value for the organisational culture. Satu Teerikangas and Olivier Irrmann (2016) argue that it needs to be well managed to be effective. We saw in Chapter 1 that Blockbuster's blitzscaling strategy proved disastrous for the company. Disney's acquisition of Pixar Animation Studios took place in 2006 for $7.4 billion. According to Gasparini, Vieira, and Dias (2025), Pixar was nervous during negotiations that Disney would destroy its unique culture, despite strong contractual agreements that guaranteed the organisation's independence. The Disney-Pixar merger turned out to be a "strategic triumph", strengthening both brands and leading to renewed profitability. Gasparini, Vieira, and Dias (2025) consider it a strong merger model that

maintains creative autonomy. It has also proved to be an effective template for future Disney acquisitions.

3. Top-down mandates and decrees
The classic example of a top-down mandated change is the infamous 1300-word "burning platform" memo from Nokia's CEO, Stephen Elop, in 2011. Nokia's market share steadily declined throughout the 2010s, and Elop was brought in to turn things around for the Finnish mobile phone giant. Within a short time of his appointment, he issued a highly directive, alarmist memo that used a burning platform metaphor. He wrote, "We too, are standing on a 'burning platform', and we must decide how we are going to change our behaviour" (cited in Arthur 2011). Elop explains in the memo that the company was losing the smartphone war to Apple iOS and Google Android, blaming internal factors.

   Juha-Antti Lamberg and coauthors (2019) believe the problems with Nokia were not just technological choices, but ran deep in its organisational design, with "sluggish decision-making" (575) and unhealthy internal competition. Georges Y. Maalouf and Issam Jallad (2024) identify a chronic strategic blind spot in Nokia, saying it failed to understand the rise of the smartphone over the traditional mobile phone, which led to its rapid decline in market share.

   The point to emphasise here is that the top-down mandate approach spectacularly backfired. Stephen Elop thought he could cut through the sluggish culture by not consulting with the business or testing ideas. The memo leaked, markets got jittery amid the panic-driven language of burning platforms, and employees felt blindsided and were understandably mistrustful. The strategy failed to deliver a turnaround; morale fell to an all-time low, investor confidence eroded, and Nokia ultimately exited the mobile-phone business.

   This kind of experience has led authors, such as Bryan Walker and Sarah A. Soule (2017), to question this mandate-driven approach.[15]

Shaping Organisational Culture through Indirect Intervention

Imposed cultural transformation through leadership directives, mergers, and mandates has dominated organisational practice for decades. However, this model often produces compliance rather than genuine commitment, which undermines the cultural transformation. There is a growing recognition that culture is better shaped through indirect and informal practices, grounded in social norm research, adaptability theory, organisational design, and strategic alignment. Jennifer Chatman and her coauthors (2014), for example, view organisational culture as a set of social norms and values that develop over time through socialisation, alignment, and systems. Let's explore several ways culture can be built indirectly.

1. Building culture indirectly through social and cultural normalisation
   Changing an organisation's default culture through social norms and systems, an approach that Chatman and Cha (2003) term "normalisation", has become a growing area of research. This approach views cultural transformation as an incremental process that occurs through gradual socialisation and internalisation. Joanne Martin and Caren Siehl (1983) describe this as a form of "counterculture", where culture evolves organically rather than through forced transformation. The underlying assumption is that "culture develops gradually" (Rani and Srivastava 2015, 18) and cannot be mandated or enforced. Joerg Esser (2021) characterises adaptability as a form of cultural infusion:

   > The real issue is not successfully transforming your organization on a one-time basis – it's writing the ability to adapt and transform into the company's DNA. It's developing a mechanism or reflex for dealing with whatever crisis comes along, be it financial, technological, environmental, or health related.

From this perspective, organisational cultures and behaviours gradually emerge through processes of "norm formation", in which cultural norms are transmitted rather than imposed (Arrow and Burns 2004, 186–187).

This is not a new idea, Chester Barnard (1968) discussed the notion of social processes in informal organisations. O'Reilly and Chatman, along with their co-researchers, are pioneers in this method, defining culture as a "normative order, operating through informational and social influence, that guides and constrains the behavior of people in collectives" (O'Reilly and Chatman 1996, 160). Their work has influenced a generation of thinkers who conceptualise culture as a social system.[16] Within this framework, the terms "norms" and "normalisation" are central. Holly Arrow and K.L. Burns define social norms as "collective expectations about how to behave that are enacted in the patterned behavior of members over time" (Arrow and Burns 2004, 174). Socialisation plays a pivotal role in the transmission of organisational culture (Maanen et al. 1978; Pereira Da Silva et al. 2023), as it supports the formation of shared norms. Organisational socialisation is defined as "the process by which an individual acquires the social knowledge and skills necessary to assume an organizational role" (Maanen and Straw 1978, 3). Talya N. Bauer and coauthors (2007) describe how in organisational socialisation, newcomers transition from being "outsiders" to "insiders". The effectiveness of this transition depends on the organisation's capacity to support it, argue Bauer and Erdogan (2011), which can lead to higher job satisfaction, engagement, innovation, and collaboration. In *The Oxford Handbook of Organizational Socialization,* Connie Wanberg (2012) links the subject to overall organisational performance.

2. Building culture indirectly at the level of organisational design

   Another indirect way of building an adaptive culture is through organisational design. Chapters 4, 5, and 6 will explore how to build adaptability at the level of business architecture, which must be reconfigured to create an enduring adaptive culture (essential for the adaptive organisation). David Costanza and his team (2016) refer to this as intentionally developing organisational "infrastructure and capabilities that allow adaptation to such environmental changes" (361). The organisational design/business architecture comprises three coactive drivers: structure, governance, and workflow (see Figure 3.2).

   The cultural shift required for each of these business architecture pillars is highlighted in Table 3.1.

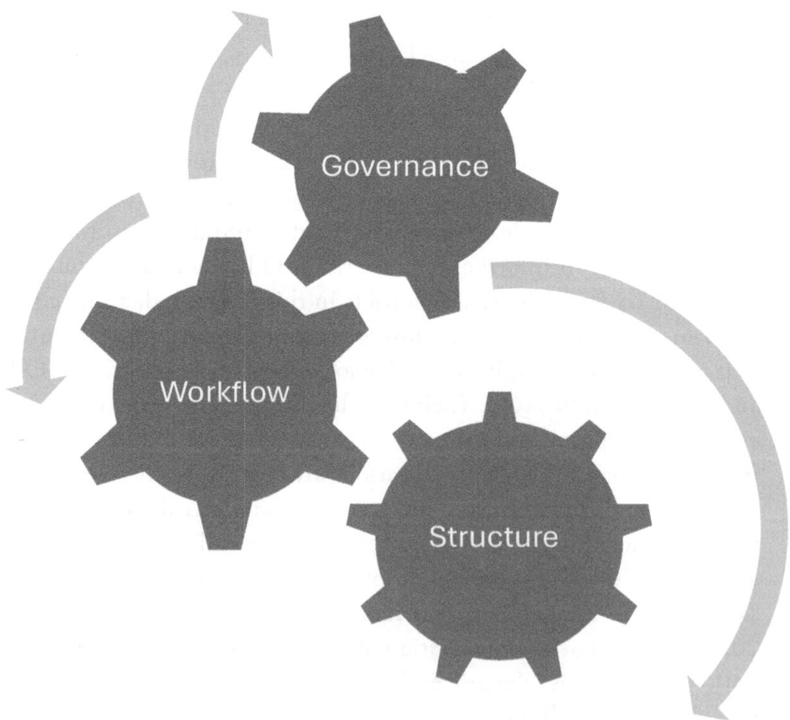

Figure 3.2 The three coactive drivers of the organisational design.

The following three sections explain table 3.1 and show how each organisational design pillar can indirectly influence culture.

i. Organisational structure and ecosystem cultures

Adaptive cultures thrive within ecosystems. Sergio Caredda (2024) emphasises their importance within organisational systems theory. Business strategist James Moore introduced the concept of business ecosystems in his influential 1993 *Harvard Business Review* article, and the term has gained popularity over the last 30 years. Inspired by biological ecosystems, business ecosystems are interlinked entities that encourage an outward (rather than inward) organisational focus. James Moore (1993) writes:

> I suggest a company be viewed not as a member of a single industry but as part of a business ecosystem that crosses a variety of industries. In a business ecosystem, companies coevolve capabilities around a new innovation: they work cooperatively and competitively to support new products, satisfy customer needs, and eventually incorporate the next round of innovations.

Elizabeth Altman and coauthors (2021) define workforce ecosystems as "a structure that consists of interdependent actors, from within the organization and beyond, working to pursue both individual and collective goals". An ecosystem culture thrives on relationships, boundaries, and interfaces between interdependent parts. John Geraci (2016) eloquently describes it in this way:

> Ecosystems, by contrast, are boundless, constantly able to grow, absorb new entities, adapt, react, and transform. They don't acquire new elements by ingesting them, but by absorbing new components at the edges of the network. And when they do that, they create new value for the whole ecosystem.

Nathan Furr and Andrew Shipilov (2018) believe this will encourage businesses to "collaborate in new ways with unlikely partners". Walter Shraiber (2023) notes that ecosystems highlight "the need to understand the relationships and dynamics between different parts of the organization and how they contribute to overall flexibility and resilience".

Chapter 2 introduced the STEP-WIDE wheel that supports organisations in developing their ecosystem quotient and mindset. Research by Gartner identifies eight dimensions of a business ecosystem (Panetta 2017). James Moore (1993) cites Apple, IBM, Ford, and Walmart as successful business ecosystem leaders. A more recent example is Netflix, which has had to navigate both emerging streaming competitors and

Table 3.1 A Cultural Comparison of Closed Versus Open Organisational Designs

	From...	*To...*
Structure	Monoculture • Hierarchical structures	Ecosystem • Modular structures
Governance	Managed • Status leaders (executive decision-making)	Self-organising • System leaders (collaborative decision-making)
Workflow	Programmatic • Process-led	Emergent • Business intelligence-led
Closed → Open		

traditional entertainment providers, such as network television, cable TV, and cinemas. Netflix's business ecosystem also extends to streaming service providers, content producers, and payment partners.

ii. Organisational governance and self-organising culture

An adaptive, self-organising culture thrives in an environment of decentralised governance. Adaptability cannot flourish in a top-down decision-making culture; it needs collective decision-making and peer accountability. At the governance level, culture shifts from command-and-control leadership to self-organising system leadership, and from centralised hierarchy to more open and adaptive self-organising systems. Eugene Pleasants Odum and Gary W. Barrett provide a helpful definition of self-organising systems:

> Self-organization can be defined as the process whereby complex systems consisting of many parts tend to organize to achieve some sort of stable, pulsing state in the absence of external interference. (Odum and Barrett 2005, 355)

Erich Jantsch's pioneering text, *The Self-Organizing Universe,* defines self-organisation as "the dynamic principle underlying the emergence of a rich world of forms manifest in biological, ecological, social and cultural structures" (Jantsch 1980, 19). It is a complex term that encapsulates dynamic systems that coevolve with the environment:

> The central aspects of the emerging paradigm of self-organisation are: *primo,* a specific macroscopic dynamics of process systems;

> *secondo*, continuous exchange and thereby co-evolution with the environment, and *tertio*, self-transcendence, the evolution of evolutionary processes (Jantsch 1980, 9)

A classic example of a self-organising system in business is the US-based manufacturing company *W.L. Gore & Associates*. Since its launch in 1958 by Bill and Vieve Gore, the company has embraced a unique self-managing culture. Daniel Roberts (2015) observes that the "lattice" structure at *W.L. Gore & Associates* eliminates rigid hierarchies, allowing workers (referred to as "associates") to operate with self-determination and to contribute to key decision-making.

iii. Organisational workflow and a culture of emergence

At the workflow level, culture shifts from a programmatic, process-led approach to a more emergent flow of business intelligence throughout the organisation. The concept of emergence, central to the philosophies of John Stuart Mill and Charles Darwin, is attributed to the psychologist George Henry Lewes, who reflected on "Life being an emergent" (Lewes 1874, 190). Comparable to self-organising systems, the term has a wide application, including in the natural world where organisms evolve "from low-level rules to higher-level sophistication" (Johnson 2001, 18). The term fell out of currency for a while but resurfaced during the rise of complexity theory. Many commentators resisted defining it until the 1990s. Kevin Mihata calls it "the process by which patterns or global-level structures arise from interactive local-level processes" (Mihata 1997, 31). Ralph Stacey provides a more comprehensive definition:

> Emergence is the production of global patterns of behavior by agents in a complex system interacting according to their own local rules of behavior, without intending the global patterns of behavior that come about. In emergence, global patterns cannot be predicted from the local rules of behavior that produce them. To put it another way, global patterns cannot be reduced to individual behavior. (Stacey 1996, 287)

Starbucks is a strong example of an organisation that embraces emergent practices. Its mission statement reflects this, aspiring "to be the premier purveyor of the finest coffee in the world, inspiring and nurturing the human spirit – one person, one cup and one neighbourhood at a time" ("Our Starbucks Mission" 2025). Airbnb is another compelling example of an emergent company. It grew from a simple idea into a global hospitality provider valued at billions. Zachary Weston (2023) recounts how two unemployed graduates rented an air mattress in their apartment to conference attendees in 2007. This small venture evolved into a worldwide network of hosts, known as Airbnb. Brian Chesky, co-founder and CEO of Airbnb, reportedly said when welcoming the company's first guest, Amol Surve, "We have to put a dent in the universe with this concept" (Stone 2017, 19). Chesky conceptualised the platform as a way for ordinary people to become "citizen hoteliers" by renting out personal space (Gallagher 2017, 70). Airbnb's rise reflected the broader zeitgeist of the late 2000s, shaped by the internet, smartphones, venture capital, the sharing economy (Kashanizadeh et al. 2024), and "informal tourism" (Guttentag 2015). As Brad Stone (2017) notes, companies like Uber and Airbnb emerged from this surge of technology and investment as "twin giants of a new era" (Stone 2017, 242). Brian Chesky places strong emphasis on organisational culture and explicitly discusses it with employees (Chesky 2014). Airbnb's adaptive and emergent culture, exemplified by its resilience during the Covid-19 pandemic, embodies its brand ethos of "Belong Anywhere".

The shift from a rigid to an adaptive organisation at the design and business architecture levels is an indirect way to develop and evolve the culture from a managed, top-down, and closed monoculture to a self-organising, emergent, open ecosystem. Figure 3.3 represents this as a conveyor belt.

Transforming from a closed to an open system requires an adaptive structure, governance and workflow. In Figure 3.3, the rollers symbolise the coactive systems that propel the cultural conveyor belt, enabling organisations to shift from a closed to an open system. These core organisational business architecture systems are interconnected, working in unison to drive organisational adaptability.

3. Building culture indirectly through transformational strategies

A final way of indirectly changing an organisation's default culture is through the alignment of transformational strategies. Recent research by Culture Partners and Stanford University shows that companies with an aligned culture, strategy, and purpose outperform organisations where these elements are misaligned (Kriegel 2023). There is broad consensus in the literature on the importance of aligning culture and strategy (e.g., Mutai 2015).[17] Many commentators highlight that organisational culture is often derailed if culture and strategy are misaligned.[18] The three strategic enablers presented in this book (digital, people, and change process) act as mobilisers of adaptive culture. Cultural transformation at the organisational design level can only be effective when it is reinforced and aligned with these strategic enablers or mobilisers. In other words, adaptability

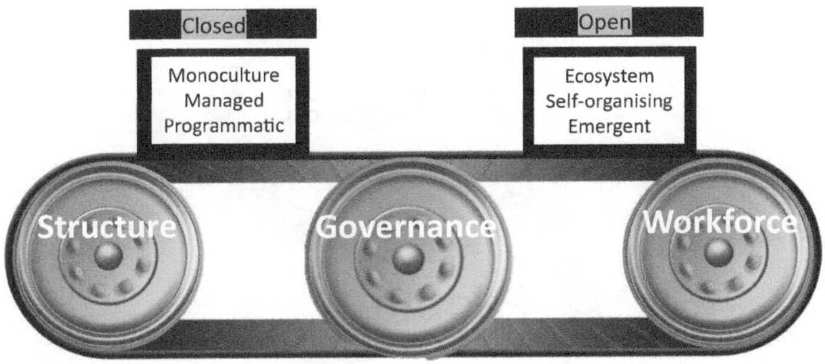

Figure 3.3 An overview of culture transformation at the level of organisational design.

must be ingrained not only in the organisation's architecture but also in its strategic approach to digital transformation, people development, and the change process (see Figure 3.4).

If the structure, governance, and workflow are the rollers that drive the cultural conveyor belt (from Figure 3.3), the strategic enablers are the levers that power and steer it. Let's explore each of these levers.

i. Digital strategy and culture
Karl Treacher (2023) observes how technology plays a significant role in shaping culture. Chapter 7 will explore digital strategy and digital transformation, directly linking digital strategy with organisational culture. Effectively, the organisation's digital wiring greatly shapes the company, its operations, and its culture (Matt, Hess, and Benlian 2015; Warner and Wäger 2019). Moreover, as Michael Wade and Jialu Shan (2020) remind us, cultural barriers are a key factor in digital transformation failure. Rahawarin, Mukhlis, and Murwani (2024), comment, "The number one barrier to digital transformation is culture" (189). Adama and Okeke (2024) confirm this when they say, "Organizational culture plays a critical role in enabling or inhibiting digital innovation and transformation" (259).
ii. People strategy and culture
Chapter 8 will develop the idea that an adaptive culture is shaped not only by an adaptive organisational design but also by an adaptive people-and-workforce strategy. As Vineesh Vijayan (2019) asserts, "the success

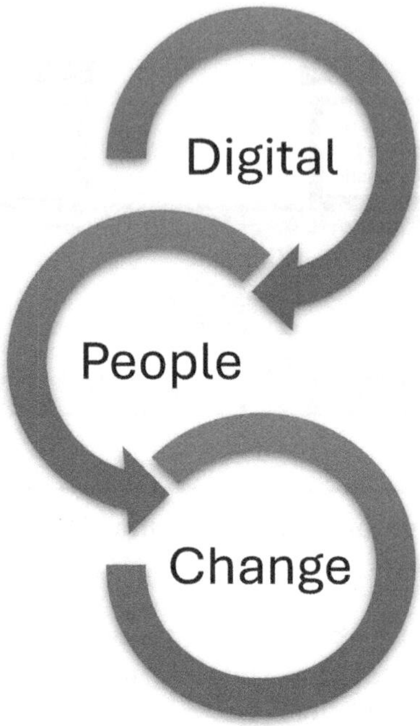

Figure 3.4 3 strategic enablers that help mobilise transformational change.

of building an agile and adaptive culture in your organisation will not come only from great ideas and plans, but it will happen through the employees". Cultivating adaptive employee mindsets is therefore essential to creating an adaptive organisational culture. Chapter 8 will explore how adaptive workforces can be developed through system and skill-based interventions.

iii. The change process and culture
There are two distinct cultural transformation methods discussed in this chapter: a direct intervention (often led by directive leaders, mergers, and top-down mandates) and an indirect intervention, an emergent transformational change process through cultural infusion and normalisation, adaptive organisational design, and organisational strategic alignment. For this approach to be effective, one that creates an enduring and lasting "strong" organisational culture, it requires an adaptive change process. Chapter 9 explores different change models and presents the hybrid change approach as a highly adaptive and practical means to support organisational behavioural change.

Synthesis: Developing Adaptive Cultures

This chapter explores culture as one of the five system levers introduced in Chapter 1. It posits that organisations must adopt and embed a normalised culture of adaptability to become truly adaptive. Culture is the backbone or glue that holds an organisation together; without an adaptive culture, no amount of structural or strategic change can create enduring adaptability in the workplace.

The chapter distinguishes between two approaches to shaping culture. The first is direct intervention, such as through directive leadership, mergers, and mandates. While these imposed methods may produce short-term compliance, they rarely generate genuine commitment. The culture created through direct intervention is seldom lasting.

The second, and more sustainable, approach is indirect intervention, which nurtures adaptability gradually through culture, design, and strategy. This includes socialisation, shared norms, and ingraining adaptability into the organisational design (its structure, governance, and workflow), as well as ensuring adaptive alignment with the strategic mobilisers of transformational change, namely technology, people, and the change process.

Crucially, this chapter argues that for a culture to be enduring and sustainable, it cannot be imposed; it must be built systemically. Within such a system, the organisation becomes an emergent, self-organising ecosystem in which adaptive behaviours arise naturally rather than being forced. This cultivates authentic commitment and forms a primary condition for building enduring adaptive organisations.

Coda (Chapters 1–3)

The first three chapters have focused on the diagnostic phase of the 3Ps Systems Model introduced in Chapter 1. When building an adaptive organisation, it is essential to understand what adaptability means and why it matters within the context of Work 4.0 and the future workplace. This requires examining how adaptive your organisation is in terms of the flow of business intelligence, decision-making processes, and the execution of work within the organisational design.

Equally important is assessing your organisation's readiness to adapt, including people's mindsets, digital transformation maturity, and the overall appetite and capability for change. A systems approach facilitates this analysis by applying an external lens (the 3P System Model of perspective, patterns, and proactivity) to understand wider industry shifts and organisational responses. The STEP-WIDE systems wheel is an excellent tool to support this process.

A close examination of culture is essential in the diagnostic phase. A rigid or closed culture will significantly block any shift towards adaptability. Developing an open, emergent, self-organising ecosystem cannot be achieved through mandates or top-down directives; it must evolve gradually through systemic cultural infusion (a culture system), shaped by organisational design, social norms, and strategic alignment.

The diagnostic phase is often overlooked in organisational change. Organisations cannot progress to later stages without first understanding their adaptive capacity in terms of clarifying the case for change, forming a compelling vision for the organisation in the context of the Work 4.0 landscape, assessing company's openness and responsiveness as a system, and considering the cultural transformation required to support this shift.

Having completed this deep reflection on adaptability, systems, and culture, we are now ready to move to the next stage in the journey: the design phase.

Notes

1. The cultural backstory of Starbucks began with a Dutch immigrant named Alfred Peet, who introduced the European coffee experience to the United States. Peet inspired the early founders of Starbucks, who preserved his culture and traditions, such as using authentic roasters to prepare coffee beans.
2. Cisco calls this "conscious culture" (Moorhead 2019). Brian Chesky, co-founder and CEO of Airbnb, also emphasises the importance of organisational culture (Chesky 2014).
3. Publications that support this view include Wilke and Cocks (2015); Gallop (2025); and Nzuva (2022).
4. This is according to Geert Hofstede et al. (1990).
5. Originating from E. Jacques' 1951 factory study, which explores factory culture as the "customary traditional way of thinking and of doing things" (Jaques 1987, 251).
6. Rose Hollister and her coauthors (2021) believe "We define *culture* as a shared set of values (what we care about), beliefs (what we believe to be true), and norms of behavior (how we do things). Cultures exist to align effort, engender shared sensemaking, increase predictability, and encode organizational lessons about what does and doesn't work".
7. These include the Organizational Culture Assessment Instrument (OCAI), the Culture Gap Survey (CGS), Organizational Beliefs Questionnaire (OBQ), the Corporate Culture Survey (CCS), Denison's Organizational Culture Survey, and the Great Place To Work Institute methodology. Source: Nold and Michel (2021).
8. Comparable terms for adaptive culture include adaptability (Daft 1986) and organisational ambidexterity (Duncan 1976).
9. Authors that reflect this perspective include Denison and Mishra (1995); Tuominen et al. (2004); and Franczak and Weinzimmer (2022).

10. Here are some references associated with this passage. An adaptive culture offers several key advantages: it encourages diversification (Sørensen 2002), enhances financial performance (Chatman et al. 2014; Kotter and Heskett 1992), improves customer services (Denison et al. 2003), strengthens overall business performance (Ghimire, Rai, and Dahal 2021), drives innovation (Tuominen, Rajala, and Möller 2004; Verdu-Jover et al. 2018), and boosts employee motivation, satisfaction, and productivity (Patel 2024). More recently, adaptability has been instrumental in ensuring that organisations are better prepared to undergo digital transformation (Bonnet and Westerman 2020).
11. To achieve this, organisations need to be very honest about their culture and avoid "culture washing", where they mislead themselves and others about their true values and practices.
12. Stephen Haeckel labels direct and indirect as a "planned response" versus a "sense and respond" approach (Haeckel 1999).
13. For example, see Ford et al. (2008); Klein (2011); Warrick (2017); Berson, Oreg, and Dvir (2008); Schulze and Pinkow (2020); Uhl-Bien and Arena (2018); Kerr (2014); and Raguž and Zekan (2017).
14. Authors who assert this view include Balthazard, Cooke, and Potter (2006); Stahl and Voigt (2008); and Weber, Shenkar, and Raveh (1996).
15. Studies exploring cultural mandates and mission-driven change include works by Lee (2011), Mallinger, Goodwin, and O'Hara (2009), and Vele (2013). Publications on central planning include Ford et al. (2008), Murunga and Karugu (2019), and Struwig and Smith (2002).
16. Researchers in this area include Coates and Atkinson (1993); Yarbrough, Morgan, and Vorhies (2011); and Whalen (2014).
17. Kulwant Singh (2007) argues against this position and suggests there is little relevance of culture to strategy.
18. Commentators include Balthazard, Cooke, and Potter (2006); Dimitrov (2018); Gupta (2011); Mutai (2015); Salamzadeh et al. (2012); Tosti (2007); Yarbrough, Morgan, and Vorhies (2011); Omuga (2009); and Kaul (2019).

Bibliography

Adama, Henry Ejiga, and Chukwuekem David Okeke. 2024. 'Digital Transformation as a Catalyst for Business Model Innovation: A Critical Review of Impact and Implementation Strategies'. *Magna Scientia Advanced Research and Reviews* 10 (2): 256–64. https://doi.org/10.30574/msarr.2024.10.2.0066.

Adler, Nancy J. 1986. *International Dimensions of Organizational Behavior.* 1st edition. The Kent International Business Series. Kent Pub. Co.

Altman, Elizabeth J., David Kiron, Jeff Schwartz, and Robin Jones. 2021. 'The Future of Work Is Through Workforce Ecosystems'. *MIT Sloan Management Review*, January 14. https://sloanreview.mit.edu/article/the-future-of-work-is-through-workforce-ecosystems/.

Arrow, Holly, and K.L. Burns. 2004. 'Self-Organizing Culture: How Norms Emerge in Small Groups'. In *The Psychological Foundations of Culture*, edited by Christian S. Crandall and Mark Schaller. L. Erlbaum, 171–199.

Arthur, Charles. 2011. 'Nokia's Chief Executive to Staff: "We Are Standing on a Burning Platform"'. Technology. *The Guardian*, February 9. https://www.theguardian.com/technology/blog/2011/feb/09/nokia-burning-platform-memo-elop.

Asiedu, Elvis. 2015. 'Supportive Organisational Culture and Employee Job Satisfaction: A Critical Source of Competitive Advantage. A Case Study in a Selected Banking Company in Oxford City-UK'. *International Journal of Social Sciences and Management* 2 (3): 290–300. https://doi.org/10.3126/ijssm.v2i3.12551.

Balthazard, Pierre A., Robert A. Cooke, and Richard E. Potter. 2006. 'Dysfunctional Culture, Dysfunctional Organization: Capturing the Behavioral Norms That Form Organizational Culture and Drive Performance'. *Journal of Managerial Psychology* 21 (8): 709–32. https://doi.org/10.1108/02683940610713253.

Barnard, Chester Irving. 1968. *The Functions of the Executive*. 30th anniversary edition. Harvard University Press.

Barney, Jay. 1991. 'Firm Resources and Sustained Competitive Advantage'. *Journal of Management* 17 (1): 99–120. https://doi.org/10.1177/014920639101700108.

Bauer, Talya N., Todd Bodner, Berrin Erdogan, Donald M. Truxillo, and Jennifer S. Tucker. 2007. 'Newcomer Adjustment during Organizational Socialization: A Meta-Analytic Review of Antecedents, Outcomes, and Methods'. *Journal of Applied Psychology* 92 (3): 707–21. https://doi.org/10.1037/0021–9010.92.3.707.

Bauer, Talya N., and Berrin Erdogan. 2011. 'Organizational Socialization: The Effective Onboarding of New Employees'. In *Apa Handbook of Industrial and Organizational Psychology, Vol 3: Maintaining, Expanding, and Contracting the Organization*, edited by Sheldon Zedeck. American Psychological Association. https://doi.org/10.1037/12171–002.

Bersin, Josh. 2015. 'Culture: Why It's The Hottest Topic In Business Today'. Leadership strategy. Forbes, March 13. https://www.forbes.com/sites/joshbersin/2015/03/13/culture-why-its-the-hottest-topic-in-business-today/.

Berson, Yair, Shaul Oreg, and Taly Dvir. 2008. 'Ceo Values, Organizational Culture and Firm Outcomes'. *Journal of Organizational Behavior* 29 (5): 615–33. https://doi.org/10.1002/job.499.

Bonnet, Didier, and George Westerman. 2020. 'The New Elements of Digital Transformation'. *MIT Sloan Management Review* 62 (2): 82–89. https://sloanreview.mit.edu/article/the-new-elements-of-digital-transformation/.

Brons, Lajos Ludovic. 2005. *Rethinking the Culture-Economy Dialectic*. University of Groningen. https://philpapers.org/archive/BRORTC-9.pdf.

Brown, Andrew. 1995. *Organisational Culture*. Pitman.

Brown, N Derek, Yixi Chen, Hope Harrington, et al. 2024. *How Have Organizational Cultures Shifted During the COVID-19 Pandemic*. California Review Management.

Cameron, Kim S., and Robert E. Quinn. 2011. *Diagnosing and Changing Organizational Culture: Based on the Competing Values Framework*. 3rd edition. The Jossey-Bass Business & Management Series. Jossey-Bass.

Caredda, Sergio. 2024. 'Organisation Ecosystem: The Theory and the Practice'. Organisation Ecosystem: The Theory and the Practice, August 25. https://sergiocaredda.eu/organisation/organisation-ecosystem-the-theory-and-the-practice.

Carlin, Shannon. 2022. 'The True Story Behind We Crashed'. *Time Magazine*, March 18. https://time.com/6158804/wecrashed-true-story/.

Carpenter, Reid, Varya Davidson, Christopher Hannegan, and Bhushan Sethi. 2021. 'Global Culture Survey 2021: The Link Between Culture and Competitive Advantage'. PwC. https://www.pwc.com/gx/en/issues/upskilling/global-culture-survey-2021/global-culture-survey-2021-report.html.

Chatman, Jennifer A., David F. Caldwell, Charles A. O'Reilly, and Bernadette Doerr. 2014. 'Parsing Organizational Culture: How the Norm for Adaptability Influences the Relationship Between Culture Consensus and Financial Performance in High-Technology Firms': *Journal of Organizational Behavior* 35 (6): 785–808. https://doi.org/10.1002/job.1928.

Chatman, Jennifer A., and Sandra Eunyoung Cha. 2003. 'Leading by Leveraging Culture'. *California Management Review* 45 (4): 20–34. https://doi.org/10.2307/41166186.

Chesky, Brian. 2014. 'Don't Fuck Up the Culture'. Business. Medium, April 20. https://medium.com/@bchesky/dont-fuck-up-the-culture-597cde9ee9d4.

Claydon, Richard, and Geoff Marlow. 2022. 'Towards an Adaptive Organisational Culture'. *EQLAB*, February 15. https://www.eqlab.co/blog/towards-an-adaptive-organisational-culture.

Coates, Dave, and Philip E. Atkinson. 1993. 'Creating Culture Change: The Key to Successful Total Quality Management'. *The Journal of the Operational Research Society* 44 (5): 525–526. https://doi.org/10.2307/2583919.

Costanza, David P., Nikki Blacksmith, Meredith R. Coats, Jamie B. Severt, and Arwen H. DeCostanza. 2016. 'The Effect of Adaptive Organizational Culture on Long-Term Survival'. *Journal of Business and Psychology* 31 (3): 361–81. https://doi.org/10.1007/s10869-015-9420-y.

Daft, Richard L. 1986. *Organization Theory and Design*. 2nd edition. West Pub. Co.

Davidson, Varya, and Paul Leinwand. 2016. *How Starbucks's Culture Brings Its Strategy to Life*. Business. Harvard Business Review, December 30. https://hbr.org/2016/12/how-starbuckss-culture-brings-its-strategy-to-life.

Davis, Stanley M. 1984. *Managing Corporate Culture*. Ballinger Pub. Co.

Denison, Daniel R. 1990. *Corporate Culture and Organizational Effectiveness*. Wiley Series on Organizational Assessment and Change. Wiley. https://openlibrary.org/books/OL2205896M/Corporate_culture_and_organizational_effectiveness.

Denison, Daniel R., Stephanie Haaland, and Paulo Goelzer. 2003. 'Corporate Culture and Organizational Effectiveness: Is There a Similar Pattern Aournd the World?' *Organizational Dynamics* 33 (1): 98–109. https://doi.org/10.1016/j.orgdyn.2003.11.008.

Denison, Daniel R., and Aneil K. Mishra. 1995. 'Toward a Theory of Organizational Culture and Effectiveness'. *Organization Science* 6 (2): 204–23. https://doi.org/10.1287/orsc.6.2.204.

Dimitrov, Kiril. 2018. *Exploring the Nuances in the Relationship 'Culture-Strategy' for the Business World*. Version 1. https://doi.org/10.48550/ARXIV.1810.02613.

Duncan, Robert B. 1976. 'The Ambidextrous Organization: Designing Dual Structures for Innovation'. In *The Management of Organization Design: Strategies and Implementation*, edited by Ralph H. Kilmann, Louis R. Pondy, and Dennis Patrick Slevin, vol. 1. North Holland.

Ertosun, Oznur Gulen, and Zafer Adiguzel. 2018. 'Leadership, Personal Values and Organizational Culture'. In *Strategic Design and Innovative Thinking in Business Operations*, edited by Hasan Dincer, Ümit Hacioglu, and Serhat Yüksel. Contributions to Management Science. Springer International Publishing. https://doi.org/10.1007/978-3-319-77622-4_3.

Esser, Joerg. 2021. *The Secret of Adaptable Organizations Is Trust*. Business Management. Harvard Business Review, March 15. https://hbr.org/2021/03/the-secret-of-adaptable-organizations-is-trust.

Fein, Paul. 2019. 'Creating an Evolving Future-Focused Organizational Culture'. Organisational Behavior. *Association for Talent Development (ATD)*, April 22. https://www.td.org/content/atd-blog/creating-an-evolving-future-focused-organizational-culture.

Ford, Robert C., Celeste P. M. Wilderom, and John Caparella. 2008. 'Strategically Crafting a Customer-Focused Culture: An Inductive Case Study'. *Journal of Strategy and Management* 1 (2): 143–67. https://doi.org/10.1108/17554250810926348.

Franczak, Jennifer, and Laurence Weinzimmer. 2022. 'How SMEs Leverage Adaptability, Risk-Taking, and Action Into Positive Performance: A Moderated Mediation Model'. *Journal of Small Business Strategy* 32 (4): 1–18. https://doi.org/10.53703/001c.40318.

Furr, Nathan, and Andrew Shipilov. 2018. 'Building the Right Ecosystem for Innovation'. *MIT Sloan Management Review*, May 15. https://sloanreview.mit.edu/article/building-the-right-ecosystem-for-innovation/.

Gallagher, Leigh. 2017. *The Airbnb Story: How Three Ordinary Guys Disrupted an Industry, Made Billions... and Created Plenty of Controversy*. 1st Mariner Books edition. Houghton Mifflin Harcourt.

Gallop. 2025. 'What Is Organizational Culture? And Why Does It Matter?' Gallup.Com. https://www.gallup.com/workplace/327371/how-to-build-better-company-culture.aspx.

Gasparini, Pedro Paulo Rigoni, Keitiane Barros Vieira, and Murillo de Oliveira Dias. 2025. 'Disney's Pixar Animation Studios Acquisition Case: Revitalization or Trouble?' *GPH-International Journal of Social Science & Humanities Research* 8 (4): 46–57. https://doi.org/10.5281/zenodo.15365962.

Geraci, John. 2016. 'What I Learned from Trying to Innovate at the New York Times'. *Harvard Business Review*, April 7. https://hbr.org/2016/04/what-i-learned-from-trying-to-innovate-at-the-new-york-times.

Ghimire, Binod, Bharat Rai, and Rewan Kumar Dahal. 2021. 'Corporate Culture and Organizational Performance in the Banking Industry of Nepal'. *Management Dynamics* 24 (2): 1–8. https://doi.org/10.3126/md.v24i2.50031.

Giorgi, Simona, Christi Lockwood, and Mary Ann Glynn. 2015. 'The Many Faces of Culture: Making Sense of 30 Years of Research on Culture in Organization Studies'. *Academy of Management Annals* 9 (1): 1–54. https://doi.org/10.5465/19416520.2015.1007645.

Gupta, Bindu. 2011. 'A Comparative Study of Organizational Strategy and Culture Across Industry'. *Benchmarking: An International Journal* 18 (4): 510–28. https://doi.org/10.1108/14635771111147614.

Guttentag, Daniel. 2015. 'Airbnb: Disruptive Innovation and the Rise of an Informal Tourism Accommodation Sector'. *Current Issues in Tourism* 18 (12): 1192–217. https://doi.org/10.1080/13683500.2013.827159.

Haeckel, Stephan H. 1999. *Adaptive Enterprise: Creating and Leading Sense-and-Respond Organizations*. Harvard Business School Press.

Hald, E. Julie, Alex Gillespie, and Tom W. Reader. 2021. 'Causal and Corrective Organisational Culture: A Systematic Review of Case Studies of Institutional Failure'. *Journal of Business Ethics* 174 (2): 457–83. https://doi.org/10.1007/s10551-020-04620-3.

Hemerling, Jim, Julie Kilmann, Martin Danoesastro, Liza Stutts, and Cailin Ahern. 2018. 'It's Not a Digital Transformation Without a Digital Culture'. Business. BCG Global, April 13. https://www.bcg.com/publications/2018/not-digital-transformation-without-digital-culture.

Hofstede, Geert, Bram Neuijen, Denise Daval Ohayv, and Geert Sanders. 1990. 'Measuring Organizational Cultures: A Qualitative and Quantitative Study Across Twenty Cases'. *Administrative Science Quarterly* 35 (2): 286–316. https://doi.org/10.2307/2393392.

Hollister, Rose, Kathryn Tecosky, Michael Watkins, and Cindy Wolpert. 2021. 'Why Every Executive Should Be Focusing on Culture Change Now'. *MIT Sloan Management Review*, August 10. https://sloanreview.mit.edu/article/why-every-executive-should-be-focusing-on-culture-change-now/.

Janicijevic, Nebojsa. 2012. 'Organizational Culture and Strategy'. *Ekonomika Preduzeca* 60 (3–4): 127–39. https://doi.org/10.5937/ekopre1204127J.

Jantsch, Erich. 1980. *The Self-Organizing Universe: Scientific and Human Implications of the Emerging Paradigm of Evolution*. 1st edition. Systems Science and World Order Library. Pergamon Press.

Jaques, Elliot. 1987. *The Changing Culture of a Factory*. Repr. Original. publ.: Tavistock, 1951. Continuity in Administrative Science / Ed. by Arthur P. Brief 14. Garland.

Johnson, Steven. 2001. *Emergence: The Connected Lives of Ants, Brains, Cities, and Software*. Scribner.

Kashanizadeh, Zahra, Saeed Khanagha, Andreas Alexiou, and Henk Volberda. 2024. 'The Dynamics of New Sharing Economy Ventures Strategies and Ecosystem Legitimacy: The Case of Airbnb'. *R&D Management* 54 (5): 1166–89. https://doi.org/10.1111/radm.12649.

Kaul, Amarjeev. 2019. 'Culture Vs Strategy: Which to Precede, Which to Align?' *Journal of Strategy and Management* 12 (1): 116–36. https://doi.org/10.1108/JSMA-04-2018-0036.

Kerr, Fiona. 2014. 'Creating and Leading Adaptive Organisations: The Nature and Practice of Emergent Logic'. Thesis (Ph.D), University of Adelaide, Business School,. https://core.ac.uk/download/pdf/79084514.pdf.

Kilmann, Ralph H., M. J. Saxton, and R. Serpa, eds. 1985. *Gaining Control of the Corporate Culture*. Jossey-Bass.

Klein, Andrew. 2011. 'Corporate Culture: Its Value as a Resource for Competitive Advantage'. *Journal of Business Strategy* 32 (2): 21–28. https://doi.org/10.1108/02756661111109743.

Kotter, John P., Vanessa Akhtar, and Gaurav Gupta. 2021. 'Overcoming Obstacles to Successful Culture Change'. *MIT Sloan Management Review*, July 26. https://sloanreview.mit.edu/article/overcoming-obstacles-to-successful-culture-change/.

Kotter, John P., and James L. Heskett. 1992. *Corporate Culture and Performance*. Free Press; Maxwell Macmillan Canada; Maxwell Macmillan International. https://openlibrary.org/works/OL1932131W/Corporate_culture_and_performance?edition=key%3A/books/OL1561550M.

Kriegel, Jessica. 2023. *Adaptive Alignment on Purpose, Strategy, and Culture Is the TRUE Driver of Business Results.* With Charles O'Reilly. Stanford. https://info.culture.io/hubfs/2023_Q3_eBook_Stanford_Adaptability_Report/Culture_Partners_Stanford_Research_Report.pdf.

Lamberg, Juha-Antti, Sandra Lubinaitė, Jari Ojala, and Henrikki Tikkanen. 2019. 'The Curse of Agility: The Nokia Corporation and the Loss of Market Dominance in Mobile Phones, 2003–2013'. *Business History* 63 (4): 574–605. https://doi.org/10.1080/00076791.2019.1593964.

Latta, Gail F. 2009. 'Chapter 3 Maturation of Organizational Development in Higher Education'. *To Improve the Academy: A Journal of Educational Development* 27: 32–71. http://dx.doi.org/10.3998/tia.17063888.0027.007.

Lee, Jeremiah. 2011. 'Aligning Organizations for Positive Change: The Role of Leadership in Matching Strategy, Culture, and Social Networks to Vital Organizational Challenges'. In *Advances in Global Leadership*, edited by William H. Mobley, Ming Li, and Ying Wang, vol. 6. Emerald Group Publishing Limited. https://doi.org/10.1108/S1535-1203(2011)0000006007.

Lewes, George Henry. 1874. *Problems of Life and Mind.* Vol. 1. Houghton, Miffin and Company.

Lundy, Olive, and Alan Cowling. 1996. *Strategic Human Resource Management.* Routledge. http://archive.org/details/strategichumanre0000lund.

Maalouf, Georges Y., and Issam Jallad. 2024. 'How Nokia Missed the Smartphone Revolution: A Case Study of Strategic Failure'. *Journal of Economics and Technology Research* 5 (1): 57. https://doi.org/10.22158/jetr.v5n1p57.

Maanen, J, E Schein, and Barry Straw. 1978. 'Toward a Theory of Organizational Socialization'. In *Research in Organizational Behavior*, vol. 1, edited by Barry Staw. JIP Press. https://www.semanticscholar.org/paper/Toward-a-theory-of-organizational-socialization-Maanen-Schein/eb8b4aa450019035f8c4d72c3c19126615121d65.

Mallinger, Mark, Don Goodwin, and Tetsuya O'Hara. 2009. 'Recognizing Organizational Culture in Managing Change'. *Graziadio Business Review* 12 (1): 1–10.

Martin, Joanne, and Caren Siehl. 1983. 'Organizational Culture and Counterculture: An Uneasy Symbiosis'. *Organizational Dynamics* 12 (2): 52–64. https://doi.org/10.1016/0090-2616(83)90033-5.

Matt, Christian, T Hess, and A Benlian. 2015. *Digital Transformation Strategies.* May 14. https://doi.org/10.7892/BORIS.105535.

Midolo, Emanuele. 2020. 'Don't Blame Coronavirus for WeWork's Collapse, Blame WeWork'. *Wired*, April 6. https://www.wired.com/story/wework-coronavirus-collapse/.

Mihata, Kevin. 1997. 'The Persistence of "Emergence"'. In *Chaos, Complexity, and Sociology: Myths, Models, and Theories*, edited by Raymond A. Eve, Sara Horsfall, and Mary E. Lee. Sage Publications.

Mohelska, Hana, and Marcela Sokolova. 2015. 'Organisational Culture and Leadership – Joint Vessels?' *Procedia – Social and Behavioral Sciences* 171 (January): 1011–16. https://doi.org/10.1016/j.sbspro.2015.01.223.

Moore, James. 1993. 'Predators and Prey: A New Ecology of Competition'. Business Management. Harvard Business Review. https://hbr.org/1993/05/predators-and-prey-a-new-ecology-of-competition.

Moorhead, Patrick. 2019. 'How Cisco Fosters A "Conscious Culture" Within The Company'. Business. Forbes, March 19. https://www.forbes.com/sites/patrickmoorhead/2019/03/19/how-cisco-fosters-a-conscious-culture-within-the-company/.

Müller, Lea S., Sebastian Reiners, Jörg Becker, and Guido Hertel. 2023. 'Long-Term Effects of COVID-19 on Work Routines and Organizational Culture – A Case Study Within Higher Education's Administration'. *Journal of Business Research* 163 (August): 113927. https://doi.org/10.1016/j.jbusres.2023.113927.

Murunga, Edgar Sikuku, and Jane Esther Karugu. 2019. 'Organizational Culture and Strategy Execution at Commission for University Education, Kenya'. *International Journal of Current Aspects* 3 (V): 76–90. https://doi.org/10.35942/ijcab.v3iV.62.

Mutai, Preston Kipkemoi. 2015. *Organization Culture and Strategy Implementation at Airtel, Kenya*. MBA, University of Nairobi.

Niccol, Brian. 2024. 'Message from Brian: Back to Starbucks. An Open Letter for All Partners, Customers and Stakeholders'. Company Website. About Starbucks, September 10. https://about.starbucks.com/press/2024/back-to-starbucks/.

Nneji, Ngozi, Olalekan Asikhia, and Victoria Akpa. 2021. 'Organizational Culture and Organizational Performance: A Review of Literature'. *International Journal of Advances in Engineering and Management (IJAEM)* 3 (1): 361–72.

Nold, Herbert, and Lukas Michel. 2021. 'Organizational Culture: A Systems Approach'. In *Accounting and Finance Innovations*, edited by Nizar Alsharari. IntechOpen. https://doi.org/10.5772/intechopen.97466.

Nzuva, Silas Mutie. 2022. 'The Impact of Organisational Culture on Employees' Productivity: A Comprehensive Systematic Review'. *European Journal of Business and Management* 14 (4): 42–55. https://doi.org/10.7176/EJBM/14-4-05.

Odum, Eugene P., and Gary W. Barrett. 2005. *Fundamentals of Ecology*. 5th edition. Thomson Brooks/Cole.

Omuga, Nyarang'o. 2009. *Alignment of Strategy and Organizational Culture in the Mobile Phone Service Providers in Kenya*. University of Nairobi. http://erepository.uonbi.ac.ke/handle/11295/13061.

O'Reilly, Charles A., and Jennifer Chatman. 1996. 'Culture as Social Control: Corporations, Cults, and Commitment'. *Research in Organizational Behavior* 18: 157–200.

Our Starbucks Mission. 2025. 'Our Starbucks Mission'. About Starbucks, January 9. https://about.starbucks.com/stories/2025/our-starbucks-mission/.

Panetta, Kasey. 2017. '8 Dimensions Of Business Ecosystems'. Information Technology. Gartner, July 12. https://www.gartner.com/smarterwithgartner/8-dimensions-of-business-ecosystems.

Patel, James. 2024. 'The Role of Adaptive Culture in Organizational Success: A Comprehensive Review'. *Journal of Organizational Culture, Communications and Conflict* 28 (2S): 1–3.

Pereira Da Silva, Paulo, Darcy Mitiko Hanashiro, and Almir Martins Vieira. 2023. 'Socialização Organizacional: Um Estudo Com Trainees Da Geração Z'. *Revista Pensamento Contemporâneo Em Administração* 17 (3): 1–19. https://doi.org/10.12712/rpca.v17i3.59963.

Pettigrew, Andrew M. 1979. 'On Studying Organizational Cultures'. *Administrative Science Quarterly* 24 (4): 570. https://doi.org/10.2307/2392363.

Raguž, Ivona Vrdoljak, and Borovac Senka Zekan. 2017. 'Organizational Culture and Leadership Style: Key Factors in the Organizational Adaptation Process'. *Ekonomski Vjesnik* 30 (1): 209–19.

Rahawarin, Fazlur Rahman, Imam Mukhlis, and F. Danardana Murwani. 2024. 'Organizational Culture and Digital Transformation of Msmes: Bibliometric and Systematic Literature Analysis'. *Nusantara Economics and Entrepreneurships Journals*, May 13, 189–96. https://doi.org/10.59971/necent.v1i3.22.

Rani, Manisha, and Upasana Srivastava. 2015. 'Study of Organizational Culture and Its Impact on Employee Retention'. *Interal Res Journa Managt Sci Tech* 6 (10): 14–20.

Roberts, Daniel. 2015. 'At W.l. Gore, 57 Years of Authentic Culture'. Fortune, March 5. https://fortune.com/2015/03/05/w-l-gore-culture/.

Salamzadeh, Y, A Ahmadi, S Ali, M Daraei, and J Akbari,. 2012. 'Relationship Between Organizational Culture and Strategy Implementation: Typologies and Dimensions'. *Global Business & Management Research* 4 (January): 286–99.

Schein, Edgar H. 1999. *The Corporate Culture Survival Guide* . Jossey-Bass Inc.

Schultz, Howard, and Dori Jones Yang. 1997. *Pour Your Heart into It: How Starbucks Built a Company One Cup at a Time.* With Starbucks Coffee Company. Hyperion.

Schulze, Jonas Hermann, and Felix Pinkow. 2020. 'Leadership for Organisational Adaptability: How Enabling Leaders Create Adaptive Space'. *Administrative Sciences* 10 (3): 37. https://doi.org/10.3390/admsci10030037.

Serinkan, Celalettin, and Mehmet Kiziloglu. 2021. 'The Relationship between Organisational Culture and Job Satisfaction in Higher Education Institutions: The Bishkek Case'. *Periodica Polytechnica Social and Management Sciences* 29 (2): 168–79. https://doi.org/10.3311/PPso.15319.

Shraiber, Walter. 2023. 'The Perils of an Egosystem and the Promise of an Ecosystem'. Medium, September 25. https://magazine.eau.university/the-perils-of-an-egosystem-and-the-promise-of-an-ecosystem-6aca08a916af.

Singh, Kulwant. 2007. 'The Limited Relevance of Culture to Strategy'. *Asia Pacific Journal of Management* 24 (4): 421–28. https://doi.org/10.1007/s10490-007-9057-0.

Sørensen, Jesper B. 2002. 'The Strength of Corporate Culture and the Reliability of Firm Performance'. *Administrative Science Quarterly* 47 (1): 70–91. https://doi.org/10.2307/3094891.

Spagnoletto, Lyuba, Dianah AlabdulJabbar, Harsha Jalihal, Queenie Chan, and Ravin Jesuthasan. 2019. *HR4.0: Shaping People Strategies in the Fourth Industrial Revolution.* White Paper No. 10122019. World Economic Forum in collaboration with Saudi Aramco, Unilever, and Willis Towers Watson. https://www3.weforum.org/docs/WEF_NES_Whitepaper_HR4.0.pdf.

Stacey, Ralph D. 1996. *Complexity and Creativity in Organizations.* Berrett-Koehler Publishers.

Stahl, Günter K., and Andreas Voigt. 2008. 'Do Cultural Differences Matter in Mergers and Acquisitions? A Tentative Model and Examination'. *Organization Science* 19 (1): 160–76. https://doi.org/10.1287/orsc.1070.0270.

Stone, Brad. 2017. *The Upstarts: How Uber, Airbnb, and the Killer Companies of the New Silicon Valley Are Changing the World.* Little, Brown and Company.

Struwig, F. W., and E. E. Smith. 2002. 'The Relationship Between Organisational Culture and Strategy Formulation in South African Firms'. *South African Journal of Business Management* 33 (1): 21–29. https://doi.org/10.4102/sajbm.v33i1.694.

Teerikangas, Satu, and Olivier Irrmann. 2016. 'Cultural Change Following International Acquisitions: Cohabiting the Tension Between Espoused and Practiced Cultures'. *Management International Review* 56 (2): 195–226. https://doi.org/10.1007/s11575-015-0276–1.

Tosti, Donald T. 2007. 'Aligning the Culture and Strategy for Success'. *Performance Improvement* 46 (1): 21–25. https://doi.org/10.1002/pfi.035.

Treacher, Karl. 2023. 'Fast-Forward to the Future: Welcome to the Workplace of 2030'. *The CEO Magazine*, March 4. https://www.theceomagazine.com/opinion/workplace-2030/.

Tsui, Anne S., Sushil S. Nifadkar, and Amy Yi Ou. 2007. 'Cross-National, Cross-Cultural Organizational Behavior Research: Advances, Gaps, and Recommendations'. *Journal of Management* 33 (3): 426–78. https://doi.org/10.1177/0149206307300818.

Tuominen, Matti, Arto Rajala, and Kristian Möller. 2004. 'How Does Adaptability Drive Firm Innovativeness?' *Journal of Business Research* 57 (5): 495–506. https://doi.org/10.1016/S0148-2963(02)00316–8.

Uhl-Bien, Mary, and Michael Arena. 2018. 'Leadership for Organizational Adaptability: A Theoretical Synthesis and Integrative Framework'. *The Leadership Quarterly* 29 (1): 89–104. https://doi.org/10.1016/j.leaqua.2017.12.009.

Väänänen, Heikki. 2023. 'How to Shape Organizational Culture for the Next Generation of Employees'. Business Management. Forbes, August 31. https://www.forbes.com/sites/heikkivaananen/2023/08/31/how-to-shape-organizational-culture-for-the-next-generation-of-employees/.

Vele, Cristian-Liviu. 2013. 'Organizational Culture and Strategy: How Does It Work? An Empirical Research'. *Annals of the University of Oradea, Economic Science* 22 (1): 1690–96.

Verdu-Jover, Antonio J., Lirios Alos-Simo, and Jose-Maria Gomez-Gras. 2018. 'Adaptive Culture and Product/Service Innovation Outcomes'. *European Management Journal* 36 (3): 330–40. https://doi.org/10.1016/j.emj.2017.07.004.

Vijayan, Vineesh. 2019. 'Agility, Adaptability and Organisation Culture'. Organisational Behavior. Medium, September 17. https://medium.com/summit-plus/agility-adaptability-and-organisation-culture-7ebe8a8c5d71.

Wade, Michael, and Jialu Shan. 2020. 'Covid-19 Has Accelerated Digital Transformation, But May Have Made It Harder Not Easier'. *MIS Quarterly Executive* 19: 213–20. https://doi.org/10.17705/2msqe.00034.

Walker, Bryan, and Sarah A. Soule. 2017. 'Changing Company Culture Requires a Movement, Not a Mandate'. Harvard Business Review, June 20. https://hbr.org/2017/06/changing-company-culture-requires-a-movement-not-a-mandate.

Wanberg, Connie R., ed. 2012. *The Oxford Handbook of Organizational Socialization*. 1st edition. Oxford University Press. https://doi.org/10.1093/oxfordhb/9780199763672.001.0001.

Warner, Karl S.R., and Maximilian Wäger. 2019. 'Building Dynamic Capabilities for Digital Transformation: An Ongoing Process of Strategic Renewal'. *Long Range Planning* 52 (3): 326–49. https://doi.org/10.1016/j.lrp.2018.12.001.

Warrick, D.D. 2017. 'What Leaders Need to Know About Organizational Culture'. *Business Horizons* 60 (3): 395–404. https://doi.org/10.1016/j.bushor.2017.01.011.

Watkins, Michael. 2023. 'What Is Organizational Culture? And Why Should We Care?' Leadership Strategy. Harvard Business Review, May 15. https://hbr.org/2013/05/what-is-organizational-culture.

Weber, Yaakov, Oded Shenkar, and Adi Raveh. 1996. 'National and Corporate Cultural Fit in Mergers/Acquisitions: An Exploratory Study'. *Management Science* 42 (8): 1215–27. https://doi.org/10.1287/mnsc.42.8.1215.

Weston, Zachary. 2023. 'Title: A Journey Through Time: The Fascinating History of Airbnb'. *Medium*, July 22. https://medium.com/@zacharywestonintech/title-a-journey-through-time-the-fascinating-history-of-airbnb-4a9fcba94606.

Whalen, Thomas Brian. 2014. 'Utilizing the Social Transaction Theory of Social Ontology to Understand Organizational Culture Change'. *Journal of Business & Economics Research* 12 (1): 6.

Wilke, Alex, and Andrew Cocks. 2015. 'Creating an Adaptive High Performance Culture'. Questback. https://www.personneltoday.com/wp-content/uploads/sites/8/2016/05/Creating-an-Adaptive-High-Performance-Culture-Whitepaper.pdf.

Yarbrough, Larry, Neil A. Morgan, and Douglas W. Vorhies. 2011. 'The Impact of Product Market Strategy-Organizational Culture Fit on Business Performance'. *Journal of the Academy of Marketing Science* 39 (4): 555–73. https://doi.org/10.1007/s11747-010-0238-x.

Yuko, Melanie Pfaff, Annika Judith Wohlleber, Christopher Münch, Christoph Küffner, and Evi Hartmann. 2023. 'How Digital Transformation Impacts Organizational Culture – A Multi-Hierarchical Perspective on the Manufacturing Sector'. *Computers & Industrial Engineering* 183 (September): 109432. https://doi.org/10.1016/j.cie.2023.109432.

Zemke, Ayme. 2025. 'Strong Organizational Cultures Attract and Retain Top Talent'. *Beehive*, May. https://beehivepr.biz/strong-organizational-cultures/.

Chapter 4

Designing Adaptive Structures for Innovative Ecosystems

Pixar Animation Studios, based in Emeryville, California, produces computer-animated films that have won an impressive number of Best Animated Feature Academy Awards, including such early classics as *Finding Nemo* (2003), *The Incredibles* (2004), and *Ratatouille* (2007). Simone Stolzoff (2022) and Gustavo Razzetti (2020) both assert that a strong company culture is not driven by mission statements but rather designed as a collective, collaborative teamworking environment.[1] Ed Catmull, co-founder of Pixar Animation, recounts the story of a large conference room table that was stifling creative collaboration. The imposing table forced the group to sit in two opposing lines, and the place cards subtly reinforced hierarchy and status (the closer a place card was to the middle of the conference table, the more central and important the attendee appeared). Once Catmull realised this setup was reinforcing and conditioning status-driven hierarchical behaviour, he removed the table and binned the place cards. Ed Catmull describes how this simple structural tweak directly improved collaborative behaviour and positively influenced the organisational culture:

> the interplay was better, the exchange of ideas more free-flowing, the eye contact automatic. Every person there, no matter their job title, felt free to speak up. This was not only what we wanted, it was a fundamental Pixar belief: Unhindered communication was key, no matter what your position.
>
> (Catmull 2014, 4)

DOI: 10.4324/9781003680345-4

This simple example shows how structure determines behaviour, and that the solution to changing an organisational culture often lies in changing the conditioning structures that shape and influence it. Woolf (2024) is clear on this point:

> To harness the power of storytelling in the workplace, we must work toward eliminating structures that only favor some for sharing authentically. By dismantling these barriers, we pave the way for a more inclusive and empowering environment where the experiences of all individuals are valued and celebrated.

The role structure plays in conditioning collaboration and creativity is a significant part of Pixar's backstory. Ed Catmull writes about their unique workplace:

> Sometimes visitors misunderstand the place, thinking it's fancy for fancy's sake. What they miss is that the unifying idea for this building isn't luxury but community. Steve wanted the building to support our work by enhancing our ability to collaborate. The animators who work here are free to—no, encouraged to—decorate their workspaces in whatever style they wish. They spend their days inside pink dollhouses whose ceilings are hung with miniature chandeliers, tiki huts made of real bamboo, and castles whose meticulously painted, fifteen-foot-high styrofoam turrets appear to be carved from stone.
>
> (Catmull 2014, ix–x)

Pixar is a progressive company that ensures the structure and environment of the organisation support and reinforce its objectives, creative vision, and core values, including sharing, providing feedback (Razzetti 2020; Razzetti 2023), collaboration, and storytelling (Woolf 2024).

Pixar is a flat organisation where everybody is "entrusted... to drive their own projects forward, at their own pace" (Catmull 2014, 24). Communication and the exchange of ideas and information at Pixar don't go through hierarchical channels:

> People talking directly to one another, then letting the manager find out later, was more efficient than trying to make sure that everything happened in the "right" order and through the "proper" channels.
>
> (Catmull 2014, 64)

Catmull criticises the "cultural delusions associated with hierarchy, chiefly those that assign personal worth based on rank" (Catmull 2014, 110). He adds:

> That does not mean there is no hierarchy here. It means that we try to create an environment where people want to hear each other's notes, even when those notes are challenging, and where everyone has a vested interest in one another's success. We give our filmmakers both freedom and responsibility.
>
> (Catmull 2014, 172)

This opening Pixar case study highlights the association between organisational structure and the development of adaptive, innovative ecosystems. Mohammed Brückner (2024) describes Pixar as a "creative ecosystem", one that would not be able to thrive in a rigid structure:

> The physical space of Pixar is designed to encourage chance encounters between employees, much like how the structure of a coral reef facilitates interactions between diverse species. This layout has led to numerous collaborations and idea exchanges that might not have occurred in a more rigidly structured environment.
>
> (Brückner 2024)

It was noted in Chapter 3 that ecosystems thrive through the interfaces and dynamic interactions between the different parts of the organisation.[2] Such interplay is central to adaptive organisational structure. This chapter argues that only adaptive forms, such as modular or network-based structures, can cultivate open and responsive ecosystems.

Organisational structures form part of the business architecture's three pillars that indirectly shape organisational culture. They are part of the design element of building adaptive organisations. To sustain an open and adaptive ecosystem, organisations need to reduce structural rigidity. Visa, for example, adopted simpler structures in the 1960s when the introduction of the credit card profoundly disrupted organisational processes (Aghina, Aronowitz, and Hewes 2019).

This chapter provides an assortment of organisational structures, ranging from rigid to adaptive, and proposes that decentralised configurations best support innovative ecosystems. It goes on to outline a set of design principles for building adaptive structures suited to fluid and evolving organisational environments.

What Is Organisational Structure?

C.K. Gomathy (2023) believes organisational structure is a "vital element of any company's success" and, according to Sinqobile Nene and Alan S. Pillay (2019), helps the organisation achieve its goals and objectives. Robert Duncan observes:

> Organization structure is more than boxes on a chart; it is a pattern of interactions and coordination that links the technology, tasks and human components of the organization to ensure that the organization accomplishes its purpose.
>
> (Duncan 1979, 59)

Organisational structures are a "set of methods" by which "organizational activities are divided, organized and coordinated" (Ahmady et al. 2016, 455). Buchanan and Huczynski (2019) usefully compare organisational structures to the skeleton of an animal.

An effective organisational structure supports and shapes key elements of the organisation including organisational culture, strategy, digital transformation, knowledge management, innovation, communication, employee engagement, and change transformation.[3]

Adaptive Structures

Martin Reeves and Mike Deimler (2011) argue that an adaptive structure is a powerful lever for increasing adaptability. According to Benjamin Laker (2024), traditional rigid structures impede the flow of ideas and creativity. Adaptive structures come from an organisational theory that holds firms with flexible designs are better able to respond to changes in their external environment. Adaptive structures support a smoother flow of business intelligence (workflow) and collective decision-making (governance), resulting in emergent, self-organising ecosystems. This promotes higher customer responsiveness and gives organisations a competitive edge (Reeves and Deimler 2011).

An important theory for adaptive organisations is wirearchy. Coined in 1999, Jon Husband (2013) defined wirearchy as "a dynamic two-way flow of power and authority, based on knowledge, trust, credibility and a focus on results, enabled by interconnected people and technology". Adaptive structures are underpinned by this kind of dynamic flow of intelligence and knowledge.

A crucial decision for organisations is selecting the right adaptive structure that aligns with organisational culture and objectives. The following section provides a perspective on the history of organisational structures alongside a range of contemporary models.

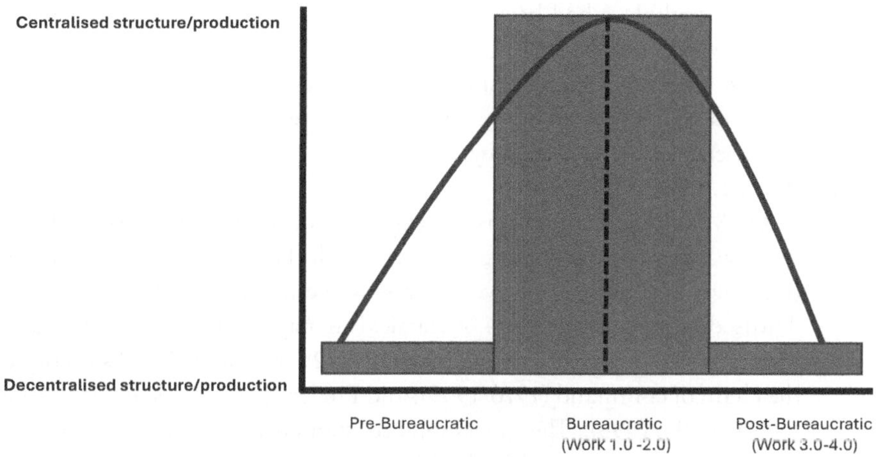

Figure 4.1 The inverse U-curve and organisational structure

Notes: This model uses pre-bureaucracy, bureaucracy, and post-bureaucracy as labels. Weber uses the term bureaucracy and pre-bureaucracy (Weber, 1944/2014), and others, such as Marsh (1961) and Dischner (2015) also use these terms. Henry Mintzberg calls it "the machine bureaucracy" and "the professional bureaucracy" in his model of organisational structure (Mintzberg et al. 1984).

Organisational Structure: Insights and Typologies

Organisational structure has evolved from Work 1.0 through to Work 4.0. Pre-industrial structures were clan-based with no centralised focus. Work 1.0 and 2.0 covered a period of centralised production. During Work 3.0, some organisations experimented with decentralising their structures to improve workflow and employee engagement. Work 4.0 is characterised by a return to fully decentralised forms. Figure 4.1 illustrates this evolution as an inverse U-curve, ranging from decentralised pre-bureaucratic structures (such as local cottage industries) to centralised bureaucratic production (the regulated factory system of late Work 1.0 and Work 2.0), and returning to decentralised post-bureaucratic structures (reflected in the shift to virtual workplaces in late Work 3.0 and Work 4.0).

Figure 4.1 shows the growth and peak of centralised production and organisational structures during Work 1.0 and 2.0, followed by the gradual decentralisation of organised work in late Work 3.0 and 4.0.

The broad idea of Work 1.0 to 4.0 was introduced in Chapter 1. Here are some further reflections.

1. Work 1.0 Centralisation

   In Work 1.0, production slowly transitioned from small cottage industries overseen by craft guilds to mills and factories. By the late Work 1.0

era, the workplace had become highly structured and centralised, with a clear division of labour. Rules and regulations were reinforced by conditioning structures such as sirens, centralised timing, and harsh factory discipline. This centralised workplace structure produced insular mindsets and a sense of being owned by the factory.

2. Work 2.0 Standardisation

   By Work 2.0, organisations had expanded beyond single mills and factories towards a more corporate structure, with the separation of production (factories) and administrative centres (offices). The workplace was standardised largely on the basis of classical management theories, including Max Weber's theory of bureaucracy (1944/2014), Henri Fayol's theory of the chain of command (1916/1949), and Frederick Taylor's standardisation theory (1911/1998). The era embraced standardised assembly-line mass production, transactional leadership, and bureaucratic structures such as pyramidal hierarchies (common in large organisations). A standardised workplace structure produced standardised mindsets and behaviours, in which workers were defined by their tasks.

3. Work 3.0 Globalisation

   Work 3.0 was a more global phenomenon. It included the rise of the digital age. This led to a natural reorganisation of internal structures to create better flows of information and decision-making to accommodate this information- and knowledge-driven era. Work environments underwent radical restructuring (General Motors called it "rightsizing"). Many organisations tried to flatten and decentralise their structures to increase engagement, accountability, and productivity among their knowledge workers.

4. Work 4.0 Personalisation

   As the world of work grows more complex and volatile and advances further into Work 4.0, organisations are revising their structures, just as they did at key moments in the past. Work will no longer be a physical place where you go to do structured tasks, but a virtual networked hub, an adaptive and organic point of connection. Dave Urich views the future workplace as a nexus of shared values and customised offerings: "Work is no longer a place – it's a way to think; it's a set of values... The boundary of work is the value I'm creating for my customer" (cited in Vander Wier 2021). Dave Macnee (2021) writes that the hybrid workplace trend involves "reconceptualizing a 'workplace' not as a building but as a network of equally important nodes". In Work 4.0, simplifying and reducing structures enhances the flow of business intelligence to support collective action, engagement, and system leadership.

Each of the Work 1.0 to 4.0 periods has its own unique set of structural challenges and solutions. Figure 4.2 provides a summary of organisational structures, grouped into pre- and post-bureaucratic clusters.

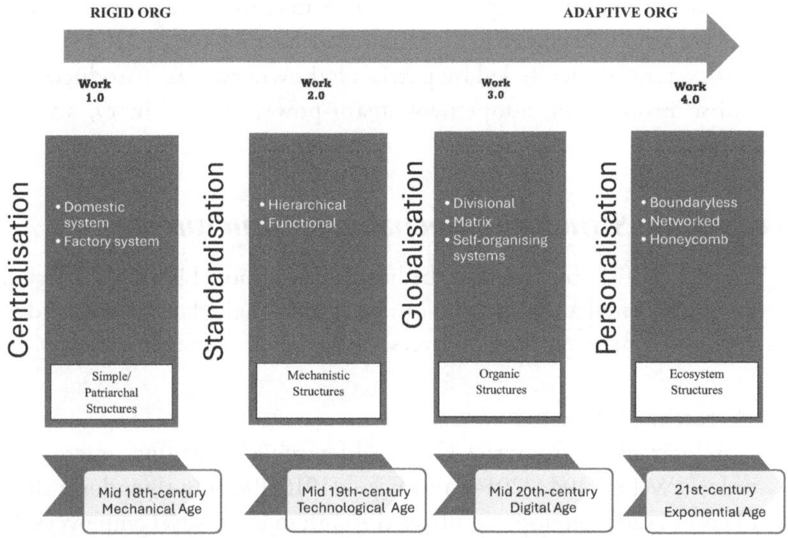

Figure 4.2 Organisational structures grouped into pre-bureaucratic/post-bureaucratic streams.

The following section explores the various structures from Work 1.0 to Work 4.0 that are shown in Figure 4.2.

Pre-bureaucracy Structure (Simple/Patriarchal Structures)

The two dominant organisational and work systems during the pre-bureaucratic period (extending up to the early phase of Industry 1.0) were the domestic system, including the cottage industry, and the factory system.

i. Domestic system (cottage industry)

   These were pockets or networks of artisans and producers who sold their products to travelling "clothiers" (cloth merchants) who visited the villages on pack horses. This domestic industry, supported by the Guilds, meant that workers could determine their own hours (often after working in the fields) and proceed at their own pace. Okechukwu E. Amah and Marvel Ogah (2023) characterise this as a family clan structure.

ii. Factory system (simple structure)

   The factory was a simple structure, a term popularised by Henry Mintzberg (1984), with production housed in a single-storey brick building, a central engine room, and machines dispersed throughout the factory. Okechukwu E. Amah and Marvel Ogah (2023) note that this system, typically led by patriarchal owners, was introduced to centralise production, adopt new steam-powered machinery, and reduce costs.[4]

Bureaucratic Structure (Mechanistic Structures)

Jarle Trondal (2017) observes that the bureaucratic model is a rigid, mechanistic structure with formal and functional rules, impersonal relationships, and hierarchies that suited mass production overseen by a paid management class.

i. Hierarchical structure

   Hierarchy is from the Greek "hierarchia" meaning "sacred rule of order". Weber (1944/2014) and Fayol (1916/1949) both endorse the chain of command from top executives through to lower-level employees. Carole Crumley (1979) defines hierarchy as a form of ranked subordination. Benjamin Laker (2024) believes hierarchies suppress and silence ideas and voices. The classic hierarchical structure is the pyramid, a line-and-staff process with degrees of authority pushing down from the apex to the base (Takahashi 1987). The hierarchical structure has survived into the modern workplace and some still champion it.[5]

ii. Functional structure

   Another way of grouping people within a hierarchical structure is by organising workers according to business function (for example, finance or human resources). It is also known as the role-based structure. This type of structuring, based on F.W. Taylor's scientific management and functional foremanship model (1911/1998) is one of the most common organisational structures with "clear chains of command and well-defined roles and responsibilities" (O'Reilly 2025). This hybrid of function and hierarchy led to the classic multi-divisional form structure (M-form), devised by Alfred Chandler (1962).

Post-bureaucratic Structures (Organic Structures)

The terms "mechanistic" and "organic" were introduced by Tom Burns and G.M. Stalker in their seminal 1961 text, *The Management of Innovation*. They observed that a mechanistic management system is effective in stable conditions, while an organic management system is suited to changing environments. Although mechanistic structures persisted in major corporations such as 3M and US Steel, many organisations in this period evolved their structures to become more organic. Examples of organic forms that emerged at this time include divisional structures, matrix structures, and various self-organising frameworks such as the Lattice, Teal, and Holacracy models.

i. Divisional structure (1940s–60s)

   The divisional structure is a hybrid model that became popular in the post-World War II era as companies expanded into international markets and diversified their product portfolios. Its design underpinned the early stages of globalisation by allowing firms to manage different regions, products, or business lines more effectively. This period also saw a rise in mergers and acquisitions, which required a more accommodating and decentralised structure. In a divisional structure, each division operates as a semi-autonomous unit, often referred to as a Strategic Business Unit (SBU), with its own profit-and-loss responsibility. This is designed to give large organisations flexibility, focus, and accountability within individual business domains. While divisions can make many independent strategic decisions, they are typically part of a formal umbrella structure with a divisional head who reports to the corporate headquarters or group CEO. Notable examples of SBUs include Procter & Gamble (P&G), which organises its SBUs by product line, and General Electric (GE), which historically structured its SBUs by industry segment.

ii. Matrix (1950s–70s)

   This form combines functional structures with product structures. It is a cross-functional organisational structure in which employees have dual reporting lines, typically reporting to both a functional manager (e.g., in marketing, finance, or engineering) and a project, product, or regional manager. Companies such as Philips and Nestlé have historically used matrix structures to manage complex operations across functions and markets.

iii. Self-organising systems

   Self-organising systems lie at the extreme end of the spectrum of organic organisational structures. One of the earliest examples is the lattice structure, which was introduced by *W.L. Gore & Associates* in the mid-twentieth century. Founder Bill Gore envisioned an organisation functioning like a living organism, not a machine. The lattice model, an early form of networked structure, has no formal hierarchy or job titles (employees at *W.L. Gore & Associates* are called "associates"), and instead relies on peer-to-peer accountability, and direct communication.

Contemporary self-organising models include Teal and Holacracy. Holacracy was developed by Brian Robertson and formalised in his 2015 book, *Holacracy: The New Management System for a Rapidly Changing World*. It replaces job titles with roles that are grouped into self-governing circles. Each circle has a lead that oversees a distributed authority. Companies like Zappos initially embraced Holacracy but later scaled back due to its complexity and rigid rules. Teal organisations, outlined by Frédéric Laloux in *Reinventing Organizations* (2014), follow principles of self-management, wholeness, and evolutionary purpose. Teal structures avoid traditional hierarchy and use distributed decision-making processes. Laloux profiles the Dutch healthcare provider Buurtzorg as an example of a Teal organisation.

Post-bureaucratic Structures (Business Ecosystem Structures)

Ecosystems were defined earlier as interdependent, system-wide, external collaborations distributed across multiple autonomous organisations. This chapter presents three ecosystem structures: boundaryless, networked, and honeycomb. Innovative business-ecosystem structures are useful organising principles for navigating the complexity and dynamism of Industry 4.0. They offer adaptability, resilience, and a form of collaborative innovation that traditional structures often cannot provide.

i. Boundaryless organisations

   The boundaryless workplace concept was pioneered at GE under CEO Jack Welch. Ronald Ashkenas and coauthors wrote a definitive book on the subject, *The Boundaryless Organization: Breaking the Chains of Organizational Structure* (1998). Their work embraced ideas of business ecosystems. Larry Hirschhorn and Thomas Gilmore (1992) observe that boundaryless organisations "break down the boundaries that make organizations rigid and unresponsive". Organisational hierarchy and geographical barriers are removed to encourage open communication, a free flow of ideas, self-accountability, continuous improvement, collaboration, and cross-functional teams. Ronald Ashkenas and his author team (1998) demonstrate how GE used a "work-out" model that brought people together in the same room across functions, levels, and geographies to have structured conversations that led to problem-solving real-time decisions.

ii. Network organisational structure

   An organisation with a network structure actively connects with other actors in the ecosystem to collectively accomplish goals. Robyn Keast and coauthors observe:

> A network structure forms when these people realize they (and the organizations they represent) are only one small piece of the total picture. It is a recognition that only by coming together to actively work on accomplishing a broad, common mission will goals be accomplished. (Keast et al. 2004, 364)

The emphasis here is on external collaborations, partnerships, outsourcing, and alliances, which has been characterised as a "business superorganism" (Kelly 2022). Work 4.0 and the workplace of the future will develop robust networks and connections through technology. Work that flows through networks rather than supervised centres of production is an ideal organisational structure for virtual working, which, according to Sean Goggins and Giuseppe Valetto (2014), flourishes on "structural fluidity". A great example of a network organisation which nurtures ecosystems is the Haier Group. It does this using the Rendanheyi model, a management approach that gives employees more freedom to make decisions and connects them directly with customers.

iii. Honeycomb structure

A honeycomb structure is a modular, networked ecosystem of interconnecting hexagons. Each self-governing hexagonal cell is collaborative, has a clear purpose, acts independently, and as Jacobides, Cennamo, and Gawer (2018) show, contributes to a broader strategic ecosystem.

Figure 4.3 outlines this.

Reeves, Morieux, and Deimler (2010) argue that each hexagon cell is an intact, self-organising cell that can reconfigure:

> Standardized (plug-and-play) interfaces enable the organization to recombine parts and rapidly introduce variations in products and processes at low cost and risk, as well as rapid shifts in resource allocation.

Cells can dock with other independent cells to begin developing a cross-functional ecosystem. They can replicate within the organisation or through external systems. Ideas flow through the connected parts of the hexagon (represented in Figure 4.3 by the thick lines). Richard Kelly observes, "organisations are wired together through the interconnections of people and technology rather than through alpha leadership and hierarchy" (Kelly 2022, 130), a process that Jon Husband (2013) termed Wirearchy, meaning "the power and effectiveness of people working together through connection and collaboration".

The honeycomb structure is an emerging concept. Some organisations are using honeycomb-like principles, including IBM, which has

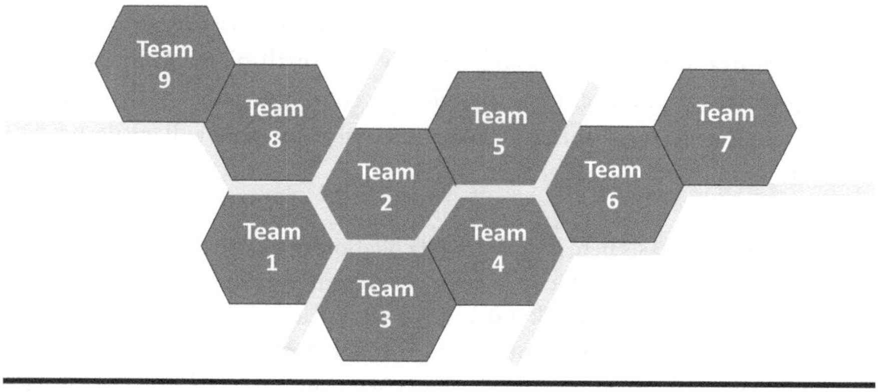

Figure 4.3 Typical hexagon structure.

experimented with aspects of the honeycomb organisational structure, particularly in its approach to innovation, agility, and cross-functional collaboration. IBM developed the idea of a "hypergrowth honeycomb" structure, which Garrick Keatts, Managing Partner at IBM Consulting (2018), explains "reflects a connected team with equally important parts. It illustrates that we are all working together in the honeycomb, not necessarily 'for' one another or 'above' one another". The IBM Garage Model (a collaborative innovation framework used to design, develop, and scale digital solutions) is perhaps the clearest reflection of honeycomb principles, which has cross-functional, agile, and customer-centric teams known as "pods". Each pod functions as an autonomous unit and includes designers, developers, architects, and business consultants. This works in both physical and virtual environments. The cell quickly connects with other cells to form a dynamic, global. and adaptive network.

The point of the honeycomb model is its cell-like structure that has the potential to replicate like a natural organism or like DNA. David Gray and co-author Thomas Vander Wal popularised the idea of the podular structure because it "focuses on modularizing work: making units more independent, adaptive, linkable, and swappable". (Gray 2012, 153). Reeves, Morieux, and Deimler (2010) also endorse modular structures for their "flexibility in a changing environment".

The honeycomb structure and model will be used in a fictionalised case-study in Chapter 9.

This section has been exploring pre-bureaucratic, bureaucratic, and post-bureaucratic structures. Each historical epoch developed organisational structures to suit their evolving work culture. Organisations have been using organic organisational structures for over 50 years, which has helped them evolve into what Senge and others call the learning organisation. As we move into uncertain times, with increased complexity and volatility, organic structures (which formally helped insular organisations to be more flexible, agile, and collaborative) are no longer fit-for-purpose. Ecosystem are dominating the business landscape in Industry 4.0.

Chapter Debrief: Presenting Some Guiding Principles Using the 4 O Framework

The introductory chapter noted that in building adaptive organisations, guiding principles replace detailed operating procedures (Reeves et al. 2010). There is no "one-size-fits-all" approach in a complex adaptive system. Having carefully established the connection between adaptive structures and organisational ecosystems, this final section outlines a set of general design principles aimed to help decision-makers create truly adaptive structures. An original model that helps structure this debrief is the 4 O Framework (see Figure 4.4), an acronym for Objective, Options, Orientation, and Outlook.

1. Objective

   Cooke and Rousseau (1988) argue that structure is an "important culture-bearing mechanism in organisations" (247). When thinking about organisational structures, it is important to begin by clarifying the organisational culture you aspire to develop. Rather than focusing solely on managing systems, organisations should focus on their goals, as this enables the effective flow of information, insight, and decision-making throughout the organisation.

   A helpful starting point is to appraise the existing organisational culture using a recognised diagnostic model, such as Cameron and Quinn's *Competing Values Framework* (2011), and then project forward to identify the cultural characteristics required for a successful adaptive organisation. Defining the desired organisational direction in terms of purpose, goals, and outcomes will helps determine which models and pathways to adopt.

   Consider how the organisation connects with customers and partners, and establish how it should operate on a day-to-day basis, including the degree of employee input, the preferred decision-making style, and the and

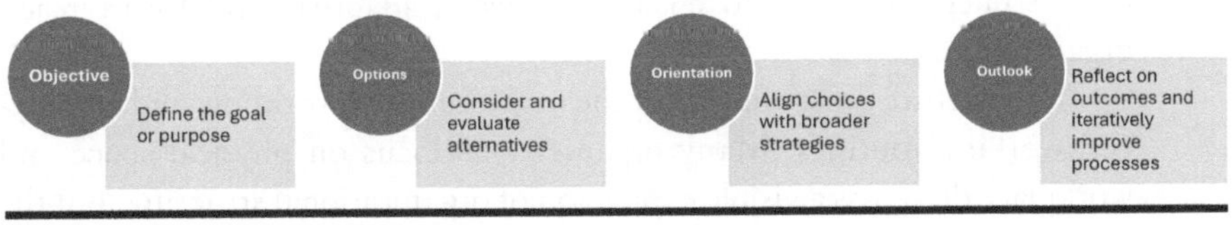

Figure 4.4 The 4 O Framework.

the required level of adaptability. This reflective stage is vital because many organisations claim they want to be more adaptive, yet they haven't always considered the full implications of moving in this direction.

2. Options

   Organisational structures serve different objectives and generate different outcomes, so it is essential for the enterprise to familiarise itself with the available options to determine which structure best supports its purpose. Table 4.1 summarises the structures discussed in the previous section and their typical applications.

   Review the range of organisational structures and select the one best suited for the operating environment. This reflects the logic of contingency theory, which holds that there is no single best way to organise or manage a system; instead, the effectiveness of any structure depends on how well it fits with the surrounding conditions. Diane Hamilton (2024) says every organisation must find its own balance. For example, a stable environment may support a highly structured system, whereas a more turbulent environment calls for flexibility, decentralisation, and adaptability. As summarised in Table 4.1 different structures come with different applications and trade-offs. If an organisation is committed to becoming truly adaptive, a modular structure provides the greatest potential to flex and thrive in complex, dynamic environments.

3. Orientation

   Organisational structures should be designed to support overall objectives and remain aligned with the organisation's governance, workflow, digital, people, and change processes. As Eva Hartl and Thomas Hess observe:

   > Firms need to transform and digitalize their entire business models and the accompanying existing organizational conditions, such as structures, processes and culture. (Hartl and Hess 2017, 1)

The link between strategy and structure is well established in the research. As noted earlier, C.K. Gomathy (2023) said, "structure must align with the company's strategic goals to ensure its success" (2). When considering organisational structure, decision-makers should account for these strategic enablers to ensure a holistic, adaptive, and future-ready organisation.

The structure must align with the organisational workflow and employees' working routines. Many organisations focus on physical space and workplace design as a visible expression of organisational structure, but the underlying culture must be properly aligned.

Table 4.1 Organisational Structures from Work 1.0 to Work 4.0 with Examples

Organisational Structure	*Best for...*	*Select Examples*
Domestic system	Small family-run businesses or platform-based businesses where self-employed workers operate under a franchise or distributed model	Small family-run businesses
Factory system	Plant-based, standardised, mass-production manufacturing	Ford
Hierarchical organisation	Large, highly regulated organisation requiring a clear chain of command defined authority	McDonald's, 3M, US Steel
Functional organisation	Small to mid-sized organisations with a narrow product or service focus, often in regulated environments	General Motors, JP Morgan
Divisional Structure	Large, diversified organisations, operating across multiple markets or product categories	PepsiCo, Amazon, Apple
Matrix	Complex organisations operating across functions and markets simultaneously	Philips, Nestlé
Self-organising structures	Teams or individuals with autonomy to make decisions about how they work, without relying on traditional top-down management	W.L. Gore & Associates
Boundaryless structure	Organisations that need to innovate and collaborate fluidly across internal and external boundaries	General Electric (GE)
Network structure	Organisations requiring flexibility, scalability, and access to specialised external expertise	The Haier Group
Honeycomb structure	Organisations operating as part of an ecosystem with modular, cell-like units	IBM

There also needs to be digital alignment. Liu, Fang, and Ma (2025) characterise Pixar as a digital innovation ecosystem, showing how creative enterprises integrate technology and structure to sustain innovation.

4. Outlook

Organisations need to stay current with emerging theories on organisational structures and ecosystems. It is important to maintain an ongoing dialogue with employees about their working needs and expectations. The workplace is undergoing an extraordinary period of transformation, yet many organisational leaders underestimate the influence employees have in shaping the future of work. As highlighted in this chapter, the future workplace will extend beyond a physical location (Vander Wier 2021). Adaptive Structuration Theory (AST), developed by DeSanctis and Poole (1994), is particularly relevant here as it suggests organisational structures (especially technology-enabled structures) are shaped not only by their formal design but also how people use and reinterpret them in practice.

Smart factories and cyber-physical systems will revolutionise both production and human roles, while advances in AI and machine learning will redefine not only tasks but the very nature of collaboration, coordination, and organisational purpose.

These shifts underline the need to view organisational design as an ongoing evolution rather than a one-off project. This links with research on dynamic capabilities (Teece, Peteraf, and Leih 2016), which emphasises the importance of sensing change, seizing opportunities, and transforming organisational configurations.

In this context, organisational structure becomes an evolving system that must respond to technological shifts, market dynamics, and changing workforce expectations. Organisations that embrace continuous learning, experimentation, and cultural adaptability will be better positioned to thrive in increasingly interconnected, rapidly changing ecosystems.

Synthesis: Developing Adaptive Structures

This chapter examined organisational structures as one of the pillars of business architecture. Positioned within the design cluster, it argues that creating an adaptive organisation requires continually adapting the underlying organisational design. The chapter explored Pixar's use of structure to reinforce its creative ecosystem and illustrated how organisational structures enable businesses to pursue their purpose. Adaptive structures serve as powerful levers that help organisations respond effectively to changing environments.

The chapter traced the evolution of organisational structure from pre-industrial forms to the Work 4.0 era, highlighting the increasing importance of ecosystem-oriented models. Structures such as the honeycomb model were recommended as modular approaches well-suited to building adaptive organisations. The chapter concluded with a set of design principles emphasising the importance of defining organisational purpose, selecting an appropriate structural framework, ensuring alignment with strategy, and continuously evolving the structural configuration.

The next chapter examines governance as the second design pillar of building an adaptive organisation.

Notes

1. The following authors explore teamworking culture: Razzetti (2023); Nesirat (2023); and Catmull (2008).
2. Authors who explore this idea include Shraiber (2023); Geraci (2016); and Altman et al. (2021).
3. Here is the passage with added references. An effective organisational structure supports and shapes key elements of the organisation including organisational culture (Cooke and Rousseau 1988; Verdu-Jover et al. 2018) strategy (Gomathy 2023), digital transformation (Shahzad, Imran, and Butt 2025; Mustafa et al. 2022), knowledge management (Zheng, Yang, and McLean 2010), innovation and communication (Burns and Stalker 1961), employee engagement (Funminiyi 2018; Adducul-Baria et al. 2024), and change transformation (Wang, Chen, and Yang 2020).
4. Pat Hudson argues that domestic and factory coexisted in the first industrial revolution and that there wasn't a sudden break to the factory system (Hudson 2004).
5. Supporters of hierarchical structures include, Jaques 1990; Simon 1991; Desmarais 2012; Zimmerman 2014; Zitek and Phillips 2020; and The Economist 2025).

Bibliography

Adducul-Baria, Sheryl A., Kirsten Doreen C. Gatan, Ivory D. Domincel, Valdez Ednaly Jane P., and Elnora V. Adalem. 2024. 'Organizational Structure and Employees' Performance: The Case of a Multipurpose Cooperative in Nueva Vizcaya'. *International Journal of Research and Innovation in Social Science* VIII (III): 2936–64. https://doi.org/10.47772/IJRISS.2024.803203.

Aghina, Wouter, Steven Aronowitz, and Caitlin Hewes. 2019. 'Rethinking the Boundaries of Your Organizational (Eco)System'. Business. McKinsey & Company, December 16. https://www.mckinsey.com/capabilities/people-and-organizational-performance/our-insights/the-organization-blog/rethinking-the-boundaries-of-your-organizational-ecosystem.

Ahmady, Gholam Ali, Maryam Mehrpour, and Aghdas Nikooravesh. 2016. 'Organizational Structure'. *Procedia – Social and Behavioral Sciences* 230 (September): 455–62. https://doi.org/10.1016/j.sbspro.2016.09.057.

Altman, Elizabeth J., David Kiron, Jeff Schwartz, and Robin Jones. 2021. 'The Future of Work Is Through Workforce Ecosystems'. *MIT Sloan Management Review*, January 14. https://sloanreview.mit.edu/article/the-future-of-work-is-through-workforce-ecosystems/.

Amah, Okechukwu E., and Marvel Ogah. 2023. 'Leadership in the Pre-Industrial and Early Industrial Revolution'. In *Leadership and Organisational Effectiveness Post-COVID-19*, edited by Okechukwu E. Amah and Marvel Ogah. Springer International Publishing. https://doi.org/10.1007/978-3-031-32763-6_2.

Ashkenas, Ronald N., Dave Ulrich, Todd Jich, and Steve Herr. 1998. *The Boundaryless Organization: Breaking the Chains of Organizational Structure*. Jossey-Bass.

Brückner, Mohammed. 2024. 'Pixar, a Dream Machine'. *Operations Research Bit*, June 25. https://medium.com/operations-research-bit/pixar-a-dream-machine-b3145769aff5.

Buchanan, David A., and Andrzej Huczynski. 2019. *Organizational Behaviour*. 10th edition. Pearson.

Burns, Tom, and G. M. Stalker. 1961. *The Management of Innovation*. 1st edition. Tavistock.

Cameron, Kim S., and Robert E. Quinn. 2011. *Diagnosing and Changing Organizational Culture: Based on the Competing Values Framework*. 3rd edition. The Jossey-Bass Business & Management Series. Jossey-Bass.

Catmull, Ed. 2008. 'How Pixar Fosters Collective Creativity'. *Harvard Business Magazine*, September. https://hbr.org/2008/09/how-pixar-fosters-collective-creativity.

Catmull, Edwin E. 2014. *Creativity, Inc: Overcoming the Unseen Forces That Stand in the Way of True Inspiration*. With Amy Wallace. Random House.

Chandler, Alfred D. 1962. *Strategy and Structure: Chapters in the History of the American Industrial Enterprise*. MIT Press.

Cooke, Robert A., and Denise M. Rousseau. 1988. 'Behavioral Norms and Expectations: A Quantitative Approach To the Assessment of Organizational Culture'. *Group & Organization Studies* 13 (3): 245–73. https://doi.org/10.1177/105960118801300302.

Crumley, Carole. 1979. 'Three Locational Models: An Epistemological Assessment for Anthropology and Archaeolog'. *Advances in Archaeological Method and Theory* 2: 141–73.

DeSanctis, Gerardine, and Marshall Scott Poole. 1994. 'Capturing the Complexity in Advanced Technology Use: Adaptive Structuration Theory'. *Organization Science* 5 (2): 121–47. https://doi.org/10.1287/orsc.5.2.121.

Desmarais, Christina. 2012. 'Your Employees Like Hierarchy (No, Really)'. Business. Inc., August 16. https://www.inc.com/christina-desmarais/your-employees-like-hierarchy-no-really.html.

Dischner, Simon. 2015. 'Organizational Structure, Organizational Form, and Counterproductive Work Behavior: A Competitive Test of the Bureaucratic and Post-Bureaucratic Views'. *Scandinavian Journal of Management* 31 (4): 501–14. https://doi.org/10.1016/j.scaman.2015.10.002.

Duncan, Robert. 1979. 'What Is the Right Organization Structure? Decision Tree Analysis Provides the Answer'. *Organizational Dynamics* 7 (3): 59–80. https://doi.org/10.1016/0090-2616(79)90027–5.

Fayol, Henri. 1916. *General and Industrial Management*. Translated by Constance Storrs. Pitman.

Funminiyi, Adeoye K. 2018. 'Impact of Organisational Structure on Employee Engagement: Evidence from North Central Nigeria'. *International Journal of Advanced Engineering, Management and Science* 4 (8): 579–89. https://doi.org/10.22161/ijaems.4.8.1.

Geraci, John. 2016. 'What I Learned from Trying to Innovate at the New York Times'. *Harvard Business Review*, April 7. https://hbr.org/2016/04/what-i-learned-from-trying-to-innovate-at-the-new-york-times.

Goggins, Sean P., and Giuseppe Valetto. 2014. 'Assessing the Structural Fluidity of Virtual Organizations and Its Effects'. In *Socioinformatics – The Social Impact of Interactions between Humans and IT*, edited by Katharina Zweig, Wolfgang Neuser, Volkmar Pipek, Markus Rohde, and Ingo Scholtes. Springer Proceedings in Complexity. Springer International Publishing. 121-137. https://doi.org/10.1007/978-3-319-09378-9_8.

Gomathy, C. K. 2023. 'A Study on Organization Structure and Design'. *Interantional Journal of Scientific Research in Engineering and Management* 7 (6): 1–5. https://doi.org/10.55041/IJSREM20880.

Gray, David. 2012. *The Connected Company*. With Thomas Vander Wal. O'Reilly.

Hamilton, Diane. 2024. 'Thriving in a Flat Organization: Strategies for Agility and Innovation'. Business. Forbes, September 5. https://www.forbes.com/sites/dianehamilton/2024/09/05/thriving-in-a-flat-organization-strategies-for-agility-and-innovation/.

Hartl, Eva, and Thomas Hess. 2017. 'The Role of Cultural Values for Digital Transformation: Insights from a Delphi Study'. Paper presented at Proceedings of the 23rd Americas Conference on Information Systems (AMCIS 2017), Boston, USA. *ResearchGate*, August. https://www.researchgate.net/publication/330353915_The_Role_of_Cultural_Values_for_Digital_Transformation_Insights_from_a_Delphi_Study.

Hirschhorn, Larry, and Thomas Gilmore. 1992. 'The New Boundaries of the "Boundaryless" Company'. *Harvard Business Review*. https://hbr.org/1992/05/the-new-boundaries-of-the-boundaryless-company.

Hudson, Pat. 2004. 'Industrial Organisation and Structure'. In *The Cambridge Economic History of Modern Britain*, edited by Roderick Floud and Paul Arthur Johnson, 1 Industrialisation 1700–1860. Cambridge university press.

Husband, Jon. 2013. 'What Is Wirearchy ?' Wirearchy, February 16. https://wirearchy.com/what-is-wirearchy/.

Jacobides, Michael G., Carmelo Cennamo, and Annabelle Gawer. 2018. 'Towards a Theory of Ecosystems'. *Strategic Management Journal* 39 (8): 2255–76. https://doi.org/10.1002/smj.2904.

Jaques, Elliott. 1990. 'In Praise of Hierarchy'. *Harvard Business Magazine*, February. https://hbr.org/1990/01/in-praise-of-hierarchy.

Keast, Robyn, Myrna P. Mandell, Kerry Brown, and Geoffrey Woolcock. 2004. 'Network Structures: Working Differently and Changing Expectations'. *Public Administration Review* 64 (3): 363–71. https://doi.org/10.1111/j.1540-6210.2004.00380.x.

Keatts, Garrick. 2018. 'The Ride Home – The Honeycomb, Maybe Your Next Organization Model'. Business. LinkedIn, February 22. https://www.linkedin.com/pulse/ride-home-honeycomb-maybe-your-next-organization-model-keatts/.

Kelly, Richard. 2022. *The Nature of Business Transformation: A Swarm Intelligent Approach to Reinventing Organisations*. Routledge.

Laker, Benjamin. 2024. 'Why Rigid Hierarchies Might Be Killing Your Team's Creativity'. Leadership. Forbes, August 15. https://www.forbes.com/sites/benjaminlaker/2024/08/15/why-rigid-hierarchies-might-be-killing-your-teams-creativity/.

Laloux, Frédéric. 2014. *Reinventing Organizations: A Guide to Creating Organizations Inspired by the Next Stage of Human Consciousness*. Nelson Parker.

Liu, Jiamin, Yongheng Fang, and Yabing Ma. 2025. 'The Driving Impact of Digital Innovation Ecosystems on Enterprise Digital Transformation: Based on an Interpretable Machine Learning Model'. *Sustainability* 17 (13): 5898. https://doi.org/10.3390/su17135898.

Macnee, Dave. 2021. 'Building a Connected Organization'. *Future Forum*, June 15. https://futureforum.com/2021/06/15/building-a-connected-organization/.

Marsh, Robert M. 1961. 'Formal Organization and Promotion in a Pre-Industrial Society'. *American Sociological Review* 26 (4): 547. https://doi.org/10.2307/2090253.

Mintzberg, Henry, Danny Miller, and Peter H. Friesen. 1984. *Organizations: A Quantum View*. 1. [Print.]. Prentice-Hall.

Mustafa, Ghulam, Hans Solli-Sæther, Virginia Bodolica, Jon Ivar Håvold, and Anam Ilyas. 2022. 'Digitalization Trends and Organizational Structure: Bureaucracy, Ambidexterity or Post-Bureaucracy?' *Eurasian Business Review* 12 (4): 671–94. https://doi.org/10.1007/s40821-021-00196-8.

Nene, Sinqobile W., and Alan S. Pillay. 2019. 'An Investigation of the Impact of Organisational Structure on Organisational Performance'. *Financial Risk and Management Reviews* 5 (1): 10–24. https://doi.org/10.18488/journal.89.2019.51.10.24.

Nesirat, Yosef. 2023. 'To Infinity and Beyond: The Incredible Success Story of Pixar Animation Studios Through Teamwork… | by Yosef Nesirat'. Business. Medium, April 13. https://medium.com/leadership-by-design/to-infinity-and-beyond-the-incredible-success-story-of-pixar-animation-studios-through-teamwork-c86eed815b6.

O'Reilly, Dennis. 2025. '7 Organizational Structure Types (With Examples)'. With Lauren Holznienkemper . https://www.forbes.com/advisor/business/organizational-structure/.

Razzetti, Gustavo. 2020. 'How Pixar Designed a Culture of Collective Creativity'. Business. Fearless Culture, January 5. https://fearlessculture.design/blog-posts/pixar-culture-design-canvas.

Razzetti, Gustavo. 2023. '12 Examples of Powerful Cultures from Successful Companies'. Business. Fearless Culture, January 19. https://fearlessculture.design/blog-posts/11-examples-of-companies-with-powerful-cultures.

Reeves, Martin, and Mike Deimler. 2011. 'Adaptability: The New Competitive Advantage'. *Harvard Business Review*, August. https://hbr.org/2011/07/adaptability-the-new-competitive-advantage.

Reeves, Martin, Yves Morieux, and Michael Deimler. 2010. 'People Advantage'. Culture. BCG Global, March 25. https://www.bcg.com/publications/2010/strategy-behavior-culture-people-advantage.

Robertson, Brian J. 2015. *Holacracy: The New Management System for a Rapidly Changing World*. 1st edition. Business and Management. Holt.

Shahzad, Khuram, Faisal Imran, and Aurangzeab Butt. 2025. 'Digital Transformation and Changes in Organizational Structure: Empirical Evidence from Industrial Organizations'. *Research-Technology Management* 68 (3): 25–40. https://doi.org/10.1080/08956308.2025.2465706.

Shraiber, Walter. 2023. 'The Perils of an Egosystem and the Promise of an Ecosystem'. Medium, September 25. https://magazine.eau.university/the-perils-of-an-egosystem-and-the-promise-of-an-ecosystem-6aca08a916af.

Simon, Herbert A. 1991. 'The Architecture of Complexity'. In *Facets of Systems Science*, edited by George J. Klir. Springer US. https://doi.org/10.1007/978-1-4899-0718-9_31.

Stolzoff, Simone. 2022. 'Why the President of Pixar Doesn't Believe in Mission Statements'. Business. Quartz, July 21. https://qz.com/work/1385570/why-the-president-of-pixar-doesnt-believe-in-mission-statements.

Takahashi, Nobuo. 1987. *Design of Adaptive Organizations: Models and Empirical Research*. Lecture Notes in Economics and Mathematical Systems Ser, v. 291. Springer.

Taylor, Frederick Winslow. 1911. *The Principles of Scientific Management*. Dover Publications.

Teece, David J., Margaret A. Peteraf, and Stephan Leih. 2016. 'Dynamic Capabilities and Organizational Agility: Risk, Uncertainty, and Strategy in the Innovation Economy'. *California Management Review* 58 (4): 13–35. https://doi.org/10.1525/cmr.2016.58.4.13.

The Economist. 2025. 'The Signals of Workplace Submissiveness'. *The Economist*, January 11. https://www.economist.com/business/2025/01/09/the-signals-of-workplace-submissiveness.

Trondal, Jarle. 2017. 'Bureaucratic Structure'. In *Global Encyclopedia of Public Administration, Public Policy, and Governance*, edited by Ali Farazmand. Springer Reference Live – Living Reference Work. Springer. https://doi.org/10.1007/978-3-319-31816–5.

Vander Wier, Marcel. 2021. 'Work 4.0: The Future of Work Is Hybrid, Personalized'. Business. Features. *Talent Canada (Queens University IRC)*, April 26. https://www.talentcanada.ca/work-4-0-the-future-of-work-is-hybrid-personalized/.

Verdu-Jover, Antonio J., Lirios Alos-Simo, and Jose-Maria Gomez-Gras. 2018. 'Adaptive Culture and Product/Service Innovation Outcomes'. *European Management Journal* 36 (3): 330–40. https://doi.org/10.1016/j.emj.2017.07.004.

Wang, Xiaoling, Yan Chen, and Bo Yang. 2020. 'The Choice of Organizational Structure in the Internet Era: Flattening and Decentralization – Based on Perspective of Dynamic Capabilities'. *American Journal of Management Science and Engineering* 5 (4): 42. https://doi.org/10.11648/j.ajmse.20200504.11.

Weber, Max. 1944. *Rationalism and Modern Society: New Translations on Politics, Bureaucracy, and Social Stratification*. Translated by Tony Waters and Dagmar Waters. Palgrave Macmillan.

Woolf, Jamie. 2024. *How Pixar Fosters a Culture of Vulnerability at Work*. Harvard Business Review. https://hbr.org/2024/03/how-pixar-fosters-a-culture-of-vulnerability-at-work.

Zheng, Wei, Baiyin Yang, and Gary N. McLean. 2010. 'Linking Organizational Culture, Structure, Strategy, and Organizational Effectiveness: Mediating Role of Knowledge Management'. *Journal of Business Research* 63 (7): 763–71. https://doi.org/10.1016/j.jbusres.2009.06.005.

Zimmerman, Eilene. 2014. 'Jeffrey Pfeffer: Do Workplace Hierarchies Still Matter?' University. Stanford Graduate School of Business, March 24. https://www.gsb.stanford.edu/insights/jeffrey-pfeffer-do-workplace-hierarchies-still-matter.

Zitek, Emily M, and L Taylor Phillips. 2020. 'Ease and Control: The Cognitive Benefits of Hierarchy'. *Current Opinion in Psychology* 33 (June): 131–35. https://doi.org/10.1016/j.copsyc.2019.07.015.

Chapter 5

Designing Adaptive Governance for Self-Organising Systems

Over a period of two decades, Cisco rewired its governance model and emerged as a truly adaptive organisation and self-organising system. CEO of Cisco from 1995 to 2015, John Chambers, transformed the organisation over 20 years from a company specialising in routers and switches with an annual revenue of $1.2 billion to an internet infrastructure company with annual revenues of $47 billion (Law 2024). This was partly achieved by transforming the organisation from a rigidly centralised entity to an adaptive governance, supported by a bespoke organisational Matrix structure.

Chambers realised that the company's centralised structure no longer supported the speed and adaptability the company required (The Economist 2009). Chambers oversaw the development of cross-functional councils, boards, and self-organising committees. This decentralised, externally focused, self-organising, and collective decision-making culture formed the essence of Cisco's new adaptive governance. Reeves, Morieux, and Deimler (2010) observe:

> Cisco transformed itself from a company in which a few people made all the decisions to one with a decentralized, externally focused council structure. Employees are allowed to form boards even with out a formal leader, thereby increasing agility and exploration. The company built a culture that is more amenable to risk taking and more accepting of failure.

DOI: 10.4324/9781003680345-5

John Chambers (2016) notes that 40 per cent of the top leadership was replaced during the transformation from a silo to a collective and adaptive governance model.

Cisco is an excellent example of a large company that adjusted its traditional structures to enable more collective, adaptive governance, thereby increasing organisational speed and innovation.

This chapter defines governance using a range of well-established sources. It examines organisational governance in the context of industrial revolution legacies and considers its future in light of emerging technologies such as AI and blockchain. The traditional hierarchical and sequential governance structure, dominated by alpha decision-making, will be rejected in favour of an adaptive and digital governance suited to the future self-organising workplace. The chapter focuses on Alfred Chandler's "visible hand" of governance, which relates to the management of day-to-day business activities.[1] Strategies and design principles will also be explored in this chapter, including creating a collective decision-making culture, encouraging system leadership, nurturing local enablement, implementing flexible compliance, promoting cross-functional collaboration, and anticipating digital and ecosystem governance.

What Is Organisational Governance?

Governance is a system for managing organisations. Nick von Tunzelmann (2003) believes it to be a "fashionable but often elusive term" (366). Lynda Bourne (2014) usefully lists six functions of organisational governance, highlighting that governance is not merely about setting up frameworks but also involves the determination of objectives, ethics, culture, compliance, accountability, and the design and implementation of organisational governance frameworks.

Corporate governance has dominated the modern workplace. The Organisation for Economic Co-operation and Development (OECD) provides a current definition of corporate governance:

> corporate governance is the system by which business corporations are directed and controlled. The corporate governance structure specifies the distribution of rights and responsibilities among different participants in the corporation, such as the board, managers, shareholders and other stakeholders, and spells out the rules and procedures for making decisions on corporate affairs. By doing this, it also provides the structures through which the company objectives are set, and the means of attaining those objectives and monitoring performance.
>
> **(Cited in Khan 2011, 2).**[2]

Other commentators such as Xue Yu Chen (2024) emphasise the ethical and responsible nature of corporate governance. Lord Adrian Cadbury, who chaired the Cadbury Commission resulting in the Cadbury Report on Corporate Governance in the UK, stated that the objective of corporate governance is to "align as nearly as possible the interests of individuals, corporations and society" (cited in Rossouw 2014, 28).

M.J.B Kabeyi (2019) observes that organisations with poor governance can lack strategy and direction and can be cumbersome and bureaucratic. According to Michel West and Isobel Gowen (2017), governance is an enabler because it allows organisations to minimise uncertainty, maximise accountability, and support clear decision-making. Jacobs Henri (2018) pithily refers to corporate governance as "the hygiene of an organization".

If governance goes wrong, it can result in a spectacular business collapse and even lawsuits. For example, Backpage.com was a classified ad website where, according to Jacques Billeaud (2024), the lack of governance not only destroyed the company but also landed its founders in jail. David Crowther and Shahla Seifi (2017) cite the 2008 financial recession, the 2004 misreporting of oil reserves by Royal Dutch Shell, and the 2005 corruption scandal at FIFA as examples of "bad governance".

The "visible hand" of modern organisations extends over internal and external governance structures. External governance includes bodies such as investors, shareholders, banks, owners, joint ventures and government regulation and compliance. Internal governance promotes organisational coherence and encompasses boards, CEOs, leaders, management, and peer governance. Mark Wilson (2023) notes that traditional governance models can take various forms, including advisory board, patron, corporate, management, and policy governance frameworks. Although a Board of Directors represents shareholders' interests and provides strategic oversight and guidance, it often holds substantial legal authority under corporate law, including approving major decisions, hiring or dismissing top executives, and overseeing compliance, risk, and financial health. Many boards continue to display machismo cultures and lack genuine diversity and inclusion. A recent *Global Gender Diversity 2023* report by Maya Imberg (2023) shows that women account for only 30 per cent of board members in major corporations across 20 leading economies. High-performing boards require greater diversity to encourage adaptive mindsets and behaviours in the organisation.

Adaptive Governance

Much of the literature refers to adaptive governance in sociopolitical and public policy contexts,[3] but it is also an organisational term (Van Assche 2022). According to Marijn Janssen (2022), adaptive governance (AG) is "a governance philosophy based on a range of instruments to create adaptability"(3). Marijn

Traditional Governance	Adaptive Governance
"One size fits all"	Flexible
Stand-alone (closed)	Ecosystems (open)
Human governance	Human & digital governance
Manager-led	Self-organising
Status leadership	System leadership
Top-down	Emergent
Human supervision	Digital supervision

Figure 5.1 Traditional versus adaptive governance.

Janssen and Haiko van der Voort (2016) believe adaptive governance can "deal with and adapt to changes, while protecting the same organization from becoming unstable" (1). Adaptive governance is a shared and collective decision-making approach which, as Marijn Janssen (2022) writes, "embraces uncertainty and complexity by enabling continuous learning, involving a wide range of diverse actors, and being able to react within a short time frame" (3). Kalle Matso (2016) views it as an antithesis to Frederick Taylor's scientific management. Figure 5.1 compares traditional and adaptive governance.

As we shift towards Work 4.0 and Industry 4.0 (characterised by digitally advanced, socially volatile, adaptive ecosystems), traditional governance models developed during the bureaucratic age of Work 2.0, will prove too rudimentary and inadequate a framework to manage and support modern organisational ecosystems. Marijn Janssen and Haiko van der Voort emphasise the point:

> large organizations try to manage the new developments using established mechanisms of governance, with stability and accountability as the main values. However, these mechanisms were largely not developed to adapt to changes
>
> (Janssen and van der Voort 2016, 1)

Van Assche, Valentinov, and Verschraegen (2022) observe that organisations will need to adapt to the increasingly complex social and work environments, which will require a change in the "process of governance or decision making" (Van Assche et al. 2022, 1740). They further add that "The core task of adaptive governance, for both organizations and communities, is to navigate and overcome the precariousness" (Van Assche et al. 2022, 1739).

Governance frameworks must adapt quickly to changing external realities, including legislative obligations, demographics, new technologies, sustainability, social responsibility, and evolving economic models. In light of the constant evolution of technology and ongoing digital transformation, there is a practical need to rethink governance, notably the possibility of adopting digital governance.

Why Embrace Organisational Adaptive Governance?

Marijn Janssen and Haiko van der Voort (2016) concisely lay out the case for adaptive governance:

> Adaptive governance is a way to cope with unpredictability which due to, among other things, the complexity, non-reducibility, spontaneity, variability, and collective quality of ecosystems... Adaptive governance is about being able to improve the adaptive capacity of organizations to deal with uncertainty and improve the speed of decision-making.
>
> (Janssen and van der Voort 2016, 3)

The authors argue that adaptive governance arises from "the mismatch between the characteristics of the environment and the way organizations are governed" (Janssen and van der Voort 2016, 3). A 2018 OECD report on corporate governance discusses how regulatory frameworks need to be "fit for purpose" (OECD 2018, 11) and should be allowed to evolve.

The literature on adaptive governance argues that it manages complexity, facilitates rapid organisational decision-making, supports the free flow of knowledge within the organisation, is well placed to serve as a governing model for the ecosystem economy, and supports digital transformation.[4]

The Evolution of Workplace Governance: From Work 1.0 to Work 4.0

The reason organisational governance is an "elusive term" (Von Tunzelmann 2003, 366) is that it has steadily evolved (and and continues to evolve) from Work 1.0 to Work 4.0, shifting from pre-bureaucratic to post-bureaucratic structures. Figure 5.2 represents this shifting governance picture.

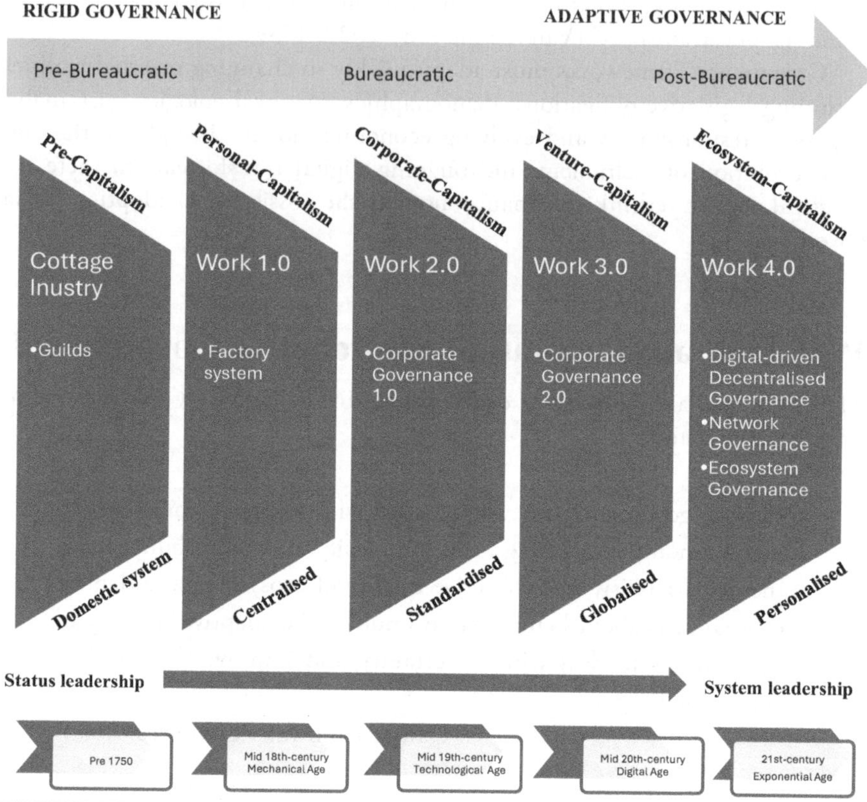

Figure 5.2 The changing face of organisational governance.

Over the past 300 years, workplace governance has transitioned dramatically through four major phases:

1. *Work 1.0* was owner-run, patriarchal, and funded largely through personal capital rather than outside investors (Cheffins 2008).[5] Leadership tended to revolve around a single powerful figure at the top, reflecting the era's "Great Man" view of leadership (Kelly, 2019).
2. *Work 2.0* marked the rise of large, centralised corporations such as Siemens in Europe and General Electric, General Motors, and AT&T in the US. During this period, the foundations of the modern corporate governance model took shape. Earlier legislative reforms paved the way for professionally managed firms. By the early twentieth century, ownership had become increasingly dispersed, formal boards of directors were established, and a command-and-control managerial culture prevailed. This period also saw the emergence of the modern CEO, with clearly defined executive

authority. Governance shifted towards bureaucratic, rule-based structures, alongside increased government intervention through regulation and legislation. This became a defining feature of the corporate environment.

3. *Work 3.0* saw the rise of venture capital-funded startups and the emergence of major tech empires. Entrepreneurial founders, often beginning with modest resources, built companies that grew to global prominence. Some startups, such as Uber, Netflix, and Microsoft, eventually went public, incorporating elements of corporate governance structure into their innovative startup culture. Throughout this period, investors and shareholders, acting through boards of directors, continued to play a central role in strategic decision-making and corporate governance.
4. *Work 4.0* is expected to rely heavily on Artificial Intelligence (AI), machine learning, and advanced data analytics, with data-enabled decision making becoming a key source of competitive advantage. Organisations that effectively use AI systems and data infrastructures, such as data lakes, are widely expected to outperform those that do not. As digital technologies reshape business models, many analysts argue that corporate governance frameworks and organisational ecosystems will need to evolve, with boards becoming more digitally literate, strategically engaged, and proactive in overseeing technological transformation. Governance discussions are also increasingly incorporating environmental, social, and governance (ESG) considerations, although the significance of ESG varies across regions and industries. The growing influence of large technology firms and AI systems raises ethical and governance questions about the concentration of power and the implications for organisational autonomy.[6] There is considerable uncertainty surrounding Work 4.0, highlighting the need for governance models that can anticipate a range of possible social and economic outcomes.

Towards an Adaptive (Ecosystem) Governance

The traditional corporate governance model has long dominated organisational practice. The OECD (2018) and others now call for a more fit-for-purpose and adaptive governance approach. This section explores these perspectives.

Centralised Governance from Pre-industrial Times to Work 3.0

A centralised (egosystem) governance, termed monocentric governance in policy-making (Termeer, Dewulf, and Lieshout 2010), is where ideas, direction, and decisions that impact the organisation originate from a rigid central authority.

Guilds were centralised domestic systems, governed by a master, two wardens, and a Court of Assistants. Robert Sabatino Lopez (1976) observes how the masters set policies, oversaw the administration of company properties, governed the distribution of charitable funds, and made decisions about promotions. This domestic system continued with the factory model where "captains of industry" controlled factory production. During the second industrial revolution, business governance evolved from founder-led enterprises to more formal corporate structures (Governance 1.0). Large firms progressively adopted boards of directors, professional executives, and multi-layered managerial hierarchies, reflecting the growing scale and complexity of industrial operations. This period marked a major shift towards the modern managerial corporation, in which ownership and day-to-day control became separated. While some legal elements of the corporate form had emerged earlier, the organisational model that underpins today's large companies took shape primarily during this era. Corporate governance continued throughout the third industrial revolution. As globalisation accelerated in the late twentieth century, organisational governance grew more complex. Companies faced diverse shareholders, cross-border regulation, and a broader range of stakeholders, driving the development of more formal, globally aligned governance frameworks (Governance 2.0).

Adaptive Governance and Work 4.0

According to Karpouzoglou, Dewulf, and Clark (2016), adaptive governance is not centralised, but multifaceted. Some of the adaptive governance models have included digitally-driven decentralised governance,[7] network governance, and ecosystem governance.

Let's explore this now.

1. *Digitally-driven decentralised governance* is an approach that moves away from traditional hierarchical structures and top-down decision making. Instead of decisions being made by a small group of leaders, technology allows communities and organisations to make decisions together. One example is Decentralised Autonomous Organizations (DAOs). These use blockchain technology and automated rules (known as smart contracts) to manage how decisions are made. Members can vote using digital tokens so people from different backgrounds can take part without relying on a central authority or leadership (Santana and Albareda 2022; Zhao and Qiu 2025). Jacobs Henri (2018) predicts that blockchain-based structures may eventually enable organisations to operate without traditional leaders. Unlike distributed systems (such as Wikipedia), decentralised governance still has a structure, but power is shared rather than concentrated at the top. Real-world examples include MakerDAO, a blockchain-based startup

where users, developers, miners, and the wider community all have a say in decisions. This approach aligns with the broader principle of collective governance, which, Niloufar Khonsari (2022) describes as the systematic distribution of power, ownership, and accountability to all participants to create more inclusive and collaborative organisations.

2. *Network governance* is defined as the "mechanism of reaching and implementing decisions whereby, instead of hierarchy and command or markets and prices, networks and cooperation are at work" (Hollstein, Matiaske, and Schnapp 2017, 1). Keith Provan and Patrick Kenis (2007) examine "multi-organizational governance" (230), which is a collaborative structure that lacks a central hierarchy and has only limited formal accountability. They identify several governance forms for such networks, including participant-governed networks, where members collectively manage activities; lead-organisation governed networks, where one organisation or member assumes a coordinating role with asymmetrical power; and network administrative organisations (NAOs), in which a separate entity acts as a neutral broker to manage and support the network (Provan and Kenis 2007).
3. *Ecosystem governance* is another form of governance that is antithetical to centralised and top-down control, embracing multiplicity (Karpouzoglou, Dewulf, and Clark 2016; Jacobides, Cennamo, and Gawer 2018). Gayan Benedict and Ina M. Sebastian (2024) observe that ecosystem governance is about providing value. Sara Brown (2024) concisely articulates ecosystem governance's role and purpose:

> Sometimes organizational goals depend on the actions of other organizations in an ecosystem. By identifying and applying the right type of governance, ecosystem participants can address shared challenges and access common resources and expertise. Effective ecosystem governance is the key to creating trust among participants and growing value.

Getting the ecosystem governance of the ecosystem right can be a critical success factor, as it requires strengthening external partnerships. Pidun, Reeves, and Knust (2021) share the story of how BlackBerry chose a closed governance model to protect its data security standards, which disincentivised app developers from joining the platform, leading them to focus their expertise on smartphone ecosystems based on Apple's iOS and Google's Android. This negatively impacted BlackBerry.

Status leaders	System leaders
Focus on status	Focus on system
Decision maker	Co-decision maker
Egocentric	Ecocentric
Alpha	Beta
Directive	Responsive
Self-advancement	Enterprise advancement
Status quo	Adaptive

Figure 5.3 Status versus system leadership.

From Status to System Leadership

Another important element represented in Figure 5.2 is the shift from status leadership to system leadership. Figure 5.3 outlines key differences between status and system leadership.

Traditional status leadership, epitomised by centralised decision-making and top-down control, rests on three key assumptions: that supervisors drive productivity, that appointed managers are necessary to oversee the organisation and "connect the dots", and that leaders must implement ideas and decisions. These assumptions worked well in the more stable producer-led economies of Industry 1.0 and 2.0, but they are increasingly outdated in today's personalised, exponential era characterised by interconnected ecosystems.

System leadership, which represents the next governance evolution, is counterintuitive to top-down and centralised chain of command leadership. It is a mindset (not a role) that supports ongoing system transformation. Senge, Hamilton, and Kania (2015) observe that system leaders help bring about "new ways of thinking, acting, and being". They add, "System leaders focus on creating the conditions that can produce change and that can eventually cause change to be self-sustaining". System leadership is a form of collective leadership, suited to complex adaptive systems. It supports self-organising behaviours, promotes collaboration, encourages cross-functional thinking, and enhances organisational adaptability. A system leadership mindset encourages the organisation to adopt an enterprise-first perspective, inspiring the wider system to cultivate engagement, innovation, and system performance. This form of leadership has been explored extensively in the business world.[8] The UK Government Office for Science (2023) is looking at adopting system leadership. The natural world, particularly honeybee colonies, can help us conceptualise system leadership. It is an important enabler for supporting organisations to transform from a rigid to an adaptive culture. System leadership will be further explored in the coming chapters.

Design Principles for Adaptive Governance

It has been observed that adaptive organisations thrive on broad guiding principles rather than rigid and prescriptive off-the-shelf processes (Reeves, Morieux, and Deimler 2010). This section mirrors the format of Chapter 4 and uses the 4 O Framework (Objective, Options, Orientation, and Outlook) as an organising system (see Figure 4.4 in Chapter 4).

1. Objective

   Bayu Prawira Hie (2019) identifies a clear link between cultural transformation and organisational governance. Any cultural transformation, such as building an adaptive organisation, requires a clearly defined objective that outlines and communicates the role governance will play. Cultural transformations can fail or be seriously derailed if stakeholders are unaware of the ramifications of organisational governance. It has been established that adaptive organisations represent a shift from centralised governance and controlled decision-making to self-organising, self-managing, and emergent systems. In such a context, a decentralised governance model will impact the perceived authority of status leaders, and this must be carefully managed to prevent possible resistance from prominent stakeholders. Stakeholders need to be aware of the implications for their daily routines, including decision-making, roles, and accountability. It is important to reflect on whether your organisation is ready for a change in governance and to review the intended and unintended consequences of such a move.
2. Options

   Options should be carefully considered in terms of the scope and speed of governance. Marijn Janssen and Haiko van der Voort (2016) believe adaptive governance requires organisations to balance stability and adaptability and align governance structures with their vision and objectives. Historical failures at Enron, WorldCom, and Royal Dutch Shell illustrate the risks of poor governance. Work 3.0 oscillated between rigid compliance and self-accountability, which created organisational uncertainty. Such ambiguity needs to be avoided in the future. In the emerging Work 4.0 era, complex technologies, environmental, social, and governance (ESG) considerations, and global ecosystems require governance models intentionally designed for adaptability. This should be done through consultation, through cultivating trust, transparency, responsiveness, and strong stakeholder relationships. Beaumier, Couette, and Morin (2025) argue, "To maintain equilibrium between order and chaos, some organisations must create bridges between otherwise homogeneous groups" (1004).

There are also options to be considered at the board level. An adaptive and responsive organisation that has improved flows of business intelligence and an evolving system leadership needs an adaptive and responsive board. This will require boards to shift from being passive overseers to strategic players. Betsy Atkins (2022) makes this point very effectively:

> In this new model of corporate governance 4.0 directors need to be a competitive asset and an accelerant for the business, adding a perspective that not only performs oversight but helps move the company forward.

Babur Mirza (2025) writing in *The Independent* makes a similar observation about boards when he says, "For boards to govern effectively in a world increasingly characterised by uncertainty, they need to abandon the incremental changes of the past in favour of bold, forward-thinking strategies". A more inclusive, strategically focused board will require a more diverse board composition.

3. Orientation

It has been observed that cultural transformation, particularly the shift from rigid to adaptive cultures, can be derailed if organisations lack clarity concerning the role of governance or if the scope and pace of governance change fall out of sync with the broader transformation. Cultural change also falters when structure and workflow redesigns are not aligned with the organisational governance. Strong business architecture and strategic alignment with governance are essential. Put simply, if the organisation expects to operate with more adaptive structures and workflows, and wants employees to contribute more ideas and participate in decision-making, it cannot maintain a rigid governance model.

One of the biggest mistakes organisations make during major transformations is failing to evolve their governance structures in line with new adaptive workflows and organisational models. Research shows that if structures and processes become more decentralised and adaptive, but the governance framework remains rigid and centralised, misalignment is inevitable. Marijn Janssen and Haiko van der Voort (2016) caution that this often leads to confusion, reduced responsiveness, disengagement, and ultimately failure. The authors go on to say that effective transformation requires adaptive governance that evolves in parallel with structural and cultural change.

A clear example of the need for rapid governance change emerged during the coronavirus pandemic. Organisations had to quickly shift to remote work and revise presentism-based governance frameworks to address new data and security risks.

4. Outlook

Marijn Janssen and Haiko van der Voort (2016) argue that it is essential for organisations to stay informed about emerging trends in corporate governance so they can remain relevant and pace their adaptive governance accordingly. Organisations are now investing billions in maturing technologies such as DAO-style blockchain governance, autonomous and quantum-enhanced AI systems, and advanced analytics. These developments will profoundly impact organisational structures and workflows, reshaping business processes and work models at speed. This will require a major change in governance. Lucy Reeve (2023) reports that the Chartered Governance Institute UK & Ireland (formerly known as ICSA) is urging companies and boards to develop digital governance policies.[9]

As machines increasingly participate in organisational decision-making, clear digital governance strategies become critical. Lisa Welchman defines digital governance as "a framework for establishing accountability, roles, and decision-making authority for an organization's digital presence" (Welchman 2015, 28). Such frameworks must establish boundaries, rules, and safeguards to manage unintended bias, opaque decision-making, misaligned incentives, and risks of technological overreach. Organisations also need to prepare for the ethical and legal implications of automation, including digital surveillance, technological unemployment, and large-scale redundancies. Without a clear digital governance strategy, organisations will struggle to transition smoothly into an augmented, machine-integrated future.

Historically, organisations have delegated their digital strategy to IT departments. But as digital technologies increasingly shape decision-making and supervision, digital governance must become a core strategic organisational imperative and not a technical afterthought.

Synthesis: Developing Adaptive Governance

This chapter, the second pillar of the business architecture, has explored how to design a governance framework that supports organisations to adapt to volatile and changing conditions, particularly as intelligent machines begin to play an increasing role in organisational life and decision-making. The corporate governance model developed in the early twentieth century has long dominated the business landscape and remains the prevailing framework. Yet, it has failed to keep pace with rapidly changing business models. Organisations now urgently need new forms of digital governance. This lack of synchronisation between governance and business processes has led to organisational failures and, in some cases, corruption and scandal.

The chapter examined Cisco as a case study of an organisation that developed an adaptive governance model that kept pace with its innovation cycle. Adaptive governance acts as an enabler, helping organisations navigate a sensible path between innovation and compliance, while managing unpredictability. It does this by cultivating collective governance, mobilising the workforce as system leaders, and integrating adaptive governance into the organisation's shared way of thinking. The chapter outlined some practical adaptive approaches that help organisations manage this complexity, along with core design principles that support the creation of truly adaptive organisations.

The next chapter looks at workflow as a final organisational design consideration.

Notes

1. This is a reference to "invisible hand", a term Adam Smith associated with markets. Nick von Tunzelmann's article helped me make this connection (Von Tunzelmann 2003).
2. Carla L. Reyes and Nizan Geslevich Packin (2016) define corporate governance as "the mechanism by which business organizations oversee, execute, and maintain a complex series of interacting agreements between the organization's different stakeholders" (14).
3. For example, Hatfield-Dodds, Nelson, and Cook 2007; Brunner 2005; May 2022; Munaretto, Siciliano, and Turvani (2014); Karpouzoglou, Dewulf, and Clark 2016; Chaffin, Gosnell, and Cosens 2016; Schultz et al. 2015; Eshuis and Gerrits 2019.
4. Here are the references to substantiate this passage. Adaptive governance manages complexity (Nelson, Howden, and Smith 2008), facilitates speedy organisational decision-making (Janssen and van der Voort 2016), supports the free flow of knowledge through the organisation (Reeves et al. 2010), is best placed to be a governing model for the ecosystem economy (Janssen and van der Voort 2016), and supports digital transformation (Tygart 2025; Li et al. 2022; Warrier 2021).
5. The early factories were seen as risky investments because of the new technology and the existence of machine saboteurs, known as the Luddites.

6. Scholars and commentators have expressed differing views on how AI will affect workplace decision-making and worker empowerment. Some, including Yanis Varoufakis (2023), propose scenarios such as "technofeudalism" to describe potential future power imbalances, while others debate the extent to which AI could create or displace jobs.
7. A close cousin of a decentralised governance is shared governance, but they have different nuances. In a business setting, shared governance involves collaborative decision-making among defined stakeholder groups within an existing hierarchy, whereas distributed governance spreads decision-making authority across autonomous teams or units that operate more independently within a networked structure.
8. Authors publishing in this area include, Kelly 2022a, 2022b; Mdluli and Makhupe 2017; Grzybowska and Łupicka 2017; Senge, Hamilton, and Kania 2015; Guzmán et al. 2020; and Steiner 2017.
9. It is clear that "effective governance of these technologies is essential to harness their benefits while mitigating potential risks" (Atladóttir 2024, 1). Some believe that boards must lead this initiative (Nandi-Ray 2025; Ghonda 2024). This may necessitate educating policymakers and developing a quantum framework (Atladóttir 2024). Maëva Ghonda believes it is essential to establish a Quantum Task Force with technical experts, senior executives and board members to advise on the company's quantum computing strategy (Ghonda 2024).

Bibliography

Atkins, Betsy. 2022. 'The 4 Eras of Corporate Governance'. Forbes. https://www.forbes.com/sites/betsyatkins/2022/01/10/the-4-eras-of-corporate-governance/.

Atladóttir, Drífa. 2024. *Navigating the Quantum Wave: A Policy Maker's Guide for the Responsible Governance of Quantum Technologies*. ICT4Peace Foundation. https://ict4peace.org/wp-content/uploads/2024/05/Atladottir-Navigating-The-Quantum-Wave.pdf.

Beaumier, Guillaume, Cynthia Couette, and Jean-Frédéric Morin. 2025. 'Hybrid Organisations and Governance Systems: The Case of the European Space Agency'. *Journal of European Public Policy* 32 (4): 1004–34. https://doi.org/10.1080/13501763.2024.2325647.

Benedict, Gayan, and Ina M. Sebastian. 2024. *Designing Ecosystem Governance to Grow Value*. XXIV–2. MIT CISR Research Briefing. MIT Center for Information Systems Research. https://cisr.mit.edu/publication/2024_0201_EcosystemGovernance_BenedictSebastian.

Billeaud, Jacques. 2024. 'Backpage.Com Founder Michael Lacey Sentenced to 5 Years in Prison for Money Laundering'. *The Independent*, August 28. https://www.independent.co.uk/news/ap-lacey-phoenix-arizona-google-b2603479.html.

Bourne, Lynda. 2014. 'The Six Functions of Governance'. *PM World Journal* 3 (11): 443–93. www.pmworldjournal.net.

Brown, Sara. 2024. '3 Approaches to Ecosystem Governance | MIT Sloan'. MIT Management Sloan School, March 5. https://mitsloan.mit.edu/ideas-made-to-matter/3-approaches-to-ecosystem-governance.

Brunner, Ronald D., ed. 2005. *Adaptive Governance: Integrating Science, Policy, and Decision Making*. Columbia University Press.

Chaffin, Brian, Hannah Gosnell, and Barbara A. Cosens. 2016. 'A Decade of Adaptive Governance Scholarship: Synthesis and Future Directions'. SSRN Scholarly Paper No. 2717757. Social Science Research Network, January 18. https://papers.ssrn.com/abstract=2717757.

Chambers, John. 2016. *Cisco's John Chambers on the Digital Era*. Interview by Rik Kirkland. March 18. Mckinsey & Company. https://www.mckinsey.com/industries/technology-media-and-telecommunications/our-insights/ciscos-john-chambers-on-the-digital-era.

Cheffins, Brian R. 2008. *Corporate Ownership and Control*. Oxford University Press. https://doi.org/10.1093/acprof:oso/9780199236978.001.0001.

Chen, Xue Yu. 2024. 'A Literature Review of Corporate Governance'. *Edelweiss Applied Science and Technology* 8 (6): 8945–49. https://doi.org/10.55214/25768484.v8i6.3916.

Crowther, David, and Shahla Seifi, eds. 2017. *Modern Organisational Governance*. 1st edition. Developments in Corporate Governance and Responsibility, Vol. 12. Emerald Publishing.

Eshuis, Jasper, and Lasse Gerrits. 2021. 'The Limited Transformational Power of Adaptive Governance: A Study of Institutionalization and Materialization of Adaptive Governance'. *Public Management Review* 23 (2): 276–96. https://doi.org/10.1080/14719037.2019.1679232.

Ghonda, Maëva. 2024. 'Board of Directors' Quantum Computing Corporate Governance Guide | by Maëva Ghonda | The Future of Governance | Medium'. Business. Medium, July 20.

Government Office for Science. 2023. *Systems Leadership Guide: How to Be a Systems Leader*. Government Office for Science. https://www.gov.uk/government/publications/systems-leadership-guide-for-civil-servants/systems-leadership-guide-how-to-be-a-systems-leader.

Grzybowska, Katarzyna, and Anna Łupicka. 2017. 'Key Competencies for Industry 4.0'. October 11, 250–53. https://doi.org/10.26480/icemi.01.2017.250.253.

Guzmán, Valeria E, Bernd Muschard, Mateus Gerolamo, Holger Kohl, and Henrique Rozenfeld. 2020. 'Characteristics and Skills of Leadership in the Context of Industry 4.0'. *Procedia Manufacturing* 43: 543–50. https://doi.org/10.1016/j.promfg.2020.02.167.

Harari, Yuval Noaḥ. 2017. *Homo Deus: A Brief History of Tomorrow*. HarperCollins Publishers.

Hatfield-Dodds, Steve, Rohan Nelson, and David Cook. 2007. 'Adaptive Governance: An Introduction, and Implications for Public Policy'. Paper presented at 51st Annual conference of the Australian Agricultural and Resource Economics Society, Queenstown NZ. *Adaptive Governance*. https://core.ac.uk/outputs/6418177/?utm_source=pdf&utm_medium=banner&utm_campaign=pdf-decoration-v1.

Henri, Jacobs. 2018. 'The Future of Corporate Governance and the Role of Directors'. *Medium*, July 26. https://jacobshenri.medium.com/the-future-of-corporate-governance-and-the-role-of-directors-efcf0a5f7c5d.

Hie, Bayu Prawira. 2019. 'Impact of Transforming Organizational Culture and Digital Transformation Governance Toward Digital Maturity in Indonesian Bank'. *International Review of Management and Marketing* 9 (6): 51–57. https://doi.org/10.32479/irmm.8785.

Hollstein, Betina, Wenzel Matiaske, and Kai-Uwe Schnapp. 2017. 'Networked Governance: Taking Networks Seriously'. In *Networked Governance*, edited by Betina Hollstein, Wenzel Matiaske, and Kai-Uwe Schnapp. Springer International Publishing. https://doi.org/10.1007/978-3-319-50386-8_1.

Imberg, Maya. 2023. 'Global Gender Diversity 2023'. Diversity Report. *Altrata*, July 12. https://altrata.com/reports/global-gender-diversity-2023.

Jacobides, Michael G., Carmelo Cennamo, and Annabelle Gawer. 2018. 'Towards a Theory of Ecosystems'. *Strategic Management Journal* 39 (8): 2255–76. https://doi.org/10.1002/smj.2904.

Janssen, Marijn. 2022. 'Adaptive Governance for a Resilient Digital Society'. In *Electronic Governance and Open Society: Challenges in Eurasia*, edited by Andrei V. Chugunov, Marijn Janssen, Igor Khodachek, Yuri Misnikov, and Dmitrii Trutnev, vol. 1529. Communications in Computer and Information Science. Springer International Publishing. https://doi.org/10.1007/978-3-031-04238-6_1.

Janssen, Marijn, and Haiko Van Der Voort. 2016. 'Adaptive Governance: Towards a Stable, Accountable and Responsive Government'. *Government Information Quarterly* 33 (1): 1–5. https://doi.org/10.1016/j.giq.2016.02.003.

Kabeyi, MJB. 2019. 'Corporate Governance in Manufacturing and Management with Analysis of Governance Failures at Enron and Volkswagen Corporations'. *American Journal of Operations Management and Information Systems* 4 (4): 109. https://doi.org/10.11648/j.ajomis.20190404.11.

Karpouzoglou, Timothy, Art Dewulf, and Julian Clark. 2016. 'Advancing Adaptive Governance of Social-Ecological Systems through Theoretical Multiplicity'. *Environmental Science & Policy* 57 (March): 1–9. https://doi.org/10.1016/j.envsci.2015.11.011.

Kelly, Richard. 2019. *Constructing Leadership 4.0: Swarm Leadership and the Fourth Industrial Revolution*. 2019th edn. Springer International Publishing: Imprint: Palgrave Macmillan. https://doi.org/10.1007/978-3-319-98062–1.

Kelly, Richard. 2022a. *The Nature of Business Transformation: A Swarm Intelligent Approach to Reinventing Organisations*. Routledge.

Kelly, Richard. 2022b. 'Leadership 4.0 as a System Leadership'. *LinkedIN*. https://www.linkedin.com/pulse/leadership-40-ric-kelly-ph-d/.

Khan, Humera. 2011. 'A Literature Review of Corporate Governance'. *Management and Economics* 25: 1–5.

Khonsari, Niloufar. 2022. 'What Is Collective Governance?' Company Website. Niloufar Khonsari, May 30. https://www.niloukhonsari.com/blog/what-is-collective-governance.

Law, Marcus. 2024. 'How John Chambers Wired Cisco into the Internet's DNA'. Technology Magazine, October 4. https://technologymagazine.com/articles/how-john-chambers-wired-cisco-into-the-internets-dna.

Li, Chao, Wei-Xi Feng, Shuihua Han, Shivam Gupta, and Sachin Kamble. 2022. 'Digital Adaptive Governance, Digital Transformation, and Service Quality in Logistics Enterprises'. *Journal of Global Information Management* 30 (1): 1–26. https://doi.org/10.4018/JGIM.309377.

Lopez, Robert Sabatino. 1976. *The Commercial Revolution of the Middle Ages, 950–1350*. Cambridge University Press.

Matso, Kalle. 2016. 'Adaptive Governance'. In *Encyclopedia of Estuaries*, edited by Michael J. Kennish. Encyclopedia of Earth Sciences Series. Springer Netherlands. https://doi.org/10.1007/978-94-017-8801-4_39.

May, Candace K. 2022. 'Complex Adaptive Governance Systems: A Framework to Understand Institutions, Organizations, and People in Socio-Ecological Systems'. *Socio-Ecological Practice Research* 4 (1): 39–54. https://doi.org/10.1007/s42532-021-00101-7.

Mdluli, Siboniso, and Olebile Makhupe. 2017. 'Defining Leadership Competencies Needed for the Fourth Industrial Revolution: Leadership Competencies 4.0'. *Duke CE*, African Expansion Project, 13.

Mirza, Babur. 2025. 'The Future of Governance: Why the Boards of Tomorrow Need to Embrace Change Today'. Business. *The Independent* (UK), February 12. UK Edition Edition. https://www.independent.co.uk/news/business/business-reporter/governance-boards-agility-technology-artificial-intelligence-diversity-b2695264.html.

Munaretto, Stefania, Giuseppina Siciliano, and Margherita E. Turvani. 2014. 'Integrating Adaptive Governance and Participatory Multicriteria Methods: A Framework for Climate Adaptation Governance'. *Ecology and Society* 19 (2): art74. https://doi.org/10.5751/ES-06381–190274.

Nandi-Ray, Anita. 2025. *Quantum Governance: Why Boards Must Lead the Next Technological Revolution*. Institute of Directors, India, May 8. https://www.iodglobal.com/blog/details/quantum-governance-why-boards-must-lead-the-next-technological-revolution.

Nelson, Rohan, Mark Howden, and Mark Stafford Smith. 2008. 'Using Adaptive Governance to Rethink the Way Science Supports Australian Drought Policy'. *Environmental Science & Policy* 11 (7): 588–601. https://doi.org/10.1016/j.envsci.2008.06.005.

OECD. 2018. *Flexibility and Proportionality in Corporate Governance*. OECD Publishing. https://doi.org/10.1787/9789264307490-en.

Pidun, Ulrich, Martin Reeves, and Niklas Knust. 2021. *How Do You Manage a Business Ecosystem?* Boston Consulting Group, January 20. https://www.bcg.com/publications/2021/how-to-manage-business-ecosystem.

Provan, K. G., and P. Kenis. 2007. 'Modes of Network Governance: Structure, Management, and Effectiveness'. *Journal of Public Administration Research and Theory* 18 (2): 229–52. https://doi.org/10.1093/jopart/mum015.

Reeve, Lucy. 2023. 'Companies Urged to Set up AI Governance Framework | Linklaters'. Business. Linklaters, November 1. https://www.linklaters.com/en/knowledge/publications/alerts-newsletters-and-guides/2023/november/07/companies-urged-to-set-up-ai-governance-framework.

Reeves, Martin, Yves Morieux, and Michael Deimler. 2010. 'People Advantage'. BCG Global, March 25. https://www.bcg.com/publications/2010/strategy-behavior-culture-people-advantage.

Reyes, Carla L., and Nizan Geslevich Packin. 2016. 'Distributed Governance'. *SSRN Electronic Journal*, ahead of print. https://doi.org/10.2139/ssrn.2884978.

Rossouw, G. J. 2014. 'Balancing Corporate and Social Interests: Corporate Governance Theory and Practice'. *African Journal of Business Ethics* 3 (1): 28. https://doi.org/10.15249/3-1-72.

Santana, Carlos, and Laura Albareda. 2022. 'Blockchain and the Emergence of Decentralized Autonomous Organizations (DAOs): An Integrative Model and Research Agenda'. *Technological Forecasting and Social Change* 182 (September): 121806. https://doi.org/10.1016/j.techfore.2022.121806.

Schultz, Lisen, Carl Folke, Henrik Österblom, and Per Olsson. 2015. 'Adaptive Governance, Ecosystem Management, and Natural Capital'. *Proceedings of the National Academy of Sciences* 112 (24): 7369–74. https://doi.org/10.1073/pnas.1406493112.

Senge, Peter, Hal Hamilton, and John Kania.. 2015. 'The Dawn of System Leadership'. *Stanford Social Innovation Review* 13: 2733. https://doi.org/10.48558/YTE7-XT62.

Steiner, Roy. 2017. 'How Can We Create a Culture of System Leadership?' *Medium*, August 4. https://medium.com/@roysteiner1919/how-can-we-create-a-culture-of-system-leadership-66709ac8e88a.

Termeer, C.J.A.M., Art Dewulf, and Maartje Lieshout. 2010. 'Disentangling Scale Approaches in Governance Research: Comparing Monocentric, Multilevel, and Adaptive Governance'. *Ecology and Society* 15 (2010): 4. https://doi.org/10.5751/ES-03798–150429.

The Economist. 2009. 'The World According to Chambers'. *The Economist*, August 27. https://www.economist.com/briefing/2009/08/27/the-world-according-to-chambers.

Tygart, William. 2025. 'Comprehensive Framework for Agile and Adaptive Governance Structures in Global Companies'. *BCESG*, January 12. https://bcesg.org/business-continuity-esg-blog/comprehensive-framework-for-agile-and-adaptive-governance-structures-in-global-companies.

Van Assche, Kristof, Vladislav Valentinov, and Gert Verschraegen. 2022. 'Adaptive Governance: Learning from What Organizations Do and Managing the Role They Play'. *Kybernetes* 51 (5): 1738–58. https://doi.org/10.1108/K-11-2020–0759.

Varoufakis, Yanis. 2023. *Technofeudalism: What Killed Capitalism*. The Bodley Head.

Von Tunzelmann, Nick. 2003. 'Historical Coevolution of Governance and Technology in the Industrial Revolutions'. *Structural Change and Economic Dynamics* 14 (4): 365–84. https://doi.org/10.1016/S0954-349X(03)00029–8.

Warrier, Nikhil. 2021. *Adaptive Governance to Thrive in an Ever Canging Digital Ecosystem*. WIPRO, April. https://www.wipro.com/infrastructure/adaptive-governance-to-thrive-in-an-ever-canging-digital-ecosystem/.

Welchman, Lisa. 2015. *Managing Chaos: Digital Governance by Design*. Rosenfeld Media.

West, Professor Michael, and Isobel Gowan. 2017. 'Good Governance Is an Enabler, Not a Necessary Evil'. *Health Service Journal*, March 3. https://www.hsj.co.uk/delivering-change/good-governance-is-an-enabler-not-a-necessary-evil/7016116.article.

Wilson, Mark. 2023. 'What Is a Governance Model and Why Does It Matter?' Board Effect, August 4. https://www.boardeffect.com/blog/what-governance-model-why-does-matter/.

Zhao, Yangyang, and Jiajun Qiu. 2025. 'Decentralized Governance in Action: A Governance Framework of Digital Responsibility in Startups'. *Journal of Responsible Technology* 21 (March): 100107. https://doi.org/10.1016/j.jrt.2025.100107.

Chapter 6

Designing Adaptive Workflows for System Emergence

Spotify is a highly successful Swedish audio streaming platform.[1] Founded in 2006 by Daniel Ek and Martin Lorentzon, it reported Q3 2024 total revenue of €4 billion, with over 640 million active users in more than 100 countries (Spotify 2024). A key success factor has been its organisational adaptability. Spotify doesn't impose a set of pre-planned work practices; it allows the workflow culture to emerge and continuously evolve through self-organising teams. This helps sustain adaptability and enables the company to respond quickly to external events, swiftly implement new technologies and ideas, and effectively respond to customer needs.

The company is known for its "Spotify model", an adaptive workflow that Paul Hourlias (2023) says focuses on "organizing around work rather than following a specific set of practices". This adaptive workflow means that Spotify is more responsive to customer and stakeholder needs (Jonwal 2025). Spotify's personalised and adaptive culture means it can offer diverse individual music recommendations based on advanced algorithms which have learnt user preference over time and can offer collaborative playlists and educational podcasts. Spotify's successful model of organising around the work rather than organising the work has inspired traditional organisations, such as ING, to adopt the Spotify model.

This chapter, the third pillar of the business architecture which supports adaptive organisational cultures, focuses on Spotify, but there are other examples, particularly from the swarm organisation field, including Typeform, which

 DOI: 10.4324/9781003680345-6

wanted a "slice of that Spoti-pie" (Doehler 2021), and Daimler/Mercedes Benz (Kelly 2022).

This chapter presents adaptive workflows as a central component of organisational design and a key driver of adaptive organisations. It explores how adaptive cultures can be developed by rethinking workflows, shifting from fixed, rigid, rule-based systems to flexible, dynamic processes capable of withstanding rapid change, volatility, and uncertainty. It examines how organisational workflows have historically been insular, centralised, and sequential, often exemplified by the pyramid model. Despite decades of transformational efforts to promote more flexible and adaptive approaches, workplaces have largely retained linear, sequential legacies. The chapter situates organisational workflows within the context of industrial legacies, showing how organisations can cultivate greater adaptability by rethinking rigid structures and developing integrated and adaptive processes.

What Are Organisational Workflows?

The organisational workflow is the way work is organised and flows through the organisation. Workflows are closely aligned with business processes, which Meena Ramalingam (2019) describes as the "backbone" of the organisation. Jörg Becker and coauthors (1999) view organisational workflows as a process:

> Workflows are processes – temporal and logical sequences of activities that are necessary to perform operations on economically relevant objects – whose control logic lies within the control sphere of an information system.
>
> (Becker et al. 1999, 1)

Ewa Deelman and colleagues describe workflow as "a high-level specification of a set of tasks and the dependencies between them that must be satisfied in order to accomplish a specific goal" (Deelman et al. 2009, 529).

Industry 3.0 and the digital age saw an increase in the use of workflow automation systems. This is an "information system that supports the execution… of workflow models" (Becker et al 1999, 1) through "the use of IT tools and applications" (Weske, 2012 50). AI is transforming workflow automation.[2] Ahmed S. Sabah and colleagues explore the advantages of integrating AI into traditional workflows:

> AI-driven technologies are revolutionizing organizational workflows. Repetitive, time-consuming tasks such as data entry,

> scheduling, and customer inquiries can be efficiently handled by AI systems. Robotic Process Automation (RPA) and intelligent automation tools streamline these processes, reducing human error and allowing employees to focus on more strategic activities.
>
> (Sabah et al. 2024, 17)

Organisational workflow has become synonymous with digital workflow in recent times,[3] but workflow is a broader concept; it encompasses the general business process or business operating system (Kelly 2022) which evolved throughout the industrial revolutions long before the introduction of computers in the workplace. Business process optimisation and innovationwere, for example, carried out by Japanese firms from the 1970s via Total Quality Management (TQM). In discussing organisational workflows, this book adopts a broad, general definition of the term, pertaining to the flow of business process.

Towards Adaptive Organisational Workflows

Peter Jarvis and coauthors (1999) observe how adaptive workflows flex to changing conditions. Claire Anderson (2024) describes them as "systems designed to adjust dynamically in response to varying conditions or inputs. Unlike traditional workflows, which often follow a rigid sequence of steps, adaptive workflows promote flexibility".[4] Spotify is a great example of an organisation that rejected sequential rule-based work processes in favour of a flexible workflow that self-organised around the work. Akgün, Keskin, and Byrne argue that this adaptive approach allows organisations to "reconfigure resources and coordinate processes promptly in order to develop more successful products" (Akgün et al. 2012, 171). An adaptive workflow has profound implications for human and machine resourcing, business processes, customer interface, and work models.[5]

Why Adaptive Workflow?

Claire Anderson (2024) discusses how adaptive workflows allow organisations to flex and respond to rapidly changing conditions. These include internal restructuring and shifts in governance, changing customer needs (Akgün et al. 2012), major external disruptions such as pandemics, and changes in generational working values and expectations.[6] Adaptive workflows will also be crucial in the future for enabling effective human-machine interaction and collaboration. As automation and digitalisation reshape work, adaptive workflows will help integrate human and machine resources more seamlessly (Tarafdar 2025).

The ability to be adaptive will be a key survival factor for Industry 4.0 companies. Real-time responsiveness will be essential in Industry 4.0. Claire Anderson (2024) acknowledges that the ability to adjust workflows in real time will separate high-performing companies from the rest.

The Evolution of Organisational Workflows: From Work 1.0 to 4.0

Organisational business processes and workflows have adapted over three centuries from a pre-bureaucratic domestic system to a post-bureaucratic ecosystem. Each of these industrial revolution periods has produced its own unique workflow. Figure 6.1 represents this evolution.

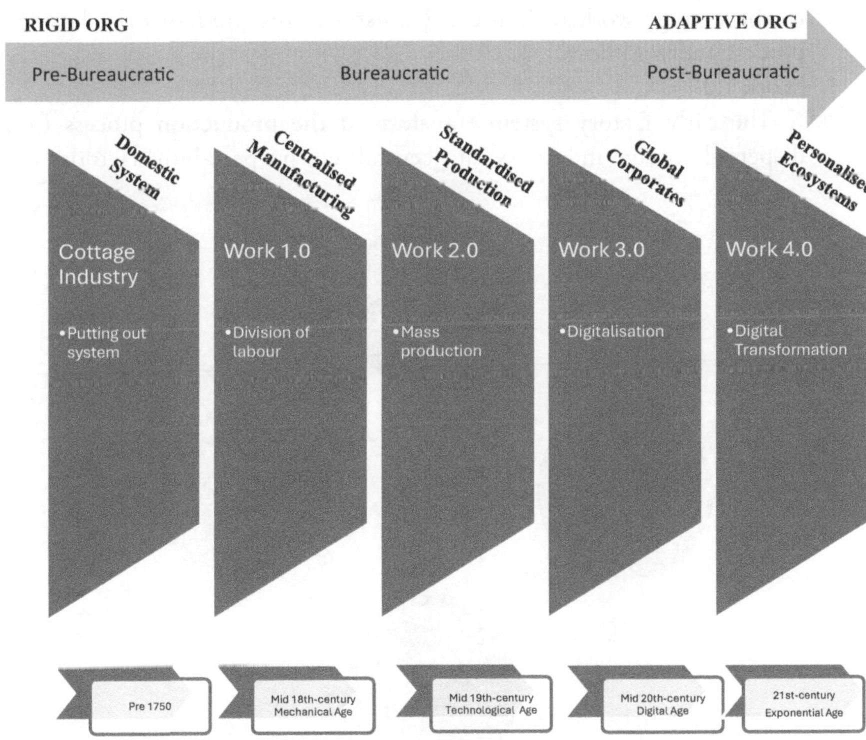

Figure 6.1 Three centuries of organisational workflow.

Let's unpack this model.

0. Pre-industrial revolution

   In the proto-industrial period spanning the seventeenth and eighteenth centuries in Europe, Rab Houston and K.D.M Snell (1984) discuss how small family-run cottage industries supplemented their income by spinning wool or weaving and washing cloth. It was a highly organised and regulated workflow using the "putting-out system" where merchants supplied raw materials to cottage workers who delivered back finished cloth. The merchants and guilds dictated production, standards, and market demands. Cottage industry workers retained some autonomy over their schedules, operating as small, self-governing enterprises within this tightly controlled framework.

   The business process was based on a transactional cycle in which the merchant supplied the raw materials, the cottage worker made the finished goods, delivered them to the merchant for payment, and the merchant sold the goods to market and procured more raw materials to supply back to the cottage worker. Figure 6.2 illustrates the pre-industrial business process and workflow.

1. Work 1.0

   The early factory system transformed the production process from dispersed cottage industries into centralised, purpose-built factories and

Figure 6.2 The pre-industrial business process/workflow model.

mills equipped with steam-powered machinery to optimise production. The workflow model was largely based on Adam Smith's 1776 division of labour theory, in which Smith asserted that when tasks are broken down into specialised components, production is more efficient. In practice this meant workers moved around the factory floor. It was noisy and highly dangerous work. Workers (including women and children) were abused and exploited at the hands of what Joshua Freeman (2018) calls a "paternal grandee". The flow of work around the factory was highly conditioned by factory clocks, sirens, and constant threats of punishment. Technological advances led to a rise in skilled workers, although the culture remained patriarchal and authoritarian, with workers viewed as bonded labour rather than employees (Pollard 1963). Though the new system increased output and created jobs over time, it did so at the cost of a regimented and dehumanising work environment that prioritised productivity over welfare.[7]

The business model is a linear process where the factory owners raise funds to construct and maintain the factory, invest in machinery, purchase and transport raw materials, and pay workers. Production is mechanised and in-house, supported by specialist employees performing specific tasks throughout the factory.[8] Finished goods are distributed to market via canals, railways, and ships. Profits go back to the factory owner and investors. Figure 6.3 illustrates this business process and workflow model.

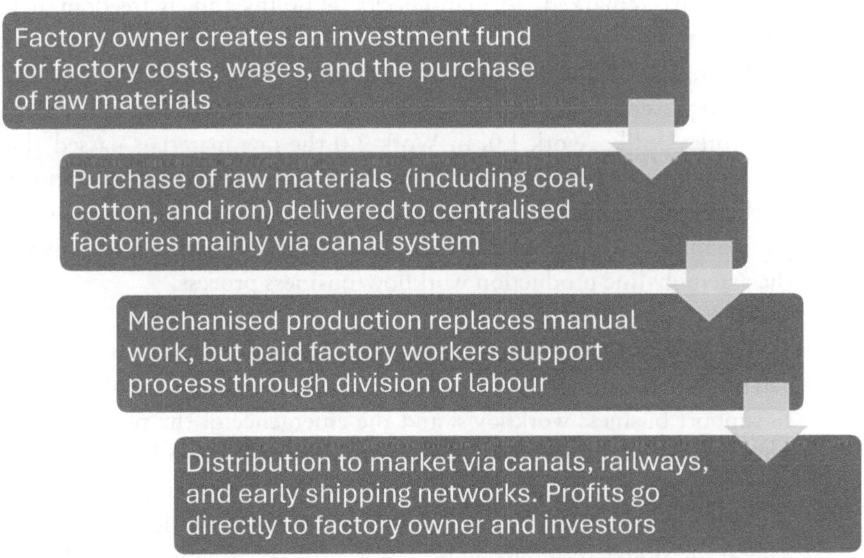

Figure 6.3 Industry 1.0 business process/workflow model.

2. Work 2.0

   Work 2.0 covers the industrial era of electric-powered machinery, mass production, and the rise of the bureaucratic corporation. Roshan Agarwal and Abhishek Pandey (2021) argue that Ford Motor's assembly-line manufacturing symbolises the era. Inspired by Frederick Taylor's *The Principles of Scientific Management* (1911/1998), labour was standardised, timed, and narrowly specialised, with workers assigned repetitive tasks along moving belts that calculated every motion. This created a command-and-control culture in both factories and offices, with a rise in a management class that supervised these standardised workflows. This period saw major advances in worker representation through trade unions and welfare reforms in the United Kingdom. David Montgomery (1987) tells how child labour and racial discrimination persisted in the US. This era is characterised by mechanical mindsets, with workers increasingly portrayed in Modernist art as alienated and controlled by machines. Cultural depictions like Chaplin's *Modern Times,* in which Chaplin plays an assembly-line worker, capture the monotony, isolation, and loss of freedom inherent in this system. Karl Marx characterised this as "barrack discipline", which served to alienate workers (Marx 1970/1887, 423–4). Joshua Freeman (2018) elegantly describes the shift from pre-industrial, seasonal, and self-directed rural work to clock-regulated industrial schedules in mills and factories. This was as transformative socially as it was economically, redefining work as a regimented and mechanised experience. One Ford factory worker is said to have remarked, "A man checks 'is brains and 'is freedom at the door when he goes to work at Ford's" (cited in Freeman 2018, 80). The workflow and business process evolved around assembly-line production, which represented a completely different way of structuring and organising work. Unlike Work 1.0, in Work 2.0 the raw materials passed along rubber conveyor belts through fixed workstations operated by stationary workers who are assigned a specific task. The finished assembled product goes to market when it reaches the end of the belt. Figure 6.4 demonstrates the assembly-line production workflow/business process.

3. Work 3.0

   The Work 3.0 era marked the transition from analogue to digital, characterised by the rise of digital automation, the increasing use of computers to support business workflows, and the emergence of the platform-based economy. Digital tools, such as the introduction of email, reshaped how tasks were organised, coordinated, and dispatched, enabling rapid gains in workplace productivity. The connected digital economy also supported the expansion of global supply chains, mass customisation, and globalisation.

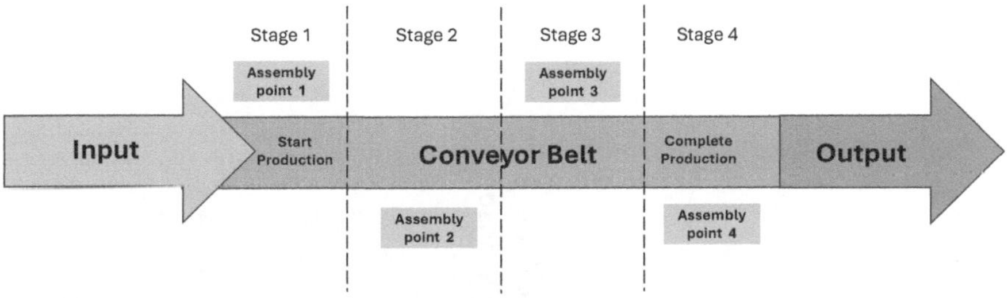

Figure 6.4 Production line workflow model.

Backed by a new generation of venture capitalists, entrepreneurial startups rapidly scaled, some becoming global brands.

That said, organisational workflows remained strangely mechanistic and linear. It was almost as if the manufacturing assembly line of Industry 2.0 had reappeared as a human assembly line in the offices of Industry 3.0, where work often followed predefined procedural logic. As Turriago-Hoyos, Thoene, and Arjoon (2016) demonstrate, some knowledge-based, decentralised, and team-oriented work cultures emerged, but most organisations in this period remained dominated by hierarchical structures and insular mindsets. Companies guarded products and brands carefully, operating as stand-alone entities rather than interconnected ecosystems.

The shift from manufacturing to service industries led to the rise of the office; however, the factory mentality of presenteeism, rigid roles, and command-and-control decision-making permeated the office environment, leading to chronic disengagement among the new knowledge workers.

During Industry 3.0, the growing emphasis on corporate governance (discussed in Chapter 5) further reinforced compliance-driven and standardised workflows. Organisations introduced linear, rule-based business processes defined by a "rigid sequence of steps" (Anderson 2024) and governed by "procedural rules" (Weske 2012, 50).[9]

A pyramid best represents the ideas presented here for Work 3.0 (see Figure 6.5).

The pyramid workflow model has dominated organisational life for nearly 150 years and remains a tenacious legacy. It is an insular, closed system that is highly standardised, rational, and rule-based, where information flows downward and outputs flow upward to the apex decision-makers. Such an approach inevitably creates roadblocks, bottlenecks, power struggles, and disengagement. A culture of control and presenteeism often permeates and ultimately defines such organisations. Closed organisations tend to be secretive, with cultures shaped by those at the top. It

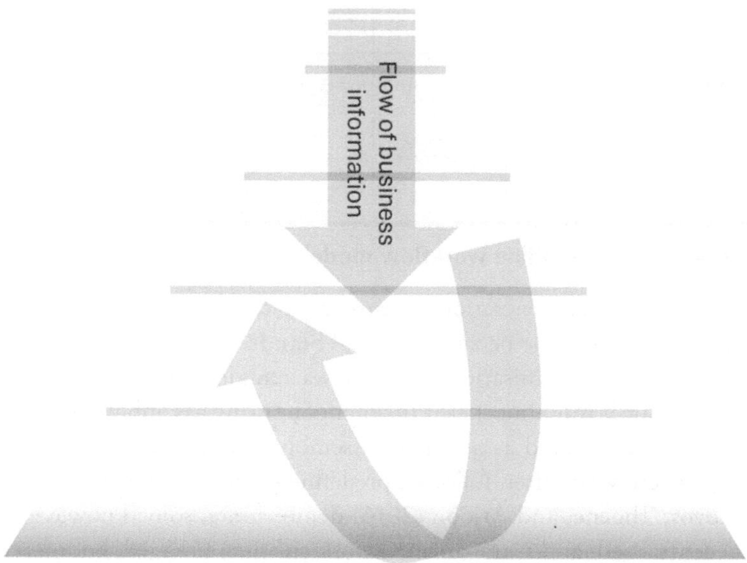

Figure 6.5 The pyramidal organisation in Work 3.0.

only takes one or two closed-minded leaders to derail, or even destroy, an enterprise, as illustrated by the failure of Blockbuster and WeWork. Ultimately, the pyramid workflow model thrives on rigidity and top-down governance, qualities that account for its endurance, yet also explains its lack of adaptability and innovation.

For almost 50 years, management theorists and consultants have sought to dismantle this pyramidal model through theories such as transformational leadership, empowerment, learning organisations, and team-based decision-making. Yet, these efforts largely failed due to the persistence of entrenched top-down cultures.

4. Work 4.0

This era is being shaped by the seismic technological shifts towards intelligent and interconnected systems, encompassing autonomous and quantum-enhanced AI, real-time data analytics, advanced automation, and green technologies. This is already reshaping the business landscape, leading to an increase in augmented workplaces, ecosystem governance and economics, a continuously restructuring business environment, and a generational shift in workers' values and attitudes. Venkat Atluri and Miklós Dietz (2022) reflect on how this will require cross-functional and networked collaboration, adaptive resourcing and performance, and continuously evolving skillsets. It is also coevolving the workflow: shifting it from mass production and consumption towards mass personalisation[10] where customers become coproducers, requiring organisations to restructure operations and workflows to accommodate personalisation and collaboration across global networks and ecosystems (Tessarini and Saltorato 2021).

Work 4.0 can be concisely characterised as an evolution towards a work environment that is highly connected, fluid, personalised, and deeply embedded in global, cross-cultural ecosystems. This has profound implications for the business process and workflow, which increasingly depends on the seamless flow of business intelligence through self-organising, emergent ecosystems. Figure 6.6 captures this complexity and flow.

Here, the business process functions as a complex adaptive system, represented as a pipeline through which business intelligence flows. In this protean and interconnected landscape, workflows continuously adapt, reconfigure, and respond in real time. This business process draws on cross-functional collaboration (Frans Johansson coined this the "Medici Effect" in 2004) and is designed to optimise what Ben Hecht (2013) terms "collective impact". It operates as an emergent, self-organising interconnected ecosystem. This makes it highly adaptive. Business intelligence is harvested through sensemaking processes across these networks and channelled directly into decision making. The continual evolution of AI

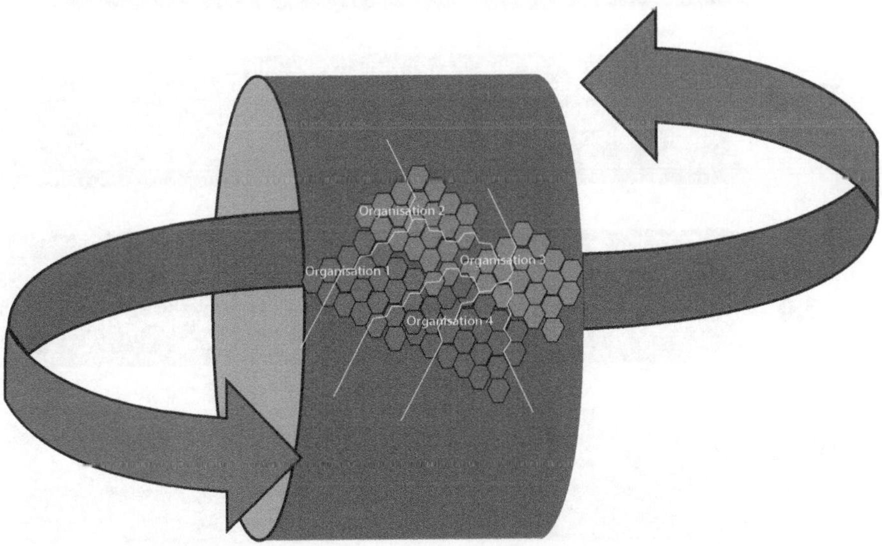

Figure 6.6 The flow of business intelligence through self-organising, emergent ecosystems.

further accelerates and enhances automated workflows, strengthening the augmented workforce.

This section on Work 1.0 to 4.0 is summarised in Figure 6.7.

Design Principles for Adaptive Workflows

Chapters 4 and 5 used the 4 O Framework of objectives, options, orientation and outlook (see Chapter 4 Figure 4.4) to organise the design principles, based on Reeves, Morieux, and Deimler (2010) who emphasised the importance of guiding principles. This section follows the same approach.

1. Objectives

   Determining objectives allows businesses to reflect on and engage in structured dialogue about their desired business model and workplace culture, and how these align with long-term mission and values. Establishing clear workflow objectives enables leaders to articulate strategic priorities,

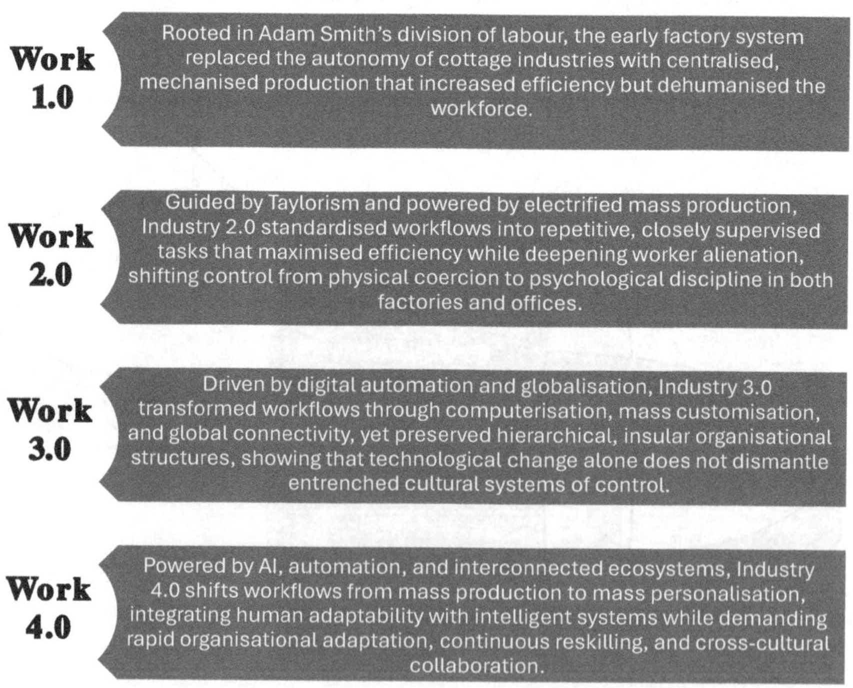

Figure 6.7 A summary of the four workflows from Work 1.0 to Work 4.0.

identify operational constraints, and describe the capabilities needed for future growth.

A recent consideration shaping the business workflow debate is the increase of smart technology in the workplace which is impacting human resourcing and innovation. Engaging with questions like these allows organisations to reflect on their business model in the context of emerging technologies, take stock of their digital transformation effort, and to strategise on the system and skill interventions needed for a successful augmented workplace. It also stimulates a broader discussion on organisational structure and governance, including how leadership, decision-making processes, and workforce development strategies must evolve to support an adaptive workflow.

This reflection and dialogue phase is a strategic checkpoint, encouraging organisations to consider workforce upskilling, ethical implications of automation, cross-functional collaboration, and mechanisms for continuous learning. Ultimately, well-defined workflow objectives act as a bridge between high-level organisational strategy and practical design considerations.

The final paragraphs of *The Nature of Business Transformation* urged organisations to appraise their business processes: "Organisations need to appraise their business processes – I call it business genome sequencing – and revitalise their creaky [business operating systems]" (Kelly 2022, 259).

2. Options

   To understand workflow options, it is critical for businesses to conduct a diagnostic of their existing business process workflow and review it against the organisational vision and objectives mentioned above. Streamlining workflows (Szhruthi 2023) in this way means "envisioning the end result, enabling it through logical steps and prototyping the process" (Butner and Ho 2019, 26). A simple model that supports this is the MARVEL model, an acronym for six steps (Map, Appraise, Redesign, Verify, Educate, and Log). This model helps organisations to investigate current workflow challenges and to explore and test future options. Figure 6.8 illustrates these steps.

3. Orientation

   A key aspect of orienting the workflow is understanding how it coevolves and aligns with the broader organisational context and system. There is a strong tie between workflow and the other business architecture pillars of structure and governance. Pidun, Reeves, and Zoletnik (2022) argue that "firms that want to successfully build business ecosystems have to rethink their operating models". The shift away from centralised governance models has encouraged greater collective decision-making and a stronger flow

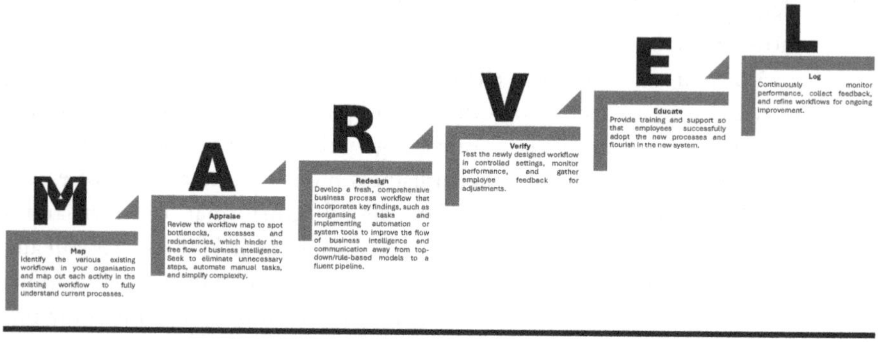

Figure 6.8 The 6-Step MARVEL model.

of business intelligence, enabling work to flow through a broader network of contributors. This has reshaped the organisational operating system. Later chapters will examine how digital transformation is rewiring organisational processes through digital workflows and how adaptive workforce strategies challenge traditional workplace attitudes and change processes.

Ultimately, adaptive workflow cannot be imposed as a fixed design; it emerges through the ongoing co-evolution of the organisational system in which it sits. Changing any aspect of the five system levers discussed in Chapter 1 (culture, design, technology, people, and process) will have a butterfly effect across the system and impact workflow and business processes.

4. Outlook

Organisational workflows are a major topic today because Covid-19 has normalised virtual and hybrid work; new technologies are reshaping how work is done; and organisations are rethinking how future work will be resourced by humans and machines. Let's explore each of these important themes.

i. The Covid-19 pandemic and the normalisation of virtual and hybrid work models

The Covid-19 pandemic marked a profound shift in the perception and organisation of work and workflows, accelerating the pace of organisational change. What began as a short-term crisis response quickly evolved into a transformation of working practices that had been gradually unfolding but had not yet fully taken hold. Since the pandemic, remote, virtual, and hybrid working models (a mix of remote working and dedicated time in the office), previously reserved for specific roles or progressive organisations, have become the norm. The pandemic accelerated the adoption of collaborative technologies and digital workflows, reducing dependence on middle management structures that historically coordinated and supervised daily activity. New working models have evolved, including the "elastic workforce" (gig and contingent working), cross-functional composable teams, compressed workweeks, and an emerging "work-from-anywhere" culture, that Julia Hobsbawm calls the "Nowhere Office" (2022).

Organisations such as Siemens have adopted flexible and mobile working policies that allow teams and individuals to select working arrangements suited to their roles and customer needs. Together, these developments show that the pandemic was not a temporary disruption, but a driver of long-term workplace cultural change. This shift has created tensions between leaders and employees. Many senior executives continue to express a desire for employees to return to pre-pandemic norms, with structured office routines and visible supervision. Surveys such as the KPMG CEO study reveal an overwhelming preference among leaders to restore in-person work (KPMG International 2024).

Organisations are redesigning physical offices as collaborative hubs to lure virtual and hybrid workers back to office-based working. But the reality is that employee expectations have shifted. Many workers now prioritise autonomy, flexibility, and meaningful engagement over physical presence. There is a shift in the psychological contract between employees and employers. Group CEO Karl Treacher (2023) argues that by 2030 employees will exercise far greater control over work arrangements, with self-managed teams becoming the norm rather than the exception.

These outlooks must be part of the organisation's thinking as it designs future workflows.

ii. Technological transformations in assisted, augmented, and autonomous Work

Rapid technological advancement, which is enabling closer human-machine collaboration, has triggered significant debates about the future of work and workflows. Technological and industrial revolutions over the past three centuries have repeatedly transformed how work is organised and resourced, and Work 4.0 continues this trajectory. DAO-style blockchain governance, digital platforms, advanced analytics, and autonomous and quantum-enhanced AI systems are rapidly reshaping workflows, business processes, and business operating systems.

At the centre of this unfolding debate lies the distinction between assisted, augmented, and autonomous intelligence.

- *Assisted intelligence,* prevalent in Work 3.0, involves technologies that support human activity (such as search engines and speech recognition) while humans retain full control and decision-making authority.

- *Augmented intelligence* describes a deeper form of interchange in which humans and machines "team" together, with AI enhancing human expertise, judgement, and productivity. This model is gaining prominence as organisations develop digital workers, cobots, and intelligent virtual assistants. Karen Butner and Grace Ho (2019) argue that this level of human-machine collaboration has strong workflow implications.[11] JP Gownder (2019) argues, "The future of work involves human employees working side by side with robots, intelligent machines from AI, automation, and robotics. And in general, your people, leaders, and organization aren't ready for this revolution".
- *Autonomous intelligence,* by contrast, refers to systems capable of performing autonomous tasks and making independent operational decisions. This development raises profound organisational, ethical, and governance considerations. Autonomous systems have the potential to restructure management hierarchies but may result in what Shoshana Zuboff (1989) describes as the redistribution of authority between humans and machines, with machines controlling humans (Dzieza 2020).

Each of these three scenarios has implications for the workflow.

iii. Future human-machine resourcing models

Forecasts by Christopher Pissarides and Anna Thomas (2018) suggest that 10–30% of human work could be replaced or reconfigured during the current industrial transformation driven by the automation of routine cognitive and physical tasks. A key strategic question for organisations is how to balance human and machine resourcing. Organisations are increasingly experimenting with an "elastic workforce" model, such as contingent labour, gig work, freelancing, and pooled resourcing via online platforms. Such resourcing models will challenge traditional managerial and governance frameworks. As machines take on more coordination and decision-making functions, organisations may reconsider the role of human management, potentially moving towards more self-managed and self-governed systems.[12]

The future labour landscape will include both risks and opportunities. Technological unemployment is becoming a reality according to Paul McClure (2018). Firms are already reducing human roles due to AI-based tools. For example, Ocado recently announced a reduction of 500 jobs, preferring to use "AI-type tools that drive up the productivity of our engineering teams" (cited in Butler 2025). CEO of Amazon, Andy Jassy (2025) has recently reflected on how AI will impact the workforce. [13]

Working time and patterns are also set to shift. There is growing support for a reduced working model, such as the four-day week.[14] Four Day

Week Global (4DWG) has conducted research on reducing work hours in 141 organisations across six countries. According to Wen Fan and coauthors (2025), the results show significant improvements in workers' wellbeing and job satisfaction.[15] Crucially, these human-machine resourcing scenarios have major implications for workflow design. As workflows become more digital, distributed, and machine-assisted, organisations will need adaptive workplaces that balance virtual and physical spaces (Bourgeois, Braier, and Garrett 2021).

Synthesis: Developing Adaptive Workflows

This chapter has explored how flexibility in organisational workflows is crucial for building adaptive organisations at the systems level. A historical perspective of Work 1.0 to 4.0 reveals that workflows never operate in isolation; they emerge through interacting with the wider system and are tightly interwoven with elements such as business architecture and transformation strategies.

Adaptive workflows are business processes designed to operate flexibly within complex adaptive environments. Developing such workflows requires ongoing adjustment of processes, working models, and resource allocations as conditions evolve. Drawing on the butterfly effect introduced in Chapter 2, the chapter emphasises the need for organisations to recognise how small workflow design changes can create significant system-wide impacts.

The chapter emphasised the value of personalisation and alignment in workflow design. A Spotify case study revealed that tailoring workflows to context rather than relying solely on rigid, rule-based processes is a powerful enabler of organisational responsiveness and adaptability.

The chapter presented several design principles that promote adaptive workflows, including setting clear objectives, assessing current workflows and future options, aligning with the evolving system. It also highlighted the importance of remaining mindful of employee expectations, technological developments, and the future implications for work models and resourcing. Critically, these design principles reinforce that adaptive workflows cannot be imposed; they must emerge organically from the evolution of the wider organisational system.

Coda

Chapters 3–6 explored the design phase of the 3Ps Systems Model introduced in Chapter 1. Taking a systems-and-culture approach to building an adaptive organisation requires drilling into the foundational business architecture pillars of structure, governance, and workflow, and embedding adaptability at this organisational design level. The historical analysis of Work 1.0 to 4.0 demonstrated the deep interconnectedness of these pillars and highlighted that developing adaptive organisations depends on cultivating adaptive cultures within the business architecture itself. This was illustrated through the case studies of Pixar, Cisco, and Spotify.

Each chapter concluded with a set of design principles for building adaptability, organised around objectives, options, orientation, and outlook (the 4 O Framework). The message is consistent: be clear about what you aim to achieve, remain open to the complex adaptive system around you, align decisions with the broader organisational system, and stay receptive to emerging ideas that strengthen your purpose.

Having diagnosed the organisation's adaptability using a systems-and-culture approach and having reviewed organisational design at the levels of structure, governance, and workflow, the final phase is to consider how to deliver an adaptive organisation by mobilising technology and people and adopting the right change process.

This is the focus of the final three chapters.

Notes

1. Spotify is known as an ethical company. It has tackled piracy and pays fair royalties to artists (Stern 2012). Although artists largely support the Spotify approach, some are critical of the streaming service, saying that "the payment model is unfair and that the service is cannibalizing album sales" (Swanson 2013, 207).
2. Artificial Intelligence is playing a key role in supporting digital workflows and the digital transformation of the organisation. See, for example, Berinder and Eckervald 2025; Pingili 2025; Ellingrud and Sanghvi 2023; Chandra 2024.
3. Authors reflecting this perspective include, Lawrence 1997; Koulopoulos 1994; and Weske 2012.
4. Adaptive workflows can be linear, parallel, looping, or automated (van Zandt 2023). They can also be swarm-based (Kelly 2019, 2022). Adaptive workflows can include "on the fly" or even "evolving" workflows (Kammer et al. 2000).
5. Similar to other workflow management systems, adaptive workflows have been significantly enhanced by automation. Samuel Tatipamula, however, distinguishes between rule-based automation and adaptive intelligence, noting that rule-based approaches have notable limitations in adaptive environments (Tatipamula 2025).
6. Workforce demographics are also driving the need for adaptability. Doug Lovelock (2018) reports that digital natives and millennials now make up roughly 75% of the workforce, a demographic that prioritises flexibility, wellbeing, and collective decision-making over rigid, centralised work models. Meanwhile, of course, many older workers have exited the labour market in post-pandemic times, contributing to a talent shortage (Boileau and Cribb 2022).

7. Andrew Ure, a contemporary physician, science writer, and business theorist wrote in 1835 in *The Philosophy of Manufactures: or, an Exposition of the Scientific, Moral, and Commercial Economy of the Factory System of Great Britain* that the greatest hurdle mill operators faced was training human beings to "renounce their desultory habits of work, and to identify themselves with the unvarying regularity of the complex automation" (Ure 1835, 15). Some contemporary workers revolted against the automatisation of humans in the workplace and smashed the machinery. They were known as the Luddites and acts of Parliament were introduced to curb their behaviour.
8. A list of job roles from this period can be found in local records of graveyards. For example, the Friends of Salford Cemeteries Trust (2025) list local graveyards in the Salford area showing a broad range of specialised job roles including Cloth Lapper (who took the cloth from the carding machine and readied it for the next process), Dyer (who coloured the fabrics), Overseer (who supervised production), Picker (who cast the shuttle on a loom), and Slubber Doffee (who removed the bobbins from the spindles in the mills).
9. Kanana Ezekiel and colleagues argue that "Almost all workflow applications are based on some sort of rule-based systems" (Ezekiel et al. 2019, 948).
10. Authors exploring personalisation include Pech and Vrchota (2022) and Wang et al. (2017).
11. Clara Murray (2025) discusses the mental strain of working with machines.
12. Authors publishing on this subject include Karl Treacher (2023) and Lynda Gratton (2011).
13. This should be considered alongside the debate that more opportunities are being developed by AI (Ball 2023) and that "AI won't replace people – but people who use AI will replace people who don't" (Goldstein et al. 2023).
14. Authors publishing on the four-day week include Barnes and Jones 2020; Ryle 2024; and Schor 2025.
15. These changes echo earlier labour transformations, including the move to a five-day workweek during Industry 2.0, the rise of flexitime during Industry 3.0, and today's emerging forms of compressed, hybrid, and omni-working in Industry 4.0 (Stirling-Wilkie 2023).

Bibliography

Agarwal, Roshan, and Abhishek Pandey. 2021. 'Industrial Revolution 2.0 — Era Of Mass Production'. *Medium - Society for Industrial Management and Engineering*, July 16. https://medium.com/spark-by-sime/industrial-revolution-2-0-era-of-mass-production-594acfa228c6.

Akgün, Ali E., Halit Keskin, and John Byrne. 2012. 'Antecedents and Contingent Effects of Organizational Adaptive Capability on Firm Product Innovativeness: Organizational Adaptive Capability'. *Journal of Product Innovation Management* 29: 171–89. https://doi.org/10.1111/j.1540-5885.2012.00949.x.

Anderson, Claire. 2024. 'What Is Adaptive Workflows?' *Focus Keeper*, August 7. https://focuskeeper.co/glossary/what-is-adaptive-workflows.

Atluri, Venkat, and Miklós Dietz. 2023. *The Ecosystem Economy: How to Lead in the New Age of Sectors without Borders*. John Wiley and Sons, Inc.

Ball, James. 2023. 'Will AI Steal My Job? Maybe – but Here Are Some Possible New Opportunities'. *The Guardian*, August 16. https://www.theguardian.com/global-development/2023/aug/16/will-ai-steal-my-job-maybe-but-here-are-some-possible-new-opportunities.

Barnes, Andrew, and Stephanie Jones. 2020. *The 4 Day Week: How the Flexible Work Revolution Can Increase Productivity, Profitability and Well-Being, and Help Create a Sustainable Future*. Little, Brown Book Group.

Becker, J., C.V. Uthmann, M. Zur Muhlen, and M. Rosemann. 1999. 'Identifying the Workflow Potential of Business Processes'. *Proceedings of the 32nd Annual Hawaii International Conference on Systems Sciences. 1999. HICSS-32. Abstracts and CD-ROM of Full Papers*, 10. https://doi.org/10.1109/HICSS.1999.772962.

Berinder, Victoria, and Elin Eckervald. 2025. 'Integrating Generative Ai into the Analytics Workflow'. MA, Uppsala University. https://www.diva-portal.org/smash/get/diva2:1965188/FULLTEXT01.pdf.

Boileau, Bee, and Jonathan Cribb. 2022. 'Decisions to Retire Early Are Driving Growing Economic Inactivity among People in Their 50s and 60s'. Institute for Fiscal Studies, June 16. https://ifs.org.uk/news/decisions-retire-early-are-driving-growing-economic-inactivity-among-people-their-50s-and-60s.

Bourgeois, Doug, Alex Braier, and Matt Garrett. 2021. *Adaptive Workplaces and Technology: Infrastructure Considerations to Support the Workforce Post-COVID*. Deloitte Development LLC. https://www.deloitte.com/content/dam/assets-zone3/us/en/docs/alliances/2024/Adaptive_Workplaces_and_Technology_-_Infrastructure_Considerations_to_Support_the_Workforce_post-COVID.pdf.

Butler, Sarah. 2025. 'Ocado to Cut 500 Technology and Finance Jobs as AI Reduces Costs'. *The Guardian*, February 27. https://www.theguardian.com/business/2025/feb/27/ocado-to-cut-500-technology-and-finance-jobs-as-ai-reduces-costs.

Butner, Karen, and Grace Ho. 2019. 'How the Human-Machine Interchange Will Transform Business Operations'. *Strategy and Leadership* 47 (2): 25–33. https://doi.org/10.1108/SL-01-2019-0003.

Chandra, Dev. 2024. 'Revolutionizing Business: Mastering Generative AI Workflows for Entrepreneurs'. *Dev Chandra*, September 13. https://theprocesshacker.com/blog/generative-ai-workflows/.

Deelman, Ewa, Dennis Gannon, Matthew Shields, and Ian Taylor. 2009. 'Workflows and E-Science: An Overview of Workflow System Features and Capabilities'. *Future Generation Computer Systems* 25 (5): 528–40. https://doi.org/10.1016/j.future.2008.06.012.

Dessein, Wouter, and Tano Santos. 2006. 'Adaptive Organizations'. *Journal of Political Economy* 114 (5): 956–95. https://doi.org/10.1086/508031.

Doehler, Tom. 2021. 'Flat Out Change: Balancing Structure with Culture'. Blog. *Typeform*, January 15. https://www.typeform.com/blog/engineering-org.

Dzieza, Josh. 2020. 'How Hard Will the Robots Make Us Work?' *The Verge*, February 27. https://www.theverge.com/2020/2/27/21155254/automation-robots-unemployment-jobs-vs-human-google-amazon.

Ellingrud, Kweilin, and Saurabh Sanghvi. 2023. *Generative AI's Impact on Jobs and Workflows*. McKinsey Global Institute, September 21. https://www.mckinsey.com/mgi/our-research/generative-ai-how-will-it-affect-future-jobs-and-workflows.

Ezekiel, Kanana, Vassil Vassilev, Karim Ouazzane, and Yogesh Patel. 2019. 'Adaptive Business Rules Framework for Workflow Management'. *Business Process Management Journal* 25 (5): 948–71. https://doi.org/10.1108/BPMJ-08-2017-0219.

Fan, Wen, Juliet B. Schor, Orla Kelly, and Guolin Gu. 2025. 'Work Time Reduction via a 4-Day Workweek Finds Improvements in Workers' Well-Being'. *Nature Human Behaviour* 9 (10): 2153–68. https://doi.org/10.1038/s41562-025-02259-6.

Freeman, Joshua Benjamin. 2018. *Behemoth: A History of the Factory and the Making of the Modern World*. 1st edition. W. W. Norton and Company.

Friends of Salford Cemeteries Trust. n.d. 'Some Old Job Titles from the Textile Industries. - Weaste Cemetery'. Weaste Cemetery Heritage Trail. Accessed 28 October 2025. https://www.weasteheritagetrail.co.uk/Resources/some-old-job-titles-from-the-textile-industries/index.htm.

Goldstein, Jill, Bill Lobig, Cathy Fillare, and Christopher Nowak. 2023. *Augmented Work for an Automated, AI-Driven World*. IBM Institute for Business Value. IBM Corporation. https://www.ibm.com/thought-leadership/institute-business-value/en-us/report/augmented-workforce.

Gownder, J.P. 2019. 'The Future Of Work Is An Adaptive Workforce'. *Forbes*, August 1. https://www.forbes.com/sites/forrester/2019/08/01/the-future-of-work-is-an-adaptive-workforce/.

Gratton, Lynda. 2011. 'The End of the Middle Manager'. *Harvard Business Review* 89 (1/2): 60–68. https://hbr.org/2011/01/column-the-end-of-the-middle-manager.

Hecht, Ben. 2013. *Collaboration Is the New Competition*. Harvard Business Review, July 10. https://hbr.org/2013/01/collaboration-is-the-new-compe?

Hobsbawm, Julia. 2022. *The Nowhere Office: Reinventing Work and the Workplace of the Future*. Basic Books.

Hourlias, Paul. 2023. 'Agile Team Organization: A Deep-Dive on the Spotify Model'. Medium, February 9. https://medium.com/found-ation/agile-team-organization-a-deep-dive-on-the-spotify-model-f5b32dfc37dd.

Houston, Rab, and K. D. M. Snell. 1984. 'Proto-Industrialization? Cottage Industry, Social Change, and Industrial Revolution'. *The Historical Journal* 27 (2): 473–92. https://doi.org/10.1017/S0018246X0001791X.

Jarvis, Peter, Jonathan Moore, Jussi Stader, Ann Macintosh, Andrew Casson-du Mont, and Paul Chung. 1999. 'Exploiting AI Technologies to Realise Adaptive Workflow Systems'. Paper presented at Artificial Intelligence Application Institute, University of Edinburgh. *AAAI Workshop on Agent-Based Systems in the Business Context*.

Jassy, Andy. 2025. *Message from CEO Andy Jassy: Some Thoughts on Generative AI*. Amazon, June 17, 2025. Amazon corporate news. https://www.aboutamazon.com/news/company-news/amazon-ceo-andy-jassy-on-generative-ai.

Johansson, Frans. 2004. *The Medici Effect: Breakthrough Insights at the Intersection of Ideas, Concepts, and Cultures*. Harvard Business School Press.

Jonwal, Sakshi. 2025. 'Spotify Case Study 2025: Innovation, Strategy and Growth'. Marketing Case Study. *Young Urban Project*, May 24. https://www.youngurban-project.com/spotify-case-study/.

Kammer, Peter J., Gregory Alan Bolcer, Richard N. Taylor, Arthur S. Hitomi, and Mark Bergman. 2000. 'Techniques for Supporting Dynamic and Adaptive Workflow'. *Computer Supported Cooperative Work (CSCW)* 9 (3–4): 269–92. https://doi.org/10.1023/A:1008747109146.

Kelly, Richard. 2019. *Constructing Leadership 4.0: Swarm Leadership and the Fourth Industrial Revolution*. 2019th edition. Springer International Publishing: Imprint: Palgrave Macmillan. https://doi.org/10.1007/978-3-319-98062-1.

Kelly, Richard. 2022. *The Nature of Business Transformation: A Swarm Intelligent Approach to Reinventing Organisations*. Routledge.

Koulopoulos, Thomas M. 1994. *The Workflow Imperative: Using Workflow Technology to Create Adaptive Organizations and Enduring Competitive Advantage*. 1st edition. Delphi Pub.

KPMG International. 2024. *KPMG Global CEO Outlook Survey*. KPMG. https://kpmg.com/xx/en/our-insights/value-creation/kpmg-global-ceo-outlook-survey.html.

Lawrence, Peter, ed. 1997. *Workflow Handbook 1997*. Wiley.

Lovelock, Doug. 2018. 'How Digital Natives Are Changing the Modern Workplace'. *Nintex*, August 14. https://www.nintex.com/blog/how-digital-natives-are-changing-the-modern-workplace/.

Marx, Karl. 1970. *Capital, Volume I: A Critique of Political Economy – Book One: The Process of Production of Capital*. English edition, Originally 1887. Edited by Friedrich Engels. Progress Publishers English Edition. Progress Publishers.

McClure, Paul K. 2018. '"You're Fired," Says the Robot: The Rise of Automation in the Workplace, Technophobes, and Fears of Unemployment'. *Social Science Computer Review* 36 (2): 139–56. https://doi.org/10.1177/0894439317698637.

Montgomery, David. 1987. *The Fall of the House of Labor: The Workplace, the State, and American Labor Activism, 1865–1925*. With Internet Archive. Cambridge [Cambridgeshire]; Cambridge University Press; Editions de la Maison des Sciences de l'Homme. http://archive.org/details/fallofhouseoflab0000mont.

Murray, Clara. 2025. 'Working with Robots Often Carries Mental Strain, Studies Find'. *Financial Times*, May 27. https://www.ft.com/content/528e3c25-22c7-4c83-b80a-dd07dae92c5d.

Pech, Martin, and Jaroslav Vrchota. 2022. 'The Product Customization Process in Relation to Industry 4.0 and Digitalization'. *Processes* 10 (3): 539. https://doi.org/10.3390/pr10030539.

Pidun, Ulrich, Martin Reeves, and Balázs Zoletnik. 2022. *Are You Ready to Become an Ecosystem Player?* BCG Global, June 23. https://www.bcg.com/publications/2022/major-shifts-to-become-successful-ecosystem-strategy-player.

Pingili, Ramesh. 2025. 'Generative AI Unlocking Adaptive Workflow Design'. *Journal of Next-Generation Research 5.0* 1 (2): 1–13. https://doi.org/10.70792/jngr5.0.v1i2.72.

Pissarides, Christopher, and Anna Thomas. 2018. *The Future of Good Work: The Foundation of a Modern Moral Economy – A Discussion Paper*. Institute for the Future of Work. https://assets-global.website-files.com/64d5f73a7fc5e8a240310c4d/64d5f73b7fc5e8a240310e92_Full%2Bpaper%2B-%2BThe%2BFuture%2Bof%2BGood%2BWork-v7-2.11.18.pdf.

Pollard, Sidney. 1963. 'Factory Discipline in the Industrial Revolution'. *The Economic History Review* 16 (2): 254. https://doi.org/10.2307/2598639.

Ramalingam, Meena. 2019. 'Business Process - Backbone of an Organization'. LinkedIn, November 7. https://www.linkedin.com/pulse/business-process-backbone-organization-meena-ramalingam/.

Reeves, Martin, Yves Morieux, and Michael Deimler. 2010. 'People Advantage'. BCG Global, March 25. https://www.bcg.com/publications/2010/strategy-behavior-culture-people-advantage.

Ryle, Joe. 2024. *The 4 Day Week Handbook: Your Guide to Happier Staff and Smarter Working*. Canbury Press.

Sabah, Ahmed S., Ahmed A. Hamouda, Yasmeen Emad Helles, Sami M. Okasha, Bassem S. Abu-Nasser, and Samy S. Abu-Naser. 2024. 'Artificial Intelligence and Organizational Evolution: Reshaping Workflows in the Modern Era'. *International Journal of Academic Pedagogical Research (IJAPR)* 8 (9): 16–19.

Schor, Juliet B. 2025. *Four Days a Week: The Life-Changing Solution for Reducing Employee Stress, Improving Well-Being, and Working Smarter*. Harper Business.

Spotify. 2024. 'Spotify Reports Third Quarter 2024 Earnings'. Company website. *For the Record*, November 12. https://20230524t095215-dot-pr-newsroom-wp.uc.r.appspot.com/2024-11-12/spotify-reports-third-quarter-2024-earnings/.

Stern, Joanne. 2012. 'Spotify Founder Daniel Ek Wanted to Create Something "Better than Piracy"'. *ABC News*, December 10. https://abcnews.go.com/blogs/technology/2012/12/spotify-founder-daniel-ek-wanted-to-create-something-better-than-piracy/.

Stirling-Wilkie, Gwen. 2023. *Omni-Working: In All Ways, From All Places — Work Effectively in All Ways from All Places*. Practical Inspiration Publishing. https://omni-working.com/our-book.

Swanson, Kate. 2013. 'A Case Study on Spotify: Exploring Perceptions of the Music Streaming Service'. *Journal of the Music and Entertainment Industry Educators Association* 13 (1): 207–30. https://doi.org/10.25101/13.10.

Szhruthi, B. 2023. 'The Complete Guide to Business Process Workflows'. ManageEngine Blog, September 20. https://blogs.manageengine.com/corporate/general/2023/09/20/the-complete-guide-to-business-process-workflows.html.

Tarafdar, Rajarshi. 2025. 'Human-AI Collaboration in Workflow Optimization: A Framework for Hybrid Decision Systems in Automation-Heavy Industries'. *International Journal of Scientific Research in Computer Science, Engineering and Information Technology* 11 (1): 3594–613. https://doi.org/10.32628/CSEIT251112384.

Tatipamula, Samuel. 2025. 'The Evolution of AI Workflow Automation: From Rules to Adaptive Intelligence'. *International Journal on Science and Technology* 16 (2): 1–15.

Taylor, Frederick Winslow. 1911. *The Principles of Scientific Management*. Dover Publications.

Tessarini, Geraldo Junior, and Patrícia Saltorato. 2021. 'Workforce Agility: A Systematic Literature Review and a Research Agenda Proposal'. *Innovar* 31 (81): 155–67. https://doi.org/10.15446/innovar.v31n81.95582.

Treacher, Karl. 2023. 'Fast-Forward to the Future: Welcome to the Workplace of 2030'. *The CEO Magazine*, March 4. https://www.theceomagazine.com/opinion/workplace-2030/.

Turriago-Hoyos, Alvaro, Ulf Thoene, and Surendra Arjoon. 2016. 'Knowledge Workers and Virtues in Peter Drucker's Management Theory'. *Sage Open* 6 (1): 2158244016639631. https://doi.org/10.1177/2158244016639631.

Ure, Andrew. 1835. *The Philosophy of Manufactures: An Exposition of the Scientific, Moral, and Commercial Economy of the Factory System of Great Britain.* Charles Knight. https://babel.hathitrust.org/cgi/pt?id=hvd.32044010389476&view=1up&seq=11&q1=exposition.

Wang, Yi, Hai-Shu Ma, Jing-Hui Yang, and Ke-Sheng Wang. 2017. 'Industry 4.0: A Way from Mass Customization to Mass Personalization Production'. *Advances in Manufacturing* 5 (4): 311–20. https://doi.org/10.1007/s40436-017-0204-7.

Weske, Mathias. 2012. *Business Process Management.* Springer Berlin Heidelberg. https://doi.org/10.1007/978-3-642-28616-2.

Zandt, Paul van. 2023. 'What Is a Workflow? Definition, Types, Benefits, Examples, Advantages and Management Systems'. *IdeaScale*, July 26. https://ideascale.com/blog/what-is-a-workflow/.

Zuboff, Shoshana. 1989. *In the Age of the Smart Machine: The Future of Work and Power.* Reprint Paperback ed. Heinemann Business Paperbacks. Heinemann Professional.

Chapter 7

Digital Transformation Strategies for Adaptive Organisations

The "Kodak Moment" was an Eastman Kodak Company advertising slogan encouraging people to capture memorable moments using analogue cameras and roll film. More recently, the phrase has come to signify organisations that lack a digital transformation strategy, leaving them exposed to digital disruption.

The term originates from a much-studied case involving Eastman Kodak, where the company missed an opportunity to become a market leader in digital photography. Scott Anthony (2016) convincingly debunks a common misconception that Eastman Kodak entirely ignored the rise of pixel-based technology that enabled digital photography. Eastman Kodak's downfall was not that it failed to grasp the potential of digital imaging or to invest in it (it did); rather, the company lacked a cohesive, well-defined digital strategy. Eastman Kodak invested in R&D for digital technology, but they didn't know what to do with it and failed to capitalise on it.

As new pixel technology developed, Eastman Kodak leadership tasked employees to explore the potential of digital photography. This led to the development of the first digital camera developed in Eastman Kodak laboratories in 1975 by Eastman Kodak employee Steven Sasson (who is in the National Inventors Hall of Fame in Alexandria, USA).[1] As Clark Gilbert and Joseph Bower (2002) report, Eastman Kodak's CEO George Fischer invested over $2 billion in research and development for digital imaging in the mid-nineties.

Where Eastman Kodak became unstuck is that its core business model and commercial opportunity was developing roll film (which founder George Eastman invented). Gilbert and Bower (2002) note that even as late as the

DOI: 10.4324/9781003680345-7

mid-nineties, the company was still trying to "make the new business fit the old model". It suffered from the Blockbuster syndrome of viewing its brand and market lead as invincible. An anonymous Eastman Kodak senior executive is reported to have said:

> Kodak's monopoly was the problem ... It always believed it had a God-given right to 100% of the market... It never bothered to look over its shoulder at what was coming up from behind.
>
> (cited in Tokyo 2012)

Scott Anthony (2016) notes that if executives in the mid-seventies downplayed the new pixel technology, the executives of the mid-nineties feared it. This lack of a coordinated digital strategy, combined with leadership's unwillingness to adopt a new business model beyond roll film ultimately led to Eastman Kodak's spectacular downfall and bankruptcy in 2012. At the heart of Eastman Kodak's problems was a lack of cultural adaptability.

The STEP-WIDE model is a helpful tool here. Eastman Kodak leadership ignored the STEP-WIDE events playing out around them. In the 1970s, the US was slowly embracing recycling (Eschner 2017); the developing pixel technology made digital photography technically plausible; globalisation and the digital economy were emerging; legislators were beginning to create policy for a digital-first economy; no-frills airlines were on the rise, making leisure travel more accessible with more photo opportunities; populations were becoming increasingly mobile; and young people were being exposed to home computers and computer science at school and didn't see a future in analogue and roll film cameras. The external environment and prevailing zeitgeist pointed to a golden market opportunity for digital cameras; yet Eastman Kodak, the largest camera manufacturer in the US at the time, failed to exploit it. They were oblivious to the complex web of systems unfolding around them.

Scott Anthony (2016) argues that Eastman Kodak's downfall wasn't exclusively about technology, but a failure of vision to see the emerging technology as a new business model (Eastman Kodak was so lacking in vision that they neglected to patent their new discovery). By contrast, its nearest competitor, the Japanese company Fujifilm, proved highly adaptive and technologically adept: it acquired pixel-based technology, embraced it, developed an entirely new business model around it, and went on to dominate the digital photography market. Launched in December 1989, the DS-X Fuji camera was the first digital camera on the market. Eastman Kodak did eventually produce its own digital camera, but it was all too late. The company filed for bankruptcy in 2012 because it could not establish a foothold in the digital camera industry. Fujifilm remains a multibillion-dollar trading enterprise.

The Eastman Kodak case can be compared with Google's ongoing, strategic digital transformation. A huge part of Google's commercial success has been its digital transformation from a software company to a cloud-driven technology leader. Its path to transformation began in 2000, when it migrated some of its core offerings, including Gmail, Google Calendar, and Google Docs, to the cloud. In contrast to Eastman Kodak, Google proactively adopted new technology and integrated it into its core business processes. Another part of Google's ongoing strategic transformation has been AI and machine learning, where Google has been a leader in commercialising AI. The company is an industry leader in speech recognition, image classification, prediction, intelligence tools, and is a major investor in quantum computing technology. Google's strength lies in finding applications for these digital revolutions and successfully integrating them into its business process and model. Another facet of its ongoing strategic digital transformation has been its readiness to invest in new innovations. A part of its portfolio is called "moonshot projects", where it invests in research and development for potential future technologies such as driverless cars. Unlike Eastman Kodak, Google has pursued a continuous digital transformation strategy built on constant innovation, investment, and integration. Through its 20 per cent rule, which allows employees to dedicate time to experimental projects, innovation is a measurable goal in the company. Guided by its mission to make technology universally accessible and useful, this value runs through every aspect of its digital transformation and integrates with its business workflow.

Joseph Bower and Clayton Christensen (1995) argue that "One of the most consistent patterns in business is the failure of leading companies to stay at the top of their industries when technologies or markets change". This book has already profiled some highly successful adaptive companies including Netflix and Starbucks. A key element of their success has been their approach to digital transformation. Netflix successfully transitioned its entire operation to the cloud and discovered a lucrative niche market. In 2017, Starbucks revealed a digital transformation strategy, known as the "digital flywheel" that successfully enabled in-store customer touchpoints and mobile app purchases, digitalised its customer rewards system, improved ordering, and, according to Elizabeth Mixson (2021), enabled greater personalisation through customer data organisation. Henry Adama and Chukwuekem Okeko (2024) observe how this strategy fuelled revenue growth. Other highly successful and adaptive companies, such as Uber and Airbnb, all have effective digital strategies.

This chapter, the first of three implementation chapters, will explore the role that an effective digital transformation strategy plays in supporting an adaptive organisation. The chapter presents best practices for building an adaptive digital transformation strategy. It aligns with the three pillars of organisational design that drive adaptive culture (structure, governance and workflow) and carefully shows through research and case studies how the transformation of these organisational design elements can be supported by technology.

From Digital Transformation (DT) to Digital Transformation Strategy (DTS)

Digital transformation (DT) is an elusive term. Gong and colleagues (2023) call it "fuzzy" and Thomas Ortner and his coauthors (2024) say it has many angles and variations. As this chapter will show, the root of this "fuzziness" lies in the term's evolution. The term transitioned from a narrow technological definition that focused on the shift from analogue to digital in the 1990s to a broader meaning encompassing organisational-wide transformation enabled by technology. To add to this complexity, Daniel Schallmo, Christopher Williams, and Luke Boardman (2017) discuss how the term overlaps with digitalisation. Cheng Gong and coauthors (2023) trace the term back to the 1990s, yet it remains highly current. Willem Sundblad (2020) considers DT to be a top organisational priority.

Defining Digital Transformation as an IT Upgrade

Early research on digital transformation presents it purely in technological terms as an "informational technology (IT) investment" (Zhang et al. 2023, 528) and "technological upgrades" (Dieffenbacher 2024). A 2021 literature review by Sascha Kraus and colleagues (2021), demonstrates that technology is still believed to be a "key driver as well as an instrument for achieving a competitive advantage through DT" (2). They have usefully plotted their findings in a bibliometric map (shown in Figure 7.1), which shows that digital transformation is still a technology-focused term.

Daniel Schallmo, Christopher Williams, and Luke Boardman map the pioneering technological breakthroughs into a digital radar of four areas: digital data, automation, digital customer access, and networking. Figure 7.2 visually shows their findings.

Digital Transformation as an Organisational-wide Business Strategy

More recent perspectives of digital transformation go beyond viewing it as an IT upgrade that is a "one-and-done project" (Lamarre et al. 2024) and treat it as part of what Karl Warner and Maximilian Wäger (2019) describe as an "ongoing process". It is part of a broader system transformation strategy (White 2024; Dieffenbacher 2024) which aligns with the business model and wider cultural transformation of the organisation (O'Brien, Downie, and Scapicchio 2024). This view presents digital transformation as a more holistic, organisational-wide, and strategic challenge.[2] A recent McKinsey source refers to digital transformation as "the rewiring of an organization, with the goal of creating value by continuously deploying tech at scale" (Lamarre, Robinson, and Galvin 2024).

Research shows that digital transformation spans three key dimensions: strategic change, business-model innovation, and organisational or cultural

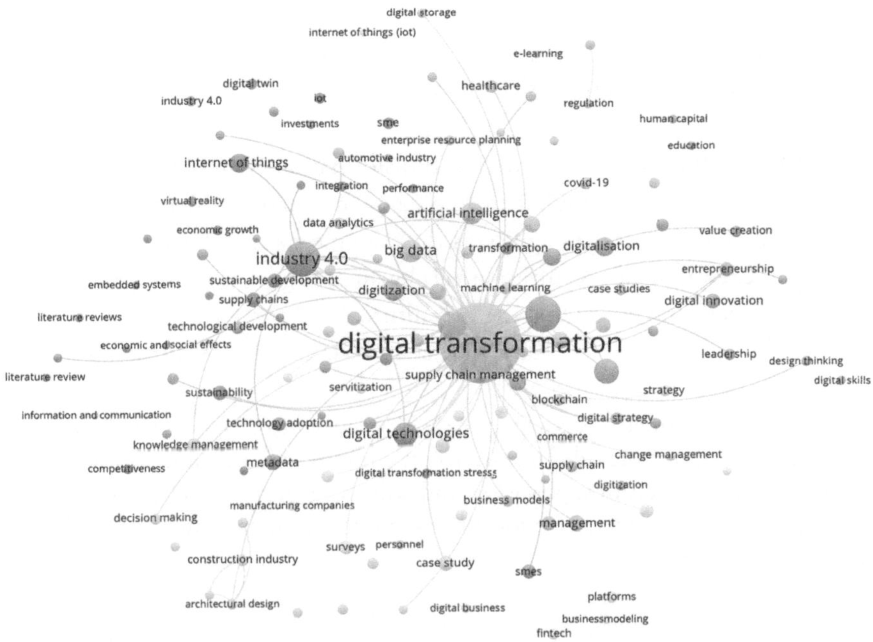

Figure 7.1 Bibliometric map of digital transformation (Kraus et al. 2021).

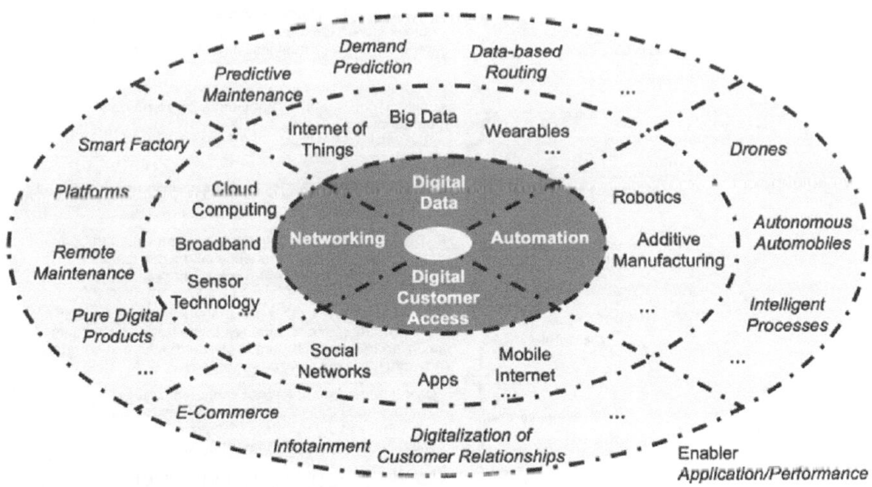

Figure 7.2 Digital radar with enablers and applications (Schallmo, Williams, and Boardman 2017).

transformation, emphasising that it is far more than a purely technological shift. Some authors such as Karl Warner and Maximilian Wäger believe all three of these systems are simultaneously at play:

> Our findings reveal that digital transformation is an ongoing process of using new digital technologies in everyday organizational life, which recognizes agility as the core mechanism for the strategic renewal of an organization's (1) business model, (2) collaborative approach, and eventually the (3) culture.
>
> (Karl Warner and Maximilian Wäger 2019 1)

Eva Hartl and Thomas Hess argue that "Firms need to transform and digitalize their entire business models and the accompanying existing organizational conditions, such as structures, processes and culture" (Hartl and Hess 2017, 1).

Figure 7.3 presents a selection of key quotes from the literature review for each of these systems.

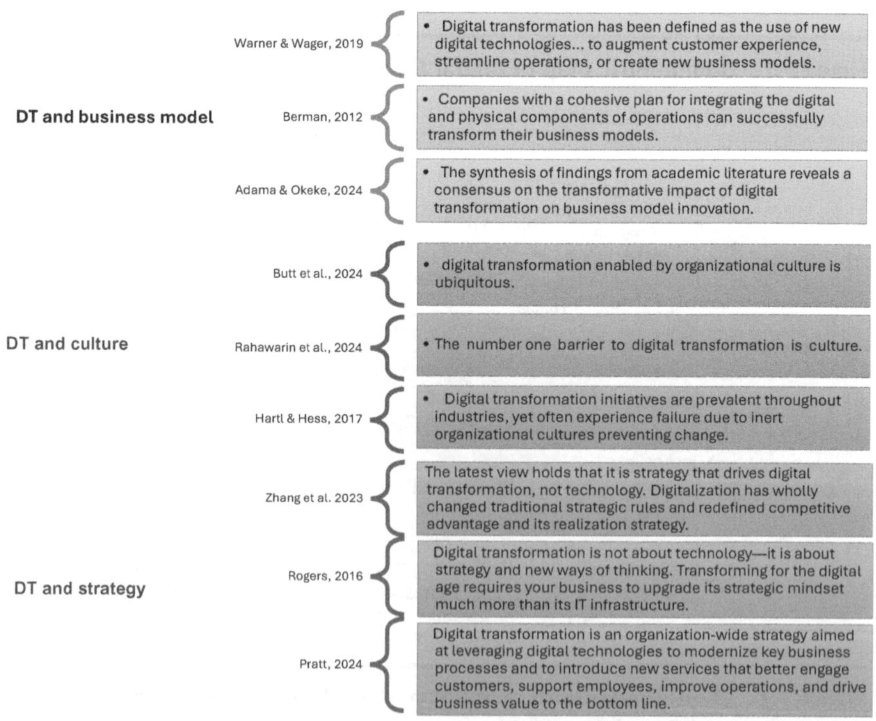

Figure 7.3 A selection of key quotations relating to DT as strategy, business model, and culture

The Role a Digital Transformation Strategy Plays in Building Adaptive Organisations

The three organisational design pillars of structure, governance, and workflow that were introduced in Chapter 1 and explored in Chapters 4–6 are key enablers of adaptive organisations. For organisations to truly evolve and sustain a culture of adaptability, they must create flexibility at the organisational design level. Digital transformation strategy is proving vital in helping organisations shift their business architecture from rigid to adaptive cultures (Sun, He, and Qian 2024). The following three sections highlight how a digital transformation strategy supports adaptability across organisational structures, governance, and workflows. Let's explore each of these in turn.

1. Digital transformation and structure

   Radhakrishnan Balakrishnan and Satyasiba Das (2020) argue that "conducive" organisational structures are essential for facilitating digital transformation. Vladimir Mirković and colleagues (2019) maintain that for digital transformation to be effective, it needs adaptive, "responsive, open and innovative" (5) flat structures. Abiodun, Rampersad, and Brinkworth (2022) concur, arguing that "digital transformation alters the organizational structure to create more agile and responsive structures" (1346). The shift from traditional pyramidal forms to what Bernd Wirtz (2021) and others describe as the digital organisation is therefore central to creating an adaptive digital ecosystem.

   Chapter 4 established that adaptive structures are crucial for cultivating organisational adaptability, showing how structures have evolved from vertical to more horizontal forms (from egostructures to ecosystems). Technology and digital transformation play a key role in enabling flatter organisational structures. They act as a digital bridge, strengthening connectivity across ecosystems by bringing ideas together, analysing data, personalising experiences for customers and stakeholders, and improving the flow of business intelligence and communication. Ghulam Mustafa and coauthors argue that "digitalization induces a faster flow of information that results in shorter time-frames for decision-making and real-time management" for both employees and customers (Mustafa et al. 2022, 675). This allows organisational actors, including employees, stakeholders, partners, and customers, to contribute to business intelligence and participate in collective decision making.
2. Digital transformation and governance

   Chapter 5 explored how adaptive governance (a self-organising framework designed to enhance self-governance and decision-making in volatile and uncertain environments) cultivates organisational adaptability by promoting the free flow of knowledge and business intelligence through system leadership. The Cisco case study from Chapter 5 illustrated how the organisation restructured its governance model to encourage self-organisation and collective decision-making. Digital transformation provides the technological infrastructure that allows organisational governance to become more adaptive, responsive, and self-governing. It creates an "organizational atmosphere that encourages innovation, embraces change and continues learning", leading to a "solid talent and cultural foundation for the long-term development of the enterprise" (He and Marcial 2024, 62).

From enhancing decision-making processes to streamlining operations, technology amplifies connectivity and shared governance. AI technology has the potential to reshape corporate governance structures. Irina Ivashkovskaya and Ilya Ivaninskiy (2020) argue that big data is enabling a stronger flow of business intelligence throughout the organisation, and that process automation through robotics is taking over everyday governance in such disciplines as auditing and improving overall organisational decision-making. This supports decision-making among employees as well as at the shareholder and board levels. Irina Ivashkovskaya and Ilya Ivaninskiy (2020) believe that the next stage of governance automation is algorithmic governance through advanced machine learning.

At an operational level, digital transformation and governance are about employee monitoring and surveillance, which Cornelius J. König (2025) maintains is a key part of the digitalisation story. Thomas Grisold and coauthors (2024) view digital surveillance in the workplace as the digital version of Taylorism and scientific management. An increase in workplace digital surveillance may well reduce the need for human supervisors.

These developments in digital governance carry risks. As Industry 4.0 progresses, AI-driven technologies will lead to greater machine-generated decisions and supervision, increasing the need for a digital or AI governance framework to establish accountability for an organisation's digital presence (Hanisch et al. 2023).

3. Digital transformation and workflow

Chapter 6 explored how the organisational workflow had evolved during the four industrial revolutions. AI and digital transformation are playing critical roles in supporting business ecosystems and cross-functional workflows. As Vijay Kotu and his coauthors observe in the 2025 AI Maturity Index, "Becoming an AI-first business means redesigning workflows so that intelligence flows seamlessly and enhances every operation" (Kotu et al. 2025, 12). AI tools can connect people, data, and processes, minimising bottlenecks and optimising workflows (Kotu 2025). As workplaces and ecosystems become increasingly augmented, with human and machine capabilities converging, connectivity and the flow of business intelligence will be supported by AI through digital workflows, often delivered as cloud-based solutions. Gita Jackson and Michael Goodwin (2024) discuss how automated processes often reduce or eliminate human input and may ultimately lead to a fully autonomous workforce.

These developments are slowly impacting work culture. Augmented workplaces and ecosystems are supporting new work models, including virtual (such as work-from-anywhere) and hybrid arrangements. A new generation of smart offices and factories is likely to emerge in the near future.

DT DRAW: A Process Tool for Developing Adaptive Digital Transformation Strategies

What this chapter has been exploring is the part digital transformation strategy plays in the adaptive enterprise story. Work 4.0 is characterised by uncertainty and complexity, and embracing technology as a strategic lever or mobiliser to navigate this evolving landscape is proving to be an organisational game changer. The DT DRAW model is an acronym for Diagnose, Resource, Adopt, and Weigh Up. It is an original process tool that helps organisations develop a system-wide, holistic, and integrated digital transformation strategy. The DT DRAW model (see Figure 7.4) provides a clear pathway for organisations to

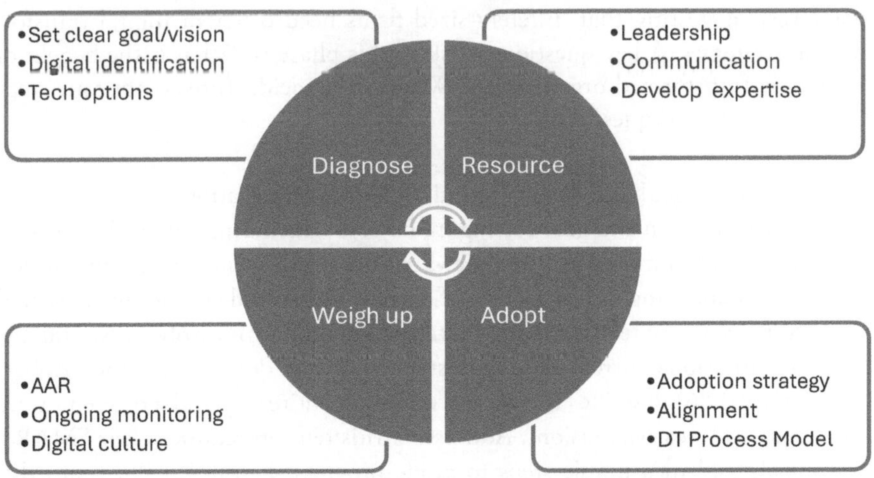

Figure 7.4 The DT DRAW model

make informed decisions about the phases or levels of digital transformation they need. This enables them to maximise digital potential, enhance adoption, and support the development of an adaptive business model and responsive business processes.

An integrated digital transformation strategy is vital because, statistically speaking, many digital transformations fail without a clear strategic focus. According to 2020 research by Boston Consulting Group (BCG), approximately 70 per cent of digital transformation projects have failed to achieve their potential (Forth et al. 2020). BCG's findings echo a 2018 McKinsey Global Survey on digital transformation, which found that "fewer than one-third of organizational transformations succeed at improving a company's performance" (Boutetière, Montagner and Reich 2018, 2). Furthermore, a 2014 study indicates that since 2000, 52 per cent of Fortune 500 companies have been taken over, gone bankrupt, or ceased to exist due to digital disruption (DXC Technology 2017).[3]

Boston Consulting Group's recommendations for an integrated digital transformation strategy, including clear goals, leadership commitment, a clearly defined DT talent pipeline, adaptive governance, monitoring, and a fit-for-purpose technology architecture, are reflected in the DT DRAW model.

Diagnose

This very important phase in the digital transformation strategy is often overlooked but is one of the major reasons for DT failure. Matt, Hess, and Benlian (2015) emphasise the significance of thinking through the digital transformation strategy and not approaching it "half-heartedly" (341). Radhakrishnan Balakrishnan and Satyasiba Das (2020) also underscore the importance of early diagnosis, suggesting that different-sized firms need different digital transformation strategies. A key question to ask in this phase is: What is the benefit of a digitally transformed organisation? What is the yield? Three diagnostic steps help us answer this question.

i. Set a clear goal and vision around digital transformation

   Most vision and goal-setting frameworks, including Robert Fritz's "creative tension model" (1986), are variations on the same underlying principle: establishing a clear picture of current reality and envisioning a desired future state. In relation to digital transformation, this involves assessing the organisation's current state against its vision and desired outcomes. Robert Fritz (1986) describes the gap between current reality and a desired future state as "creative tension". Addressing this tension requires clear SMART goals and measurable steps to guide progress. Figure 7.5 illustrates this process.

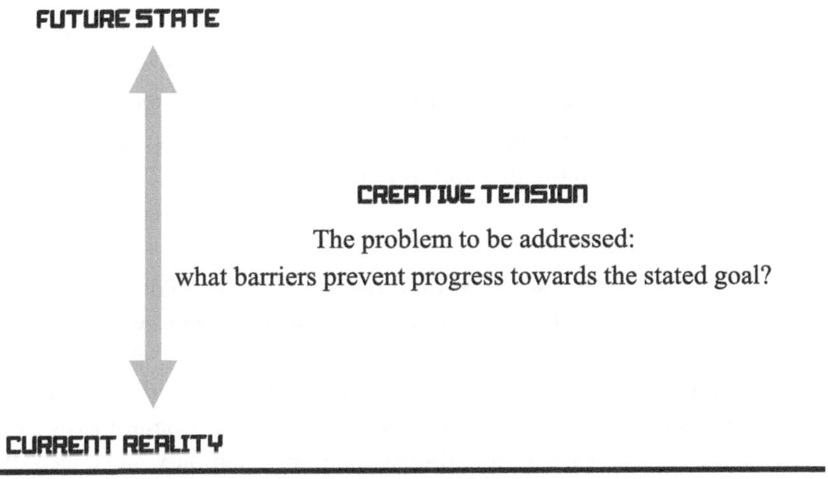

Figure 7.5 Current reality versus desired outcome

Digital transformation strategy is most effective when it begins by outlining the organisation's broader objectives rather than imposing predetermined technologies. In an adaptive organisation, the core issue is how to strengthen connectivity among people, ideas, customers, suppliers, and the wider ecosystem. Technology here serves as an enabler of this connectivity. The STEP-WIDE model from Chapter 3 is a valuable tool here; it can help people to better understand the current reality and future state in relation to external forces.

Be prepared to continuously revisit the current reality/future state concept as it may evolve and adapt over time. Consider a retail example: supermarkets originally introduced barcodes to optimise checkout speed and accuracy, while also improving store security and stock management. The introduction of portable scanners enabled customers to self-scan. As a result, the vision and the digital transformation strategy shifted from optimising checkout and inventory processes to reducing reliance on human checkout staff. This illustrates how a vision can adapt in response to changing technologies and organisational priorities.

ii. Defining transformation scope

Having set a clear digital transformation vision based on the current reality and desired outcome, the next step is to define the transformation scope. An important factor to consider here is the difference between an IT project and digital transformation. Lauri Wessel and coauthors (2021) believe that organisational value is the key determinant of whether an initiative qualifies as a digital transformation (DT) or an IT-enabled organisational transformation (ITOT):

> In DT, digital technology is central in redefining value propositions, which occasions the emergence of new organizational identity. ITOT, in contrast, involves the use of digital technology to support an existing value proposition, implying that the existing identity of an organization is reinforced.
>
> (Wessel et al. 2021, 4)

The research suggests there are three phases in any digital solution: digitisation, digitalisation, and digital transformation.[4] Figure 7.6 clearly shows this.

Digitisation (Stage 1) is the primary phase of a digital transformation and broadly means the conversion from analogue to digital. This stage involves digitising and organising information which, according to Carolyn Cordery and colleagues (2023), has the "lowest impact" (3). In the retail example, in the past, shelf workers priced items with a manual pricing gun, and the till operator entered the price manually into the cash register. The barcode converts product information into machine-readable data. An early Industry 2.0 digitisation example is the breaking of the Enigma code, which shifted from manual deciphering of intercepted German codes to machine decryption.

Digitalisation (Stage 2) broadly leads to a process change (Cordery et al. 2023). In the retail example, the digitised items (coded into the barcode) led to a change in the role of the till operator (who now scans rather than keys), a change in store security (where security gates identify unscanned

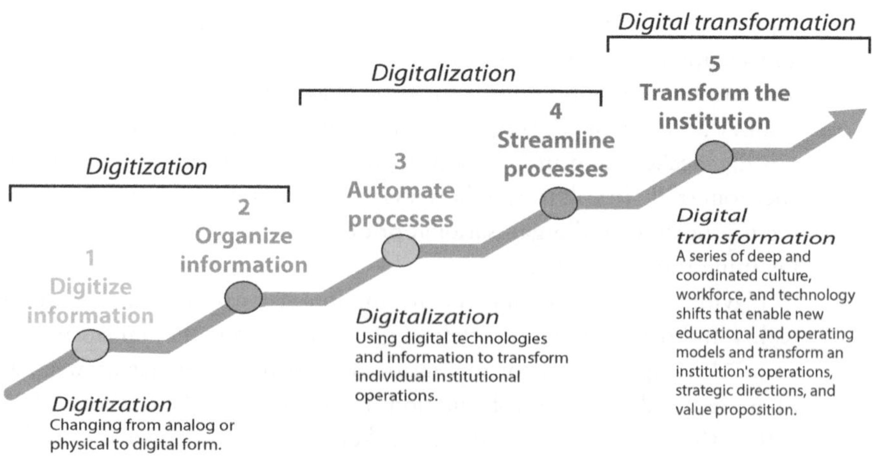

Figure 7.6 The three stages in a digital solution (Brooks and McCormack 2020)

items), a change in stock taking (where the need for new stock can be easily identified), and a change in customer experience (with hand-held portable scanners and self-service checkout tills).

Digital transformation (Stage 3) entirely transforms the system, leading to cultural and workforce changes (Alrasheedi, Sammon, and McCarthy2022). In the retail example, this would mean eliminating the human customer interface in stores, with items being processed digitally. Stage 3 will entirely transform the culture and experience of shopping, with greater emphasis on automated scanning, e-grocery, and home delivery (Eikelmann et al. 2022).

Identifying and defining the transformation scope, spanning digitisation, digitalisation, and transformation, is a crucial part of the diagnostic stage. A full digital transformation may not always be appropriate, depending on external macro forces, customer needs, and organisational values. This stage should be carefully considered and discussed even before assessing whether sufficient financial resources exist for a major transformation. It serves as the basis for setting digital milestones and requires strategic thinking about where the organisation intends to be (its vision) and the level of digital adoption that best supports it.

iii. Think about the technology that can help you (tech options)

Having established the organisational vision and the scope of the transformation, it is important to research available and feasible technologies within the allocated budget. Lack of financial means is a major obstacle to successful digital transformation adoption. Leeann Stewart (2022) advises that organisations need robust financial and technology planning for digital transformation to succeed. Patrick Forth and coauthors (2020) argue that a fit-for-purpose technological architecture is important.

A crucial point here is to have a clear view of the future of the emerging technology. There is huge investment in AI-enabled technology, but there is also ongoing discussion that it might be all hype and about to burst (Dryden, 2025). A recent report by Piero Cingari of *Euronews* (2025) discusses how the AI "bubble" is driven by the so-called "Magnificent Seven" (Nvidia, Microsoft, Apple, Alphabet, Amazon, Meta Platforms, and Tesla), which could lead to a severe setback and a possible AI winter if these organisations fail to deliver real, broad-based productivity gains that justify current valuations. Mike Walker (2021) argues for a blend of digital technology solutions, termed "digital ecosystem". Leeann Stewart (2022) says many make the mistake of seeing digital transformation as a technology-focused project that uses consultants, rather than developing capability in the organisation's DNA.

A question posed at the start of this section was: What is the benefit and yield of a digitally transformed organisation? Undertaking a diagnostic of the vision, goals, and technology plan for procuring a digital solution helps to address this question. Organisational benefits begin to emerge when a clear vision is established, the gap is identified, and defined goals are set to bridge it. Understanding what is technologically feasible, alongside an evaluation of cost versus benefit, enables organisations to assess the potential yield and determine whether investment in new technology is viable. While consultants can support this process, they should not be viewed as the primary solution. It is also important to recognise that in-house development is not always the most appropriate approach. Alternatives may include merging with organisations that already possess the required capabilities, hiring digital specialists, or forming strategic partnerships with technology providers. All of these considerations should be addressed during this critical diagnostic phase.

Resource

Developing resources to support digital transformation is another important process step in building an integrated digital transformation strategy. Becky Frankiewicz and Tomas Chamorro-Premuzic (2020) argue, "Contrary to popular belief, digital transformation is less about technology and more about people". Resource and digital transformation here include digital leadership, communication, and the development of digital literacy (or as Didier Bonnet and George Westerman (2020) term it, "digital mastery").

i. Leadership

   Patricia Forth and her coauthors (2020) maintain that leadership commitment is needed for a successful DT adoption and that this must begin at the top. Nikolaus Henke and colleagues (2021) remind us that it is crucial for board members to understand digital transformation and promote it. Senior leadership endorsement and commitment are essential for creating the vision and mobilising the organisation. We don't, however, need our leaders to be superheroes. Leaders need to quickly organise a collective effort through system leadership. Digital transformation leadership should be interwoven at every level of the organisation. As discussed throughout this book, system leadership is an organisational mindset (and not a role) that provides system-wide, collective, and responsive leadership. System leaders need to embrace digital transformation and become "digital leaders" (to use Bernd Wirtz's term) where "digital leadership is described as a contemporary, holistic, decentralized, or reciprocal form of leadership" (Wirtz 2021 477). The senior leaders' role is to get out of the way, to mentor, and be ambassadors for change.

ii. Communication

In relation to digital transformation, a McKinsey survey success rates increase when the transformation is clearly communicated. This clarity helps employees and stakeholders "understand where the organization is headed, why it is changing, and why the changes are important" (Boutetière et al. 2018, 10). Organisations that follow this practice are three times more likely to have a successful digital transformation, according to Hortense de la Boutetière and coauthors. The survey shows this is particularly effective when delivered via a change story. Developing a well-defined communication strategy is essential and all modern communication methods and digital platforms should be considered (Spagnoletto et al. 2019). Companies should avoid too many surveys or "plug-and-play" digital tools, as this can lead to information overload and employee transformation fatigue (Spagnoletto et al. 2019).

iii. Developing expertise

Recruitment and employee development plans should be continuously updated to reflect digital transformation. Satty Bhens, Ling Lau, and Hugo Sarrazin (2016) contend that a talent acquisition strategy is required to attract digital expertise. A development programme is also required to promote digital-first mindsets and quotients. This will be pursued in Chapter 8.

Adopt

The third letter of the DT DRAW model is A for Adopt. Digital transformation adoption is a vast subject. This section focuses on the importance of formulating an adoption strategy, organisational alignment, and choosing a digital transformation process model.

i. Adoption strategy

Selecting the right digital transformation adoption strategy is an important step that reconnects with the diagnostic phase, where organisations identify the digital transformation scope, budget, and support required for success. A key consideration is whether to build digital transformation capacity through a merger or through recruitment and internal development. This requires careful thought. Companies need a clear understanding of the technology required and how it fits within the organisational ecosystem. They also need to understand the available digital transformation adoption models and select the one most appropriate for their organisation.

ii. Organisational alignment

To ensure alignment, organisations should consider digital transformation in relation to adaptive structures, governance, and workflow. It is a coevolutionary relationship in which an adaptive organisational design supports digital transformation, which, in turn, reinforces the adaptive organisational design. Loonam et al. emphasise the point:

> To match the efforts made in aligning organizational structure and business processes, internal organizational systems must be integrated in order to maximize on digital transformation.
>
> (Loonam et al. 2018, 4)

iii. Digital transformation process model

There are many digital transformation process models and frameworks available, but an excellent one is Brian Solis' "Six-stage digital transformation model" (Figure 7.7)

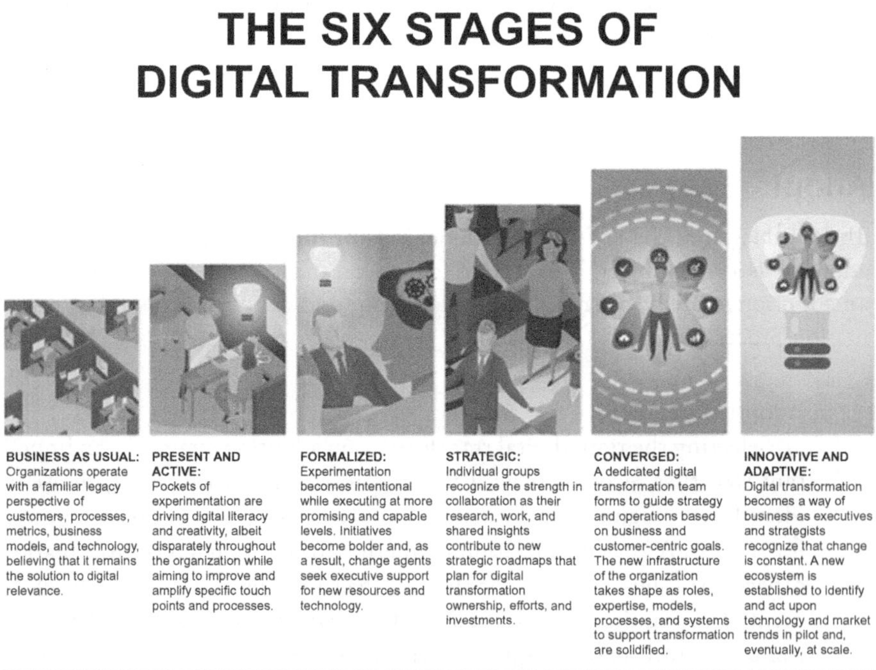

Figure 7.7 Six-stage digital transformation model (Solis,2016) with illustration by Jim MacLeod.

Solis' digital transformation model shows that digital transformation is not a one-off project; rather it is an experimental and evolutionary pathway from small, local initiatives to organisation-wide cultural and operational change that promotes core strategic capability (Solis 2016). It integrates with organisational design and people and change strategies, effectively serving as a strategic mobiliser or lever that shapes organisational direction. This emergent view aligns with contemporary discussions concerning adaptive organisations and the need for modular, iterative approaches to transformation. The case of Eastman Kodak shows the risk of experimenting with new technology without a plan to integrate and scale it: Eastman Kodak developed digital technology but failed to convert it into a sustained, company-wide strategic capability, a shortcoming discussed by Scott Anthony (2016) and others.

Weigh Up

The final letter in the DT DRAW model is W for Weigh Up, which includes an after-action review of the DT adoption, ongoing monitoring and measurement of effectiveness, and the creation of an enduring digital culture. This links to a strategic, holistic view of digital transformation as an ongoing initiative. Indeed, Brian Solis himself has recently abandoned the "digital transformation" label in favour of what he terms "business model innovation" (Solis 2024), echoing earlier discussions about expanding the notion of digital transformation to encompass business model change.[5]

In this context, weighing things up and ongoing measurement are critical for developing a strategic perspective on digital transformation.

i. After-action reviews (AARs)

   Structured reviews at the start, during, and at the close of each initiative are essential, and their outcomes should be documented and incorporated into future phases. After-action reviews (AARs) provide an effective mechanism for this. Originally developed and formalised by the US Army as a systematic debriefing tool to capture key lessons after missions, AARs offer a structured, non-threatening, and detached method for identifying insights and improvements relating to project phases. It is important to share these findings so that AARs become an integral part of the organisational feedback loop.

ii. Ongoing monitoring

   In their BCG report *Flipping the Odds of Digital Transformation Success*, Patrick Forth and his research team (2020) identify effective monitoring of transformation progress as a critical success factor in digital transformation. They recommend the use of multiple feedback loops, including both financial and non-financial performance indicators, to ensure that progress aligns with strategic outcomes. Trusted reporting mechanisms and reliable data sources are also essential, as they enable transparent and accurate tracking. Equally important is establishing clear accountabilities, with specific individuals or teams responsible for managing transformation metrics. Although not explicitly referenced in the BCG report, key behavioural indicators (KBIs) represent another important source of non-financial metrics.

iii. Develop an adaptive digital culture

Gerald Kane and coauthors (2015) assert that organisational adaptability is a key cultural driver that ensures digital transformation success, a view also shared by Nicolas Evans (2023). When the culture is digitally enabled and aligned with the organisation's technological ambitions, it can drive effective and sustainable change. Put another way, digital transformation initiatives are ineffective without alignment to strategy and culture.

Digital culture is not simply the outcome of one-off transformation projects; it is an ongoing, evolutionary process of digital adaptation, in which the organisation continuously learns, integrates new technologies, and reconfigures how people work. This reflects a broader technological progression (often framed in relation to Moore's Law[6]) where each "transformation" is only the completion of a phase, not the endpoint. Nicholas Evans (2023) argues that the word "transformation" itself is problematic because "many organizations have been on the transformation treadmill for years". Moore's Law drives rapid digital transformation in organisations, requiring constant adaptability to keep pace, a phenomenon also known as Digital Darwinism.[7] Organisations must be prepared for perpetual change, not single transformation events.

Many organisations misunderstand this, investing heavily in digital transformation programmes that focus on technology acquisition while failing to reshape mindsets, behaviours, and cultural norms. Without a digital-first mindset, characterised by curiosity, openness to experimentation, and readiness for continual change, even highly digitalised organisations struggle to realise value. An adaptive digital culture ensures that the workforce is not only equipped with digital tools but also motivated and capable of using them to drive ongoing innovation.

Synthesis: Developing a Digital Transformation Strategy

This chapter examined the role of digital transformation in creating adaptive organisations. The central argument is that digital transformation is not a "one-off" technological fix, but an ongoing system-wide process that rewires and reshapes the organisation. This involves examining how technology supports and strengthens adaptability across the business architecture and its workflows, and how it enables effective human-machine interaction and ongoing organisational evolution.

Eastman Kodak was presented as the primary case study, illustrating how an organisation can develop advanced technology yet fail to apply it strategically. To address this challenge, the chapter introduced the DT DRAW model (Diagnose, Resource, Adopt, and Weigh Up), a system-wide process tool that helps organisations to formulate a digital transformation strategy. The model encourages a shift from viewing digital transformation as a sole technological solution towards understanding it as an integrated, organisation-wide strategic framework.

Notes

1. Sasson's own perspective on the Kodak moment was reported in *The New York Times* when he said, "it was filmless photography, so management's reaction was, 'that's cute – but don't tell anyone about it'" (Gann 2016).
2. A more holistic approach (Konopik et al. 2022) and an ongoing process of strategic renewal (Kringelum et al. 2024).
3. Companies appear to be wising up to this failure. KPMG's recent Annual Tech Survey Report suggests that 88% of US businesses report improvements in profitability due to DT, compared to 45% in 2023 (Soni and Colombo 2024).
4. Researchers on this topic include: Nwaiwu (2018); Mergel, Edelmann, and Haug (2019); Brooks and McCormack (2020); Rijswijk (2020); Kelly (2022); Mapingire et al. (2022); Cordery et al. (2023). Wirtz is an outlier in the research here. He suggests four phases: digital evolution and adoption, digital extension and migration, digital transformation, and radical digital transformation (Wirtz 2021).
5. Authors publishing in this area include Warner and Wäger (2019); Berman (2012); and Adama and Okeke (2024).
6. Moore's Law, proposed by Gordon Moore in 1965, observes that transistor count (and thus computing power) roughly doubles every two years, driving the rapid growth and scaling of technology.
7. Brian Solis coined the term Digital Darwinism to mean when society and technology "are evolving faster than the ability for many businesses to adapt" (Leonard 2013).

Bibliography

Abiodun, Temitayo, Giselle Rampersad, and Russell Brinkworth. 2022. 'Driving Industrial Digital Transformation'. *Journal of Computer Information Systems* 63 (6): 1345–61. https://doi.org/10.1080/08874417.2022.2151526.

Adama, Henry Ejiga, and Chukwuekem David Okeke. 2024. 'Digital Transformation as a Catalyst for Business Model Innovation: A Critical Review of Impact and Implementation Strategies'. *Magna Scientia Advanced Research and Reviews* 10 (2): 256–64. https://doi.org/10.30574/msarr.2024.10.2.0066.

Alrasheedi, Naimah Saeed, David Sammon, and Stephen McCarthy. 2022. 'Understanding the Characteristics of Workforce Transformation in a Digital Transformation Context'. *Journal of Decision Systems* 31 (sup1): 362–83. https://doi.org/10.1080/12460125.2022.2073636.

Anthony, Scott. 2016. *Kodak's Downfall Wasn't About Technology*. Harvard Business Review, July 15. https://hbr.org/2016/07/kodaks-downfall-wasnt-about-technology.

Balakrishnan, Radhakrishnan, and Satyasiba Das. 2020. 'How Do Firms Reorganize to Implement Digital Transformation?' *Strategic Change* 29 (5): 531–41. https://doi.org/10.1002/jsc.2362.

Berman, Saul J. 2012. 'Digital Transformation: Opportunities to Create New Business Models'. *Strategy & Leadership* 40 (2): 16–24. https://doi.org/10.1108/10878571211209314.

Bhens, Satty, Ling Lau, and Hugo Sarrazin. 2016. *The New Tech Talent You Need to Succeed in Digital*. McKinsey & Company. https://www.mckinsey.com/capabilities/mckinsey-digital/our-insights/the-new-tech-talent-you-need-to-succeed-in-digital.

Bonnet, Didier, and George Westerman. 2020. 'The New Elements of Digital Transformation'. *MIT Sloan Management Review* 62 (2): 82–89. https://sloanreview.mit.edu/article/the-new-elements-of-digital-transformation/.

Boutetière, Hortense de la, Alberto Montagner, and Angelika Reich. 2018. *The Keys to a Successful Digital Transformation | McKinsey*. McKinsey & Company, October 29. https://www.mckinsey.com/capabilities/people-and-organizational-performance/our-insights/unlocking-success-in-digital-transformations.

Bower, Joseph L., and Clayton M. Christensen. 1995. 'Disruptive Technologies: Catching the Wave'. *Harvard Business Review*, February. https://hbr.org/1995/01/disruptive-technologies-catching-the-wave.

Brooks, D. Christopher, and Mark McCormack. 2020. 'Defining Digital Transformation | EDUCAUSE'. Educause, June 15. https://www.educause.edu/ecar/research-publications/driving-digital-transformation-in-higher-education/2020/defining-digital-transformation.

Cingari, Piero. 2025. 'Is the AI Bubble About to Burst, and What's Driving Analyst Jitters?' *Euronews*, November 18. https://www.euronews.com/business/2025/11/18/is-the-ai-bubble-about-to-burst-and-whats-driving-analyst-jitters.

Cordery, Carolyn J., Galina Goncharenko, Tobias Polzer, Danielle McConville, and Ataur Belal. 2023. 'NGOs' Performance, Governance, and Accountability in the Era of Digital Transformation'. *The British Accounting Review* 55 (5): 101239. https://doi.org/10.1016/j.bar.2023.101239.

Dieffenbacher, Stefan F. 2024. 'Digital Transformation Strategy Framework: 10 Key Steps'. *Digital Leadership*, January 18. https://digitalleadership.com/blog/digital-transformation-strategy/.

Dryden, Alex. 2025. 'Is the AI Bubble Ābout to Burst? What to Watch for as the Markets Wobble'. *The Conversation*, November 18. https://doi.org/10.64628/AB.ranvemta6.

DXC Technology. 2017. 'Digital Transformation Is Racing Ahead and No Industry Is Immune'. HBR, July 19. https://hbr.org/sponsored/2017/07/digital-transformation-is-racing-ahead-and-no-industry-is-immune-2#:~:text=Research%20shows%20that%20since%202000%2C%2052%20percent%20of,every%20dimension%20of%20society%2C%20commerce%2C%20enterprises%2C%20and%20individuals.

Eikelmann, Steffen, Marco Hoogenberg, Johannes Langkammer, Florian Starke, Maximilian Worm, and Joan Pujol. 2022. *The Future of Grocery Shopping – Grocery Shopping Will Change Significantly in the Decade Ahead – Traditional Food Retailers Must Adapt Fast.* Strategy& (PwC). https://www.strategyand.pwc.com/tr/en/pdf/strategyand-future-of-grocery-shopping.pdf.

Eschner, Kat. 2017. 'How the 1970s Created Recycling As We Know It'. *Smithsonian Magazine*, November 15. https://www.smithsonianmag.com/smart-news/how-1970s-created-recycling-we-know-it-180967179/.

Evans, Nicholas D. 2023. 'Why Adaptability Is the New Digital Transformation | CIO'. CIO, October 30. https://www.cio.com/article/657149/why-adaptability-is-the-new-digital-transformation.html.

Forth, Patrick, Tom Reichert, Romain de Laubier, and Saibal Chakraborty. 2020. *Flipping the Odds of Digital Transformation Success.* BCG Global, October 29. https://www.bcg.com/publications/2020/increasing-odds-of-success-in-digital-transformation.

Frankiewicz, Becky, and Tomas Chamorro-Premuzic. 2020. *Digital Transformation Is About Talent, Not Technology.* Harvard Business Review, May 6. https://hbr.org/2020/05/digital-transformation-is-about-talent-not-technology.

Fritz, Robert. 1986. *The Path of Least Resistance: Designing Your Life for Success.* Ballantine Books.

Gann, David. 2016. *Kodak Invented the Digital Camera – Then Killed It. Why Innovation Often Fails.* World Economic Forum, June 23. https://www.weforum.org/stories/2016/06/leading-innovation-through-the-chicanes/.

Gilbert, Clark, and Joseph L. Bower. 2002. *Disruptive Change: When Trying Harder Is Part of the Problem.* Harvard Business Review, May. https://hbr.org/2002/05/disruptive-change-when-trying-harder-is-part-of-the-problem.

Gong, Cheng, Vincent Ribiere, M.D. Lytras, A. Housawi, and B. Alsaywid. 2023. 'A Historical Outline of Digital Transformation'. In *Digital Transformation in Healthcare in Post-Covid-19 Times*, edited by Miltiadis D. Lytras, Abdulrahman A. Housawi, and Basim Saleh Alsaywid. Elsevier. https://doi.org/10.1016/B978-0-323-98353-2.00016-2.

Grisold, Thomas, Stefan Seidel, Markus Heck, and Nicholas Berente. 2024. 'Digital Surveillance in Organizations'. *Business & Information Systems Engineering* 66 (3): 401–10. https://doi.org/10.1007/s12599-024-00866–7.

Hanisch, Marvin, Curtis M. Goldsby, Nicolai E. Fabian, and Jana Oehmichen. 2023. 'Digital Governance: A Conceptual Framework and Research Agenda'. *Journal of Business Research* 162 (July): 113777. https://doi.org/10.1016/j.jbusres.2023.113777.

Hartl, Eva, and Thomas Hess. 2017. 'The Role of Cultural Values for Digital Transformation: Insights from a Delphi Study'. Paper presented at Proceedings of the 23rd Americas Conference on Information Systems (AMCIS 2017), Boston, USA. *ResearchGate*, August. https://www.researchgate.net/publication/330353915_The_Role_of_Cultural_Values_for_Digital_Transformation_Insights_from_a_Delphi_Study.

He, Ting E., and Dave Marcial. 2024. 'The Role and Best Practices of Digital Governance in the Digital Transformation of Enterprises'. *Theory and Practice of Science and Technology* 5 (4): 60–66. https://doi.org/10.47297/taposatWSP2633-456908.20240504.

Henke, Nikolaus, Arne Libarikian, Madhav Mysore, and Jan Soller. 2021. *How Boards Can Help Digital Transformations*. McKinsey & Company. https://www.mckinsey.com/capabilities/tech-and-ai/our-insights/how-boards-can-help-digital-transformations.

Ivashkovskaya, Irina, and Ilya Ivaninskiy. 2020. 'What Impact Does Artificial Intelligence Have on Corporate Governance?' *Journal of Corporate Finance Research / Корпоративные Финансы* 14 (4): 90–101. https://doi.org/10.17323/j.jcfr.2073-0438.14.4.2020.19-30.

Jackson, Gita, and Michael Goodwin. 2024. 'What Is a Digital Workflow? | IBM'. Company Website. IBM Think, January 8. https://www.ibm.com/think/topics/digital-workflow.

Kane, Gerald C., Doug Palmer, Anh Nguyen Phillips, David Kiron, and Natasha Buckley. 2015. *Strategy, Not Technology, Drives Digital Transformation: Becoming a Digitally Mature Enterprise*. MIT Sloan Management Review & Deloitte University Press. http://sloanreview.mit.edu/projects/strategy-drives-digital-transformation/.

Kelly, Richard. 2022. *The Nature of Business Transformation: A Swarm Intelligent Approach to Reinventing Organisations*. Routledge.

Tokyo. 2012. 'The History of the Rivalry Between Fujifilm and Kodak Is More Relevant Than Ever'. *The Economist*, January 18. https://archive.ph/WpOTb#selection-857.0-857.229.

König, Cornelius J. 2025. 'Electronic Monitoring at Work'. *Annual Review of Organizational Psychology and Organizational Behavior* 12 (1): 321–42. https://doi.org/10.1146/annurev-orgpsych-110622-060758.

Konopik, Jens, Christoph Jahn, Tassilo Schuster, Nadja Hoßbach, and Alexander Pflaum. 2022. 'Mastering the Digital Transformation through Organizational Capabilities: A Conceptual Framework'. *Digital Business* 2 (2): 100019. https://doi.org/10.1016/j.digbus.2021.100019.

Kotu, Vijay, Richard McGill Murphy, Brian Solis, and Dorit Zilbershot. 2025. *Enterprise AI Maturity Index 2025*. Index 2nd Annual Enterprise AI Maturity Index. Impact AI Series. Sevice Now and Oxford Economics. https://www.servicenow.com/content/dam/servicenow-assets/public/en-us/doc-type/resource-center/white-paper/wp-enterprise-ai-maturity-index-2025.pdf.

Kraus, Sascha, Paul Jones, Norbert Kailer, Alexandra Weinmann, Nuria Chaparro-Banegas, and Norat Roig-Tierno. 2021. 'Digital Transformation: An Overview of the Current State of the Art of Research'. *Sage Open* 11 (3): 21582440211047576. https://doi.org/10.1177/21582440211047576.

Kringelum, Louise B., Casper Gamborg Holm, Jens Holmgren, Ole Friis, and Katrine Freja Jensen. 2024. 'Digital Transformation: Strategy Comes First to Lay the Groundwork'. *Journal of Business Strategy.* ahead-of-print (ahead-of-print). world. https://doi.org/10.1108/JBS-09-2023–0199.

Kringelum, Louise B., Casper Gamborg Holm, Jens Holmgren, Ole Friis, and Katrine Freja Jensen. 2025. 'Digital Transformation: Strategy Comes First to Lay the Groundwork'. *Journal of Business Strategy* 46 (1–2): 3–10. https://doi.org/10.1108/JBS-09-2023-0199.

Lamarre, Eric, Harry Robinson, Jeff Galvin, et al. 2024. 'What Is Digital Transformation?' Consulting. *McKinsey & Company*, August 7. https://www.mckinsey.com/featured-insights/mckinsey-explainers/what-is-digital-transformation.

Leonard, Jay. 2013. 'Could Your Business Die From Digital Darwinism? Brian Solis Reveals'. Business 2 Community, Business2Community, April 16. https://www.business2community.com/expert-interviews/could-your-business-die-from-digital-darwinism-brian-solis-reveals/.

Loonam, John, Sally Eaves, Vikas Kumar, and Glenn Parry. 2018. 'Towards Digital Transformation: Lessons Learned from Traditional Organizations'. *Strategic Change* 27 (2): 101–9. https://doi.org/10.1002/jsc.2185.

Mapingire, Kudzai, Hanlie Smuts, and Alta Van Der Merwe. 2022. 'Components of a Digital Transformation Strategy: A South African Perspective'. In *Proceedings of Sixth International Congress on Information and Communication Technology*, edited by Xin-She Yang, Simon Sherratt, Nilanjan Dey, and Amit Joshi, vol. 236. Lecture Notes in Networks and Systems. Springer Singapore. https://doi.org/10.1007/978-981-16-2380-6_38.

Matt, Christian, T Hess, and A Benlian. 2015. *Digital Transformation Strategies.* May 14. https://doi.org/10.7892/BORIS.105535.

Mergel, Ines, Noella Edelmann, and Nathalie Haug. 2019. 'Defining Digital Transformation: Results from Expert Interviews'. *Government Information Quarterly* 36 (4): 101385. https://doi.org/10.1016/j.giq.2019.06.002.

Mirković, Vladimir, Jelena Lukić, Snežana Lazarević, and Željko Vojinović. 2019. 'Key Characteristics of Organizational Structure That Supports Digital Transformation'. Paper presented at 24th International Scientific Conference Strategic Management and Decision Support Systems in Strategic Management. *Proceedings of the 24th International Scientific Conference Strategic Management and Decision Support Systems in Strategic Management*, May 17. https://doi.org/10.46541/978-86-7233-380-0_46.

Mixson, Elizabeth. 2021. 'Starbucks: A Masterclass in Digital Transformation'. Intelligent Automation Network, April 27. https://www.intelligentautomation.network/transformation/articles/starbucks-digital-transformation.

Mustafa, Ghulam, Hans Solli-Sæther, Virginia Bodolica, Jon Ivar Håvold, and Anam Ilyas. 2022. 'Digitalization Trends and Organizational Structure: Bureaucracy, Ambidexterity or Post-Bureaucracy?' *Eurasian Business Review* 12 (4): 671–94. https://doi.org/10.1007/s40821-021-00196–8.

Nwaiwu, Fortune. 2018. 'Review and Comparison of Conceptual Frameworks on Digital Business Transformation'. *Journal of Competitiveness* 10 (3): 86–100. https://doi.org/10.7441/joc.2018.03.06.

O'Brien, Keith, Amanda Downie, and Mark Scapicchio. 2024. 'What Is Digital Transformation? | IBM'. IBM Think Topics, September 9. https://www.ibm.com/think/topics/digital-transformation.

Ortner, Thomas, Julia Hautz, Christian Stadler, and Kurt Matzler. 2024. 'Open Strategy and Digital Transformation: A Framework and Future Research Agenda'. *International Journal of Management Reviews*, August 22, ijmr.12379. https://doi.org/10.1111/ijmr.12379.

Rijswijk, Kelly. 2020. *Digital Transformation: Ongoing Digitisation and Digitalisation Processes*. https://desira2020.agr.unipi.it/wp-content/uploads/2020/05/DESIRA_article_rijswijk_digitisation.pdf.

Schallmo, Daniel, Christopher A. Williams, and Luke Boardman. 2017. 'Digital Transformation of Business Models – Best Practice, Enablers, and Roadmap'. *International Journal of Innovation Management* 21 (8): 1740014. https://doi.org/10.1142/S136391961740014X.

Solis, Brian. 2016. 'DMN: The 6 Stages of Digital Transformation'. Consulting. *Brian Solis*, July 27. https://briansolis.com/2016/07/dmn-the-6-stages-of-digital-transformation/.

Solis, Brian. 2024. 'The End of Digital Transformation and the Rise of Business Model Innovation'. Executive. *CIO*, August 20. https://www.cio.com/article/3487701/the-end-of-digital-transformation-and-the-rise-of-business-model-innovation.html.

Soni, Bobby, and Matteo Colombo. 2024. *2024 Kpmg Us Technology Survey Report: The Digital Dividend*. KPMG. https://kpmg.com/us/en/articles/2024/us-tech-survey-2024-gated.html.

Spagnoletto, Lyuba, Dianah AlabdulJabbar, Harsha Jalihal, Queenie Chan, and Ravin Jesuthasan. 2019. *HR4.0: Shaping People Strategies in the Fourth Industrial Revolution*. White Paper No. 10122019. World Economic Forum in collaboration with Saudi Aramco, Unilever, and Willis Towers Watson. https://www3.weforum.org/docs/WEF_NES_Whitepaper_HR4.0.pdf.

Stewart, Leeann. 2022. 'How Can Company X Effectively Make a Transition from Digitisation to Digital Transformation?' Doctorate of Business thesis, University of Liverpool. file:///D:/Books/Work%204.0/Resources/Chapter%207%20digitial%20transformation/stewart%202022.pdf.

Sun, Xinbo, Zhiwei He, and Yu Qian. 2024. 'Getting Organizational Adaptability in the Context of Digital Transformation'. *Chinese Management Studies* 18 (2): 550–74. https://doi.org/10.1108/CMS-06-2022–0222.

Sundblad, William. 2020. 'CEO Insights: Will Digital Transformation Priorities Finally Stick?' Forbes, August 3. https://www.forbes.com/sites/willemsundbladeurope/2020/07/08/ceo-insights-will-digital-transformation-priorities-stick/?sh=2ed5ff641f19.

Walker, Mike. 2021. 'Three Ways To Leverage Digital Ecosystems'. Forbes, January 5. https://www.forbes.com/councils/forbestechcouncil/2021/01/05/three-ways-to-leverage-digital-ecosystems/.

Warner, Karl S.R., and Maximilian Wäger. 2019. 'Building Dynamic Capabilities for Digital Transformation: An Ongoing Process of Strategic Renewal'. *Long Range Planning* 52 (3): 326–49. https://doi.org/10.1016/j.lrp.2018.12.001.

Wessel, Lauri, Abayomi Baiyere, Roxana Ologeanu-Taddei, Jonghyuk Cha, and Tina Blegind Jensen. 2021. 'Unpacking the Difference Between Digital Transformation and IT-Enabled Organizational Transformation'. *Journal of the Association for Information Systems* 22 (1): 102–29. https://doi.org/10.17705/1jais.00655.

White, Nancy. 2024. *Digital Transformation Strategy: The 7 Critical Tenets*. PTC, January 17. https://www.ptc.com/en/blogs/corporate/digital-transformation-strategy.

Wirtz, Bernd W. 2021. *Digital Business and Electronic Commerce: Strategy, Business Models and Technology*. Springer Texts in Business and Economics. Springer International Publishing. https://doi.org/10.1007/978-3-030-63482-7.

Zhang, Xin, Yao Yu Xu, and Liang Ma. 2023. 'Information Technology Investment and Digital Transformation: The Roles of Digital Transformation Strategy and Top Management'. *Business Process Management Journal* 29 (2): 528–49. https://doi.org/10.1108/BPMJ-06-2022-0254.

Chapter 8

Developing Systems and Skills for an Adaptive People Strategy

Other chapters have led with business examples. There will be plenty of industry case studies in this chapter, too, but let's begin with a pet fish. Picture a goldfish swimming in circles in a round goldfish bowl.[1] Suppose we want to encourage it to swim differently. We could train the goldfish to adopt a new routine, but the chance of success is slim. A better option is to approach the problem from a systems perspective. The goldfish swims in circles because its behaviour is shaped by its structure and environment (in this case, the shape of the bowl). To change the goldfish's behaviour, we need to change the system that shapes it; we need to change the bowl.

The same principle applies to organisations. When employees need to learn new skills and behaviours, the default organisational response is to send them on residential training programmes. The problem is that whatever positive attitudes and behaviours participants develop during the training programme quickly fade once they return to the workplace. They are re-immersed in the same reinforcing system that supported their old habits and ways of operating in the first place. Stephanie Crouppen (2024) makes a similar point:

> This is also why most existing learning and development initiatives fail. In the traditional workplace, employees often leave training or an all-hands meeting feeling inspired, but when they go back to their day-to-day, everything is the same. Their behavior doesn't change because there's nothing reinforcing new habits.

 DOI: 10.4324/9781003680345-8

To achieve enduring organisational transformation, it is essential to redesign the conditioning structures and cultural norms that perpetuate the toxic habit or behaviour. A strong systems-based people strategy focuses on changing the environment that sustains entrenched behaviours. It introduces skill-based learning interventions to support adaptation and growth.[2]

Building Adaptive Organisations is a systems and culture approach to developing organisational adaptability. Previous chapters explored how adaptability can be engineered at the organisational design level by remodelling structure, governance and workflow (Chapters 4–6). The digital transformation strategy also shapes an adaptive business innovation process (Chapter 7). This chapter presents two people strategies that drive adaptive workforces: a systems-led approach, in which experiencing and interacting with the transformed environment naturally shapes new mindsets and behaviours through cultural normalisation; and a personal skills-led strategy, in which formal learning interventions support new ways of working. This chapter will explore both approaches as part of an overall people strategy to help build adaptive workforces.

Two Organisational Approaches

Industry case studies were promised. The following are two different organisational approaches to developing an adaptive workforce. The first is Adobe, which primarily built a system-based people strategy; the second is Zappos, which mainly cultivated a skills-based people strategy.

Adobe

Founded in 1982 in Mountain View, California, by ex-Xerox PARC employees John Warnock and Charles ('Chuck') Geschke, Adobe began life in Warnock's garage, next to Adobe Creek (hence the company name). In 2018, the computer software company exceeded $100 billion in market cap and joined the Fortune 500 (Michelman 2018). Today, Adobe has more than 30,000 global employees and is listed in the PWC Global Top 100 companies by Market Capitalisation (PWC UK 2025).

Shantanu Narayen (2025) observes that from the start, the company was a highly innovative, people-led organisation with a strong adaptive workforce. It regularly ranks among the top global employers (Peachman 2024).

Adobe has four system-based people strategies which encourage self-organising, adaptive mindsets at every level of the organisation. These are cultivating learning, encouraging innovation, developing a growth mindset, and supporting risk taking. Let's explore these in detail.

1. Cultivating an environment of learning and curiosity
   Adobe inspires adaptive thinking through continuous reskilling, cross-functional collaboration, job rotations, stretch assignments, creative jams, and self-reflection. The company provides a constant learning infrastructure financed from a central "Adobe Learning Fund" that promotes professional and academic development and lifelong learning for all employees. Teams freely collaborate across functions, enabling system-wide awareness and adaptability. "Creative jams" are regular internal problem-solving hackathons. Adobe creates an environment of appreciative inquiry and reflection through its "Life Blog", where employees are encouraged to publicly share stories of curiosity, change, and growth. Adobe leaders model vulnerability and adaptability by talking openly about their mistakes and how they learnt from them.
2. Encouraging Innovation
   The company is committed to creativity and innovation. Adobe is renowned for its "Kickbox Innovation Program", which promotes self-directed innovative thinking and experimentation. Employees receive a red "Kickbox" toolkit that includes a prepaid card worth $1,000 to fund ideas of their own choosing. The toolkit includes instructions, templates, and tools to develop a concept, along with full autonomy for the employee to experiment and innovate without supervision. Since 2013, Michael Kan (2016) reports that the take-up for Kickbox has been 10 per cent of all employees, with at least twenty three ideas moving to the investment phase. The initiative has led to an open-source Kickbox foundation with freely available resources and templates. This establishes Adobe as an externally focused organisation that shares its best practices with the broader business ecosystem community.
3. Developing a Growth Mindset
   Adobe is a recognised for its growth mindset. It has been at the vanguard of rethinking organisational appraisals and feedback, shifting from (conditioning) performance reviews to (personalised) coaching and a growth mindset. In 2012, the company replaced the annual performance review with a process known as "check-in" (Miller 2022), which is an ongoing employee-driven performance and growth discussion that is increasingly utilising digital technology. Adobe also has a strong culture of customer and peer feedback. The company aims to cultivate a growth mindset, moving the focus from "prove yourself" to "improve yourself", encouraging frequent feedback, self-reflection (reinforcing learning over perfection),

and empowering employees to own their professional development. Gloria Chen (2023) reports that Adobe regularly holds "roundtables" to gather employee input. Karan Saini, growth product manager at Adobe, says, "Adobe, in particular, is one of those companies that really supports you. It's a place where they want you to learn and grow while you're there. It's more of a give-and-take dynamic, rather than just a one-way street" (cited in Kefford 2025).

4. Reward Risk Taking

   Jim Ludema and Amber Johnson (2019) discuss how Adobe encourages its employees to take risks by providing a culture of psychological safety and trust. Employees at all levels (but especially leadership) focus on output and outcomes, rather than micromanaging workflows. This provides the space and confidence for personal risk-taking and creative problem-solving. The culture at Adobe is to view mistakes as learning opportunities, and management is encouraged to reward risk-taking and curiosity and to regularly check in on employee wellbeing and development. This reduces the fear of failure and supports positive behaviours such as personal confidence, honesty, reflection, and experimentation. Initiating psychological safety and inclusion is critical for creativity and ideas to flourish.

Zappos

Zappos, which was briefly mentioned in Chapter 1 in connection with Holacracy, is a good example of a company with a clear, interventionist people strategy that seeks to align employees with its strong company culture and values (almost in a cult-like way). Founded in 1999 by Nick Swinmurn, Zappos is an online shoe retailer that was at the forefront of the e-commerce tide. Backed by the late entrepreneur Tony Hsieh (who later became Zappos' CEO), the company was acquired by Amazon in 2009 for $1.2 billion. Zappos underwent a much-publicised system transformation in 2013, becoming the first major company to adopt Holacracy. It scaled back its commitment to the circular structure after the untimely death of CEO Tony Hsieh, a strong champion of Holacracy.

Unlike Adobe, the system transformation at Zappos was abrupt and highly interventionist, with an imposed skills-based people strategy of ultimatums, direct learning interventions, and culture-fit recruitment. There was a clear sense of urgency to adopt the new governance framework.

1. Ultimatum

   Ultimatums are a form of direct intervention. CEO Tony Hsieh sent a 4,700-word email on 24 March 2015 to all staff, with what Aimee Groth (2016) calls an "ultimatum" to commit to Holacracy or resign from the organisation with a generous severance package worth approximately half their annual salary. Bryan Golden, Anusheel Pandey, and James O'Rourke (2017) report that 18 per cent of the Zappos staff accepted the offer. As a result, approximately 260 employees left the company, with six per cent citing Holacracy as the reason for their departure.

2. Direct learning interventions

   Susan Heathfield (2021) observes that Zappos uses several direct interventions to reinforce its company culture. As part of their onboarding, new employees spend three to four weeks in call centres learning about the core business and customer needs. After this induction, employees are offered $3,000 to leave the company, because Zappos only wants committed people. Learning and development is done through on-the-job training and intensive learning interventions, including culture camps. Heathfield (2021) reports how managers are hands-on in supporting development needs, career paths, and cultural assessments. Employees are encouraged to document their company experience in culture books.

3. Culture-fit recruitment

   Hiring at Zappos can take months due to its culture-fit recruitment process, which, according to Susan Heathfield (2021), is "more like a courtship than traditional recruitment".

It is evident that Adobe and Zappos have different people strategies for developing an adaptive workforce. Adobe assumes a highly systems and culture-oriented approach where employees are integrated into the culture over time; Zappos, on the other hand, uses direct interventions such as culture camps, exit incentives, and "cultural fit" recruitment.

Allowing employees to naturally self-organise and acclimatise to the culture through normalisation and infusion, rather than selecting and moulding them into being the "right" employee is a delicate balance. Progressive adaptive organisations achieve the optimal blend between steering employees and allowing employees to self-organise and develop over time.

A blended approach to developing an adaptive workforce is recommended for organisations seeking to build adaptability at scale. This approach combines emergent forms of socialisation and the normalisation of the environment (the "fishbowl") with structured, programmatic support to build the adaptive performance and mindsets for individuals (the "fish") to thrive in the new environment.

Developing an Adaptive Workforce and Mindset

It has been established that building an adaptive workforce is a systems challenge, but cultivating adaptive mindsets is a skill-based challenge. Systems and skills will be further unpacked in the next section, but some basic definitions for the adaptive workforce and mindsets are necessary.

1. Adaptive Workforce

   Workers need to be increasingly adaptive to thrive in changing workplaces and uncertain environments. Recent definitions of this term appear on company websites. Here is a good example:

   > Adaptive Workforce stands for a personnel strategy in which companies flexibly and dynamically adapt their resources to actual needs. Instead of relying on rigid team structures, adaptive companies create variable capacities, which can be booted up or down as needed.
   >
   > (Hartmann 2025)

   Another company website discussing the notion of an adaptive workforce observes, "As your company adapts to uncertain times, you need to organize your staff according to market trends" (Maervoet 2024).

   The central question here, posed by Lyuba Spagnoletto and coauthors (2019) and Vineesh Vijayan (2019), is not simply whether companies have the right organisational design (structure, governance, and workflow) and the right digital strategy to survive in uncertain times, but do they have an adaptive workforce to make these designs and strategies successful?

   The term "agile workforce" is widely used, but its emphasis differs from that of an adaptive workforce. An agile workforce is typically associated with the Agile Scrum framework, which focuses on specific, team-level process improvements and project delivery. In contrast, an adaptive workforce refers to a broader, system-wide capability that helps organisations to remain flexible and responsive to environmental and organisational uncertainty. The term "adaptive performance", coined by Hesketh and Neal (1999), is also widely used in the literature, but it primarily refers to an individual rather than organisational or system-wide adaptability. Another related concept is the "elastic workforce", which Michael Vaynerman (2022) as being used primarily in contingent and hourly labour contexts to describe an organisation's ability to quickly scale its workforce up or down.

Why do we need adaptive workforces?

If the design is the engine of the organisation and the strategy is the steering mechanism, an adaptive workforce is the fuel that powers momentum and enables the organisation to move forward across difficult terrain. J.P. Gownder (2019) says, "To build an adaptive enterprise, build an adaptive workforce". As a general principle, for organisations to adapt, workforces need to be adaptive. Pulakos, Dorsey, and White (2006) concur when they say, "Today's organizations are characterized by changing, dynamic environments in which the need for adaptive workers has become increasingly important" (612). Sohee Park and Sunyoung Park (2021) link this back to recruitment, arguing that as global and technological environments become dynamic, ambiguous, and complex, organisations must recruit and develop employees who can work effectively within this adaptive context. A recent McKinsey study identified adaptability as a leading factor in securing employment. Data reveals that candidates who are proficient in adaptability are 24 per cent more likely to be hired (Dondi et al. 2021). Also, adaptive workforces ease the passage of digital transformation:

> This new adaptive workforce taps into technology innovations – particularly AI and automation – to become more flexible, responsive, and productive and to support the broader adaptive enterprise strategy.
>
> (Gownder 2019)

2. Adaptive mindsets

Adaptive mindsets are defined as the ability of employees and organisations to adjust to different situations quickly and effectively (Sabet and Christofely 2026). Cultivating adaptive mindsets is a teachable skill (Prince 2019) that supports adaptive workforces in an era of Work 4.0, where "Workers need to be increasingly adaptable, versatile, and tolerant of uncertainty to operate effectively in these changing and varied environments" (Pulakos, Dorsey, and White 2006, 612). Research identifies several key components of adaptive mindsets. Mental flexibility is critical for the future of work (Dondi et al. 2021) while adaptive mindsets also help employees flex with changing workflows and build resilience (Brassey, De Smet, and Maor 2024;[3] Epstein 2022). They cultivate proactivity and role flexibility (Park and Park 2021) and can enhance work engagement (Saptarini and Mustika 2023). Evidence suggests that mindset shifts can improve productivity, with one study reporting an eight per cent increase over six months (Crouppen 2024). Experts argue that adaptive mindsets are not just skills but also attitudes and ways of thinking that enable employees to find new ways to bring out the best in any situation

(Sabet and Christofely 2026) Organisations such as Google develop adaptive mindsets using simulations, psychometric assessments, reflection, and coaching. Similarly, Natalie Fratto (2019) introduces the idea of adaptability quotient (AQ) in a TED talk, explaining how it can be measured, tested, and improved through practices like "unlearning".

The system initiative to build an adaptive workforce and the individual skills initiative to develop adaptive mindsets are two interconnected interventions that progressive organisations use to create an adaptable people strategy. The following section explores how this is realised through eight system-led initiatives designed to nurture an adaptive workforce, alongside eight skills-led interventions that help individuals cultivate adaptive mindsets. Together, these form a powerful people strategy that reshapes the environment to reinforce new behaviours and equips individuals with the skills they need to thrive in a continually changing workplace.

Building an Effective Adaptive Workforce through Systems and Skills

The content of this book has naturally shaped the people strategy. The first three chapters focused on sensemaking and adaptability as systems and culture lenses that drive sustained change. Chapters 4–6 examined how to incorporate adaptability in the organisational design, creating a normalised adaptive culture. Chapter 7 demonstrated how digital transformation supports this process by enabling people to navigate the organisation more effectively using technology.

These attributes can be developed at both a system and an individual skill-building level. This is a dual-people strategy in which system-led initiatives gradually normalise and embed behaviour through organisational socialisation, and skills-led interventions develop personal adaptive abilities. This dual approach is captured in what is being termed the people strategy steering wheel (Figure 8.1).

Figure 8.1 illustrates the broad people strategy for systems and personal skills as a steering wheel. It is known as the people strategy steering wheel because it helps organisations navigate and steer through the changing workplace.[4] At the centre of the steering wheel are the three architectural pillars (structure, governance, and workflow). Eight system interventions or enablers that support the organisational design are plotted in the inner ring. The outer rim represents eight personal skills or quotients that steer the adaptive workforce at an individual adaptive mindset level. Let's look more closely at this people strategy steering wheel, starting with the inner ring: systems.

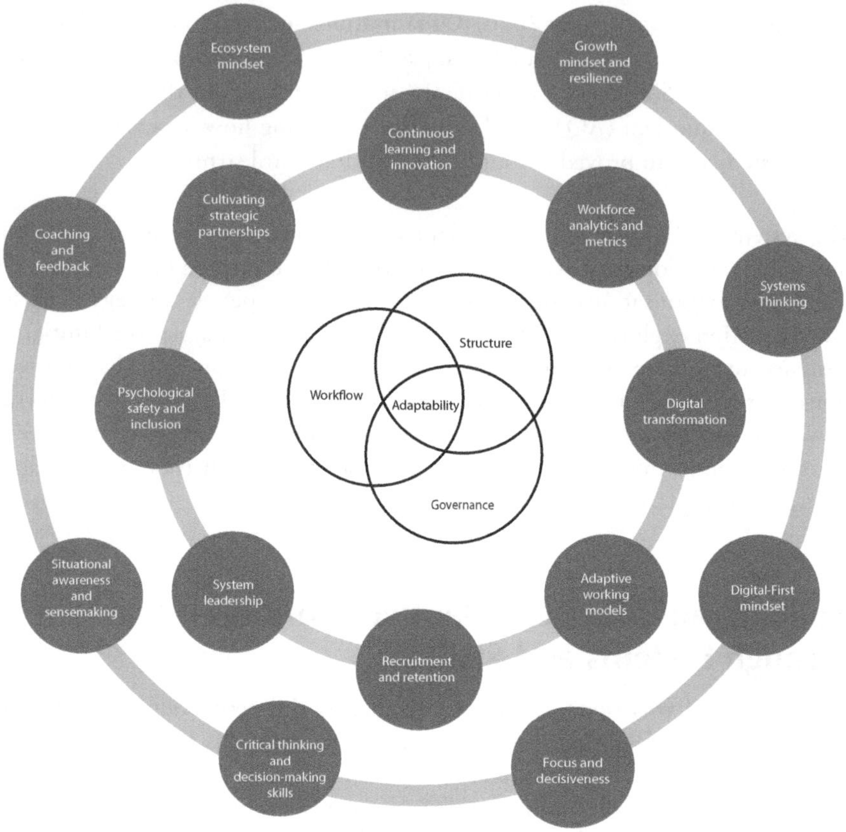

Figure 8.1 People strategy steering wheel.

Building an Adaptive Workforce at the Systems Level

The people strategy systems approach emerges through organisational socialisation. David Buchanan and Andrzej Huczynski characterise this as "the process through which an employee's pattern of behaviour, values, attitudes and motives are influenced to conform to those of the organization's" (Buchanan and Huczynski 2019, 114). This cultivates adaptive workforces through engagement with the organisational system. Below is a deeper dive into the eight system interventions and enablers that populate the inner ring.

1. Continuous learning and innovation

   An important system enabler to create an adaptive workforce environment is continuous learning and innovation. The link between curiosity and learning is well researched (Pluck and Johnson 2011; Cobo 2013). A compelling example of a culture of continuous learning and innovation is

WD-40 under the leadership of Garry Ridge. Serving as CEO from 1997 to 2022, Ridge worked tirelessly to build a "learning-obsessed" culture. This became central to WD-40's regeneration. Employees were invited to take the "WD-40 Maniac Pledge", committing themselves to be, in Ridge's words, "learning maniacs" (Taylor 2016). This mindset turned mistakes into opportunities for growth and fuelled the company's ongoing ability to innovate in a mature, competitive market.

2. Workforce analytics and metrics

   It is important to recognise, measure, and reward adaptability through workforce metrics and analytics. A key point in a World Economic Forum white paper on shaping people strategies in Industry 4.0 is the need to develop consistent metrics in organisations to measure workforce progress:

   > While there is almost unanimous agreement from business leaders and investors alike that human capital is a key driver of performance, the lack of a standard methodology and rigor reduces visibility both for within and outside the business on the value, health and progress of the workforce.
   >
   > (Spagnoletto et al. 2019, 20)

   Developing a culture of feedback is an excellent starting point, but using data to shape, develop, recognise, and reward adaptive behaviour in the workplace is vital. It is important not just to measure performance outputs such as sales and revenue, but also how people behave in changing situations. This can be achieved using key behavioural indicators (KBIs) and people surveys, such as Unilever's UniVoice survey. Herbert Nold and Lukas Michel (2021) question the conventional reliance on financial performance as a measure and propose a more holistic approach, assessing an organisation's success on factors such as responsiveness, alignment, capabilities, motivation, and innovation. Some digital systems help organisations with workforce analytics, such as Microsoft Viva. Organisations should research the various workforce metrics and analytical processes, tools, and software currently on the market to support adaptability at the system level.

3. Digital transformation

   An adaptive workforce is critical delivering real business value from digital initiatives. Without adaptability, organisations risk poor adoption of new systems, resistance, and missed opportunities. A McKinsey survey found that "developing talent and skills throughout the organization – a fundamental action for traditional transformations – is one of the most important factors for success in a digital change effort"

(Boutetière, Montagner, and Reich 2018, 6). This signals that digital transformation is as much a people transformation as a technological one (Frankiewicz and Chamorro-Premuzic 2020). Organisations must invest in employee upskilling, promote a culture of continuous learning, and encourage experimentation. Recently, for example, Tevye Markson (2025) reports that UK government workers have been offered courses on using AI as an augmentation tool in a bid to drive up productivity and streamline workflows.

4. Adaptive working models

   Chapter 5 explored current adaptive working models, including office, virtual, and hybrid working. The office environment has continually adapted from the late twentieth century onwards to become more dynamic. This is because there is a perceived link between adaptive working spaces and behavioural adaptability, such as creative thinking (Thoring, Desmet, and Badke-Schaub 2018, 2020). The link between environment and creativity was explored in the Pixar case study in Chapter 4. To enhance and promote adaptive workforces, organisations are encouraged to create adaptive workspaces, workflows, and working models. Google is a good example of a company that successfully employs adaptive workforce strategies. It has a hybrid-first model, allocating two days to remote work. Michelle Kaufmann (2022) remarks that Google's physical office space is continually reimagined to inspire collaboration, connection, and support adaptive and elastic thinking.

5. Recruitment and Retention

   Another way to influence adaptability at the system level is through recruitment and retention. We saw in Chapter 2 how LEGO underwent a significant recruitment drive, hiring brilliant employees, but failed to manage and develop them. Zappos took a "culture-fit" approach.[5]

   Some maintain that focus should be on retention. Jens Baier and coauthors (2023), for example, argue that "Developing new skills in your existing workforce is often far more cost-effective than recruiting and hiring new people externally. Moreover, rapid changes in the business landscape (particularly in areas of technology) mean that companies must continually refresh the skills and capabilities of their workforce." (15). Retaining staff has become increasingly complex due to emerging recruitment trends and challenges, including global competition for talent, the rise of "elastic" workforces such as contingent workers, the "Great Resignation" and the resulting loss of experienced talent, and growing workplace disengagement and "quiet quitting". Cultivating an adaptive performance culture is key to retaining staff. Linday McGregor and Neel Doshi (2017) argue that switching from a managed to an adaptive performance drives up engagement, creativity, innovation, problem-solving, and productivity.

6. System leadership

   As introduced in Chapter 5 and throughout the book, system leadership is an organisational behaviour and collective capacity in which leadership is distributed across the system rather than held in formal positions of authority. System leadership reimagines governance by shifting leadership from status-based, top-down "alpha" control (in which authority rests on persuading and commanding others), to collective, system-enabled adaptability that cultivates shared responsibility and self-organisation. System leadership is not a position or role but an organisational behaviour; system leaders are developed rather than appointed. System leadership flows through organisational structures and mindsets, promoting collaboration, collective governance, and self-sustaining systems.

   Senge, Hamilton, and Kania (1994) rightly link this to transformational change when they say, "System leaders focus on creating the conditions that can produce change and that can eventually cause change to be self-sustaining". Every member, regardless of role, contributes as a connector, enabler, or ambassador, acting in the best interests of the whole system. System leadership flourishes in cross-functional ecosystem environments, such as the honeycomb model described in Chapter 5, which creates more opportunity for self-organising and self-governing behaviours to develop. System leadership can also be developed through enterprise-wide mentoring and coaching programmes, participation in educational initiatives, and inclusion as a key performance indicator (KPI) in performance reviews. Organisational influencers can also support its development by role-modelling system leadership behaviours such as responsiveness, inclusion, and collaboration.

7. Psychological safety and inclusion

   Another system enabler is psychological safety and inclusion. It involves creating an environment where people feel valued, respected, and able to contribute fully. Amy Edmondson (1999) argues that this directly encourages employees to take risks in the workplace without fear of retribution. Kiara Booker (2025) notes that this is key for building adaptability and developing adaptive workforces. She observes, "When employees feel psychologically safe, they are more engaged, innovative, and proactive in finding solutions". Psychological safety and inclusion are "critical for building resilience and adaptability" (Brassey, De Smet, and Maor 2024). Google carried out a major research initiative a few years ago, known as *Project Aristotle*, analysing more than 180 teams to identify what makes a successful team. Charles Duhigg (2016) reveals that a key finding in the research was that psychological safety was the primary factor behind high-performing teams. This led Google to nurture group-wide psychological safety through check-ins, demonstrating vulnerability, equal airtime, and peer feedback. The need for diversity and inclusion is a key finding in the World Economic Forum white paper on people strategy in Industry 4.0 (Spagnoletto et al. 2019).

8. Cultivating Strategic Partnerships

   A final system-level intervention that supports adaptive workforces is cultivating strategic partnerships. Michael Schroeck and his coauthors (2020) argue that, in Industry 4.0, organisations should cultivate relationships and partnerships across the business ecosystem. This includes ecosystems outside of industry, such as government and education. Rachel Rosenfeldt (2024) observes, "The more people connect with diverse groups of other teams, cohorts or areas that don't typically work together, the more they can practice flexible thinking and challenge each other in ways that serve to advance their work". HubSpot is an excellent example of a company building partnership-driven ecosystems. Ellie Flanagan (2023) reports that the App Partner Program connects over 1,500 global companies.

Building Adaptive Mindsets at the Personal Skills Level

An alternative way to cultivate adaptability is through a direct interventionist approach, in which individuals are explicitly taught and guided to develop adaptive mindsets. Effective practice includes identifying the core components (or "quotients") of adaptive mindsets. The following quotients form the outer rim of Figure 8.1. Organisations need to work with their learning specialists to determine how to evolve these quotients into formal learning interventions. Below are the eight skills associated with building an adaptive mindset.

1. Systems Thinking

   Systems thinking is a foundational skill for personal adaptability. Peter Senge (1990) defines it as "a framework for seeing interrelationships rather than things, for seeing patterns rather than static "snapshots". It is a set of general principles... spanning fields as diverse as the physical and social sciences, engineering, and management" (68). At its core, systems thinking is a problem-solving approach that examines both the whole system and its interconnected parts. It encourages awareness of how structures, feedback loops, and relationships shape outcomes over time. Adaptability is the practical outcome of a systems-aware mindset. The STEP-WIDE model from Chapter 2 is a systems thinking tool that maps and navigates complexity. Systems thinking encourages responsiveness through the three Ps of Perspective, Patterns, and Proactivity (see Chapter 2, Figure 2.1). Systems thinking is essential for cross-functional collaboration and operating within an ecosystem environment. It helps individuals and teams see the big picture, anticipate consequences, and identify pivotal areas for change. *Building Adaptive Organisations* centres on moving from a closed, inward-looking system to an open, self-organising ecosystem. This shift demands a redesign of the business architecture and strategies, but it ultimately depends on people adopting a systems-thinking mindset. The Iceberg Model, presented in *The Fifth Discipline Fieldbook* (Senge et al, 1994), which illustrates the layers of events, patterns, systemic structures, and mental models, remains a powerful tool to help people visualise and practice systems thinking.[6]

2. Digital-first mindset

   Paul Leonardi and Tsedal Neeley (2022) argue in their introduction to *The Digital Mindset* that a digital mindset is a "set of approaches we use to make sense of, and make use of, data and technology. This set of attitudes and behaviors enable people and organizations to see new possibilities and chart a path for the future". Elissa Farrow (2023) argues that embracing an adaptive mindset will be key in the age of artificial intelligence. Developing a digital-first mindset is becoming increasingly important as workplaces grow more augmented and technology-driven.

   Digital literacy is a "foundation skill" in the *OECD* study of skills for the future (Bell, Espinoza, and Game 2019). A theory that supports the development of a digital-first mindset is computational thinking, a term, coined by Jeannette Wing (2006). Kristen Thorson (2018) defines it as a "prerequisite skill for understanding the technologies of the future". Steve Easterbrook (2014) says, "The computational thinker looks for problems that can be tackled with computers" (236).

3. Situational Awareness and Sensemaking

   Situational awareness and sensemaking are essential adaptive mindset skills. Situational awareness (SA) has military origins relating to knowing what is going on around you. To have good situational awareness, you need strong spatial intelligence and the ability to anticipate events, read and navigate situations, understand the bigger picture, and react appropriately.

   Karl Weick (1995) coined the term sensemaking, defining it as the process by which people make sense of the world. Klein, Moon, and Hoffman (2006) view sensemaking as a "continuous effort to understand connections" (71).

   Both these terms involve processing situations, but situational awareness is an in-the-moment reaction to events, whereas sensemaking concerns making sense of events and seeing patterns. Both are key skills for adapting to new situations and environments.

Crisis training using simulations, drills, and scenario-based exercises is designed to help develop situational awareness. Sensemaking can be developed over time through after-action reviews (AARs), systems mapping, and scenario planning. An excellent tool that directly helps develop situational awareness is Donald A. Schön and Martin Rein's "frame reflection" (1994). This conceptual framework helps people explore alternative scenarios and perspectives by suspending assumptions and challenging mental models.

4. Coaching and feedback

   Coaching and feedback are core skills for developing adaptive mindsets because they offer multiple perspectives, identify blind spots, and promote reflection and continuous improvement. This helps build personal adaptability and resilience. According to Kooh Givi Maryam (2025) a strong link exists between coaching interventions and employee adaptability and performance. Peer coaching is an effective way of creating systems-based feedback. Research by Natalia Fey and coauthors (2022), show how peer-to-peer feedback develops openness and trust among colleagues, inspiring self-leadership and initiative-taking, which can lead to feelings of proactiveness and empowerment. Psychometrics are a valuable way to develop team adaptability by revealing and shaping individual and team dynamics. The Myers-Briggs Type Indicator (MBTI) and the Belbin Team Roles Assessment are two valuable tools for enhancing team dynamics and cultivating team adaptability. 360-degree feedback is also an excellent feedback tool. The GROW model (an acronym for Goals/Reality/Options/Will), developed by Sir John Whitmore in the 1980s, is one of the most widely used coaching frameworks in the workplace for formal and peer-to-peer coaching.

5. Ecosystem mindset

   Delaine Jooste (2023) defines an ecosystem mindset as one that "Encourages experimentation, curiosity, and a continuous learning journey that emphasises connections with oneself and the broader community". An ecosystem mindset requires thinking beyond your organisation, recognising interdependencies with partners of all kinds, and, as Ulrich Pidun, Martin Reeves, and Balázs Zoletnik (2022) note, using networks to co-create and capture "prospects of joint value creation". Huang, Yang, and Kung (2022) demonstrate a proven link between employees with ecosystem-type mindsets and an adaptive "polycultural" organisation. Jeff Bennett (2021) believes that building an ecosystem mindset requires developing skill sets in altruism, empathy, openness, and inclusion.

Collaboration and co-creation are also key skills for developing an ecosystem mindset.[7]

Stakeholder mapping is a practical tool for understanding and managing ecosystems and their influence. Psychometrics such as the Cultural Intelligence Scale, the Cultural Mindset Profile (ICMI-P2), and the Organisational Culture Assessment Instrument (OCAI) support the development of cultural mindsets. The 360-degree feedback tool can help identify blind spots and biases. Christopher Earley and Elaine Mosakowski (2024) argue that a critical component of cultural intelligence (CQ)is the ability to suspend judgement, a capability it shares with emotional intelligence. Practical ways to suspend judgement can be found in *The Fifth Discipline Fieldbook* by Peter Senge and coauthors (1994).

6. Growth mindset and resilience

Developing a growth mindset is a further skill that promotes adaptive mindsets. The term growth mindset was coined by Stanford psychologist Carol Dweck (2006), who believes that abilities and intelligence can be cultivated through effort, practice, and learning. Developing a growth mindset represents a shift from an entrenched set of mental models to an open mindset that is receptive to new ideas and learning. There is a strong link to resilience, which David Yeager and Carol Dweck (2012) define as a "challenge that is positive and beneficial for development" (303). Eugene Allevato argues that "people with a growth mindset are more adaptable and persistent, recovering from mistakes and trying again. They understand that mistakes are part of the learning process. In addition, people with a growth mindset believe that intelligence can evolve through effort, so they use their mistakes to adjust their behavior and improve performance" (Allevato 2020, 448).

Many believe that growth mindsets can be developed (Hreha 2023; Freeman 2023), especially through habit-building activities (Derler 2019). Growth mindsets are closely linked to continuous learning mindsets and improvement. Johnathan Westover (2024) associates resilience, mindset shifts and continuous learning with building adaptive organisations. Under Satya Nadella, Microsoft introduced a growth mindset culture. Zappos was also very focused on cultivating growth mindsets among employees through its continuous learning programmes. A practical tool that can help us develop a growth learning mindset is the four stages of learning, conceived by Martin Broadwell (1969), which demonstrate levels of competence and incompetence and helps individuals remain in a constant learning zone and mindset. Kaizen, the Japanese word for continuous improvement, is also an effective tool for mindset growth and learning (Kelly 2019).

7. Critical thinking and decision-making skills

   The 2019 OECD Future Skills identifies critical thinking as one of the core "transformative competencies", a skill that strongly supports adaptability and adaptive mindsets (Bell, Espinoza, and Game 2019, 61). Mitashree Tripathy (2020) discusses how critical thinking, a skill that prevents people from jumping to judgements and conclusions based on limited data, cultivates adaptive mindsets and supports organisational decision-making, communication, and problem-solving. Critical thinking helps people objectively evaluate complex information, challenge assumptions, anticipate consequences, and make reasoned judgements in uncertain situations. Peter Facione writes, "Critical thinking involves actively interpreting one's experiences and self-consciously making and expressing one's analytical, evaluative and inferential judgments regarding what to believe or do" (Facione 1990, 86). Peter Facione identifies a strong link between critical thinking and decision-making, where critical thinking helps people "draw out presuppositions and project the range of possible consequences of decisions" (Facione 1990, 17). Gloria Pierce (1994) identifies core competencies, including critical reflection, perspectivism, dialoguing, and providing feedback. Watson Isaac (2023) recommends developing critical thinking skills through puzzle solving, such as jigsaw puzzles and brain teasers. The suite of personal mastery tools used by Senge and coauthors in *The Fifth Discipline Fieldbook* (1994) helps build these core competencies. Song, Roohr, and Kirova (2024) have developed a useful critical thinking framework.
8. Developing personal focus

   It has been calculated that in 2024, 402.89 million terabytes of data were generated per day, totalling 147 zettabytes per year. StatsPanda (nd), a live counter site, believes this will rise to 284 zettabytes annually by 2027. We are immersed in data and need to develop focus, or we will quickly become overwhelmed. A large part of the digital technology story is helping organisations process and manage this data, but if we are to continue to add value in an increasingly machine-processed world, we must learn the art of focus. In his landmark paper, "The Magical Number Seven, Plus or Minus Two" (Miller 1956), psychologist George A. Miller explored the limits of human short-term memory and attention. He observed that people can typically hold about seven items of information (plus or minus two) in their immediate awareness at any given time. This shows that the human mind has a limited capacity to handle multiple pieces of information. Daniel Goleman (2015) has conducted further research on this in his book on focus, and he reveals that cognitive scientists now believe that the average human being can handle only four pieces of information.

Mihaly Csikszentmihalyi's *Flow: The Psychology of Optimal Experience* is about self-focus. Flow is "the ability to focus attention at will, to be oblivious to distractions, to concentrate for as long as it takes to achieve a goal" (Csikszentmihalyi 1990, 31). A state of flow exists when "the duration of time is altered; hours pass by in minutes, and minutes can stretch out to seem like hours" (Csikszentmihalyi 1990, 49). Flow and focus are skills, according to Mihaly Csikszentmihalyi, that can be developed through goal setting, creating a clear mental and physical space for flow with no distractions, and self-monitoring your ability to flow to build positive habits. Mihaly Csikszentmihalyi advises starting with short, focused sessions and building up to longer, more concentrated periods. Cal Newport (2016) has some good tips for developing focus. Recognising that the world is highly distracting, he suggests four simple rules for achieving "deep work": create strong routines, train yourself out of boredom, quit social media, and minimise "shallow work".

Steering the People Strategy Wheel

We saw that the people strategy wheel (which helps organisations navigate STEP-WIDE disruptions) is a self-contained set of 16 systems and skills interventions. This final section provides five reflections on building a people strategy. The next chapter deals with the broader topic of transformational change.

i. *Don't overlook or make people strategy an afterthought.* Harshak, Aguirre, and Brown argue, "Change is, at its core, a people process" (Harshak et al. 2010, 5). People strategies are often underestimated in change transformations. Robert Ployhart and Scott Turner observe that "firm survival and adaptation are also a function of the people within those firms" (Ployhart and Turner 2014, 73). Be clear about the organisational culture and the skills required to support adaptive workforces and mindsets, and ensure this remains a constant priority.
ii. *Use systems and skills to develop a people strategy.* This chapter has recommended both a system and skills approach to developing a people strategy. Focus on the development need and then select the right system or skills intervention to get you there.
iii. *Mix up the methodology.* A 2021 McKinsey survey discusses the importance of blended learning approaches and a mix of formats (Billing et al. 2021). When building skills, draw on a range of methodologies to connect with different learning styles. This list could be exhaustive, but consider, in addition to formal classroom-based interventions, diverse methodologies

such as informal workplace learning (Decius, Schaper, and Seifert 2019), culture camps, bite-sized learning, online learning, networked learning, on-the-job training, buddy systems, self-directed learning, and coaching. Remember that changing behaviours requires changing the environment that shapes and conditions the behaviour.

iv. *Involve HR.* Sometimes people strategies are treated as technical exercises by change agents. Remember you are dealing with real people who are part of the organisation, and HR are best placed to support the people strategy because they have the relevant employee data. Don't create extra data and models; involve HR and rely on real people data. HR will have data and insights about who might be potential resistors and who already has adaptive mindsets. HR will also help track and monitor the people strategy.

v. *Switch from being reactive to responsive.* Organisations should not bear the sole burden of developing adaptive mindsets. Ambassadors from the organisation should be in discussion with local schools, colleges, universities, educational authorities, and national governments about building innovation and adaptability in the wider learning community. Organisations need to be part of an ecosystem solution to the Work 4.0 challenge.

Synthesis: Developing an Adaptive People Strategy

This chapter has focused on developing a system-and-skills people strategy to support the shift from a rigid to an adaptive organisation and to sustain adaptability over time. It introduced a dual approach: a system-led strategy, in which adaptive behaviours emerge through organisational socialisation and interaction with the environment; and a skills-led strategy, in which individuals receive targeted support to understand system expectations and build the capabilities needed to navigate them.

These approaches were illustrated through Adobe and Zappos case studies, and brought together in the people strategy steering wheel, which outlines eight system initiatives for building an adaptive workforce (one capable of flexing and responding to volatile, uncertain, complex, and ambiguous conditions) alongside eight skills-based initiatives that directly cultivate adaptive mindsets.

Together, these two strands form a coherent and powerful people strategy: one that reshapes the environment to reinforce new behaviours ("changing the fishbowl") and equips individuals with the skills required to thrive in a constantly changing, adaptive workplace ("changing the fish").

Notes

1. The idea of a fish in the round bowl is inspired by Derler, Abbatiello, and Garr 2017. The fishbowl analogy used to represent systems has appeared in previously published books (Kelly 2019, 2022).
2. Jesper B. Sørensen (2002) similarly makes a link between environment and behaviour/performance.
3. Jacqueline Brassey, Aaron De Smet, and Dana Maor (2024) provide five steps for building an "adaptability muscle".
4. The workplace is disrupted by the STEP-WIDE factors discussed in Chapter 2.
5. Cultural fit can indeed identify talent that already shares an organisation's values, but it can also lead to mirrortocracy where people hire based on confirmation bias (Bueno 2022). LinkedIn actively promotes a "culture add" approach.
6. The idea of events as being a visible tip of deeper systemic structures is attributed to Jay W. Forrester (MIT, 1950s–80s) in his system dynamics theory (Forrester 1961; Forrester 1968).
7. Rob Cross, Reb Rebele, and Adam Grant caution that sometimes there can be collaborative overload in an organisation, so you need to find the right balance between personal and group innovation (Cross, Rebele, and Grant 2016).

Bibliography

Allevato, Eugene. 2020. 'Organizational Culture Change: Growth Mindset, Positive Psychology, and Empowerment'. In *Social Entrepreneurship and Corporate Social Responsibility*, edited by Joan Marques and Satinder Dhiman. Management for Professionals. Springer International Publishing. https://doi.org/10.1007/978-3-030-39676-3_28.

Baier, Jens, Vinviane Beauchene, Julie Bedard, et al. 2023. 'Creating People Advantage 2023: Set the Right People Priorities for Challenging Times'. BCG Global, November 16. https://www.bcg.com/publications/collections/creating-people-advantage-reports.

Bell, Andrew, Ricardo Espinoza, Ben Game, et al. 2019. *OECD Skills Strategy 2019. Skills to Shape a Better Future*. OECD. https://doi.org/10.1787/9789264313835-en.

Bennett, Jeff. 2021. 'The Mindset, Traits, and Skills of an Ecosystem Builder'. Medium, January 24. https://medium.com/ecosystem-builder-hub/the-mindset-traits-and-skills-of-an-ecosystem-builder-d2d7b2139840.

Billing, Fabian, Aaron De Smet, Angelika Reich, and Bill Schaninger. 2021. *Building Workforce Skills at Scale to Thrive during–and after–the COVID-19 Crisis*. McKinsey & Company. https://www.mckinsey.com/capabilities/people-and-organizational-performance/our-insights/building-workforce-skills-at-scale-to-thrive-during-and-after-the-covid-19-crisis.

Booker, Kiara. 2025. 'How to Build a Resilient and Adaptive Workforce'. March 21. https://blog.rizeconsultants.com/en/intersections/how-to-build-a-resilient-and-adaptive-workforce.

Boutetière, Hortense de la, Alberto Montagner, and Angelika Reich. 2018. 'The Keys to a Successful Digital Transformation | McKinsey'. McKinsey & Company, October 29. https://www.mckinsey.com/capabilities/people-and-organizational-performance/our-insights/unlocking-success-in-digital-transformations.

Brassey, Jacqueline, Aaron De Smet, and Dana Maor. 2024. 'Fostering Workforce Resilience and Adaptability'. McKinsey Quarterly, December 6. https://www.mckinsey.com/capabilities/people-and-organizational-performance/our-insights/developing-a-resilient-adaptable-workforce-for-an-uncertain-future.

Broadwell, Martin M. 1969. 'Teaching For Learning (XVI.)'. *Gospel Guardian* 20 (41): 1–3a.

Buchanan, David A., and Andrzej Huczynski. 2019. *Organizational Behaviour*. 10. edition. Pearson.

Bueno, Carlos. 2022. 'The Next Thing Silicon Valley Needs to Disrupt Big Time: Its Own Culture'. Quartz, July 21. https://qz.com/225782/the-next-thing-silicon-valley-needs-to-disrupt-big-time-its-own-culture.

Chen, Gloria. 2023. 'How Adobe Revamped Its Company Values to Build a Resilient Future'. Fast Company, September 20. https://www.fastcompany.com/90946898/how-authentic-employee-input-drove-a-culture-overhaul-at-adobe.

Cobo, Cristobal. 2013. 'Skills for Innovation: Envisioning an Education That Prepares for the Changing World'. *The Curriculum Journal* 24 (1): 67–85. https://doi.org/10.1080/09585176.2012.744330.

Cross, Rob, Reb Rebele, and Adam Grant. 2016. 'Collaborative Overload'. Harvard Business Review, February. https://hbr.org/2016/01/collaborative-overload.

Crouppen, Stephanie. 2024. 'Interventions to Create an Adaptive Culture'. SHRM Business, February 22. https://www.shrm.org/executive-network/insights/people-strategy/interventions-to-create-adaptive-culture.

Csikszentmihalyi, Mihaly. 1990. *Flow: The Psychology of Optimal Experience*. Harper & Row.

Decius, Julian, Niclas Schaper, and Andreas Seifert. 2019. 'Informal Workplace Learning: Development and Validation of a Measure'. *Human Resource Development Quarterly* 30 (4): 495–535. https://doi.org/10.1002/hrdq.21368.

Derler, Andrea. 2019. *Growth Mindset Culture*. Idea Report. NeuroLeadership Institute. https://www.researchgate.net/publication/337772472_Growth_Mindset_Culture.

Derler, Andrea, Anthony Abbatiello, Stacia Sherman Garr, and Illustration Livia Cives. 2017. 'Five Ways to Nurture Developing Leaders in an Ecosystem for Growth'. *Deloitte Review* 20: 20.

Dondi, Marco, Julia Klier, Jörg Schubert, Frédéric Panier, and Jörg Schubert. 2021. 'Future-Citizen Skills | McKinsey'. McKinsey & Company, June 25. https://www.mckinsey.com/industries/public-sector/our-insights/defining-the-skills-citizens-will-need-in-the-future-world-of-work.

Duhigg, Charles. 2016. 'What Google Learned From Its Quest to Build the Perfect Team'. *The New York Times*, February 25. https://www.nytimes.com/2016/02/28/magazine/what-google-learned-from-its-quest-to-build-the-perfect-team.html.

Dweck, Carol. 2006. *Mindset: The New Psychology of Success: How We Can Learn to Fulfill Our Potential: Parenting, Business, School, Relationships*. 1st edition. Random House Publishing Group.

Earley, P. Christopher, and Elaine Mosakowski. 2024. 'Cultural Intelligence'. *Harvard Business Review*, October. https://hbr.org/2004/10/cultural-intelligence.

Easterbrook, Steve. 2014. 'From Computational Thinking to Systems Thinking: A Conceptual Toolkit for Sustainability Computing'. Paper presented at ICT for Sustainability 2014 (ICT4S-14), Stockholm, Sweden. https://doi.org/10.2991/ict4s-14.2014.28.

Edmondson, Amy. 1999. 'Psychological Safety and Learning Behavior in Work Teams'. *Administrative Science Quarterly* 44 (2): 350–83. https://doi.org/10.2307/2666999.

Epstein, Sophie. 2022. 'How Adaptability Helps You "Bounce Forwards" at Work'. News. BBC, September 20. https://www.bbc.com/worklife/article/20220915-how-adaptability-helps-you-bounce-forwards-at-work.

Facione, Peter A. 1990. *Critical Thinking: A Statement of Expert Consensus for Purposes of Educational Assessment and Instruction. Research Findings and Recommendations.* American Philosophical Association. https://philarchive.org/archive/faccta.

Farrow, Elissa. 2023. 'Embracing an Adaptive Mindset in the Age of Artificial Intelligence: Navigating the Future'. *Medium*, August 29. https://medium.com/@drelissafarrow/embracing-an-adaptive-mindset-in-the-age-of-artificial-intelligence-navigating-the-future-319c3352b32f.

Fey, Natalia, Emma Nordbäck, Mats Ehrnrooth, and Kirsi Mikkonen. 2022. 'How Peer Coaching Fosters Employee Proactivity and Well-Being within a Self-Managing Finnish Digital Engineering Company'. *Organizational Dynamics* 51 (3): 100864. https://doi.org/10.1016/j.orgdyn.2021.100864.

Flanagan, Ellie. 2023. 'HubSpot Invests in Platform Ecosystem by Adding 65+ Integrations to Its Connect Program'. Company Website. Hubspot, January 18. https://www.hubspot.com/company-news/hubspot-invests-in-platform-ecosystem-by-adding-65-integrations-to-its-connect-program.

Forrester, Jay W. 1961. *Industrial Dynamics*. MIT Press.

Forrester, Jay W. 1968. *Principles of Systems*. Wright-Allen Press.

Frankiewicz, Becky, and Tomas Chamorro-Premuzic. 2020. *Digital Transformation Is About Talent, Not Technology*. Harvard Business Review, May 6. https://hbr.org/2020/05/digital-transformation-is-about-talent-not-technology.

Fratto, Natalie. 2019. '3 Ways to Measure Your Adaptability and How to Improve It'. *TED Talk*, May. https://www.ted.com/talks/natalie_fratto_3_ways_to_measure_your_adaptability_and_how_to_improve_it.

Freeman, Leonard Jr. 2023. 'Developing A Growth Mindset Culture'. Forbes, April 17. https://www.forbes.com/councils/forbesnonprofitcouncil/2023/04/17/developing-a-growth-mindset-culture/.

Golden, Bryan, Anusheel Pandey, and James O'Rourke. 2017. *Zappos: An Experiment in Holacracy*. The Eugene D. Fanning Center for Business Communication, Mendoza College of Business, University of Notre Dame. https://doi.org/10.4135/9781526489968.

Goleman, Daniel. 2015. *Focus: The Hidden Driver of Excellence*. 1st edition. Harper.

Gownder, J.P. 2019. 'The Future Of Work Is An Adaptive Workforce'. *Forbes*, August 1. https://www.forbes.com/sites/forrester/2019/08/01/the-future-of-work-is-an-adaptive-workforce/.

Groth, Aimee. 2016. 'Zappos Has Now Lost 18% of Its Employees to Its Radical Buyout Offer'. Quartz, January. https://qz.com/590632/zappos-has-now-lost-18-of-its-employees-to-its-radical-buyout-offer.

Harshak, Ashley, DeAnne Aguirre, and Anna Brown. 2010. *Making Change Happen, and Making It Stick: Delivering Sustainable Organizational Change.* Strategy& / PwC. https://www.strategyand.pwc.com/gx/en/insights/archive/making-change-happen-making-stick/strategyand-making-change-happen-and-making-it-stick.pdf.

Hartmann, Tanja. 2025. *Adaptive Workforce: How to React Smartly to Scarce Resources.* Company Website. May 14. https://www.zep.de/en/blog/adaptive-workforce-strategies?

Heathfield, Susan M. 2021. 'Find Out How Zappos Reinforces Its Company Culture'. Company Website. LiveAbout, February 17. https://www.liveabout.com/zappos-company-culture-1918813.

Hesketh, B., and A. Neal. 1999. 'Technology and Performance'. In *The Changing Nature of Performance: Implications for Staffing, Motivation, and Development*, edited by D. R. Ilgen and E. D. Pulakos. Jossey-Bass.

Hreha, Jason. 2023. 'What Is A Growth Mindset And How To Develop It In 9 Steps'. Professional Development. August 16. https://www.personatalent.com/development/how-to-cultivate-a-growth-mindset/.

Huang, Hsuan-Che (Brad), Zhixu (Rick) Yang, and Franki Y. H. Kung. 2023. 'Employees' Mindset Matters: Leveraging Cultural Mindset to Harness the Benefits of Organizational Polyculturalism'. *Industrial and Organizational Psychology* 16 (3): 408–12. https://doi.org/10.1017/iop.2023.34.

Isaac, Watson. 2023. 'How to Develop Critical Thinking Skills through Puzzle Solving'. *Medium*, December 4. https://medium.com/@watson.isaac/how-to-develop-critical-thinking-skills-through-puzzle-solving-7b51bb34a030.

Jooste, Delanie. 2023. 'From Silos To Ecosystems – The Power Of An Ecosystem Mindset'. *Brainz Magazine*, September 29. https://www.brainzmagazine.com/post/from-silos-to-ecosystems-the-power-of-an-ecosystem-mindset.

Kan, Michael. 2016. 'How Adobe Sparks Innovation by Paying People to Fail'. *Fortune*, April 5. https://fortune.com/2016/04/05/adobe-innovation-risk-failure/.

Kaufmann, Michelle. 2022. 'Augmenting Physical Space Design with Flexible Digital Tools'. Company wWebsite. Google Workspace Blog, November 18. https://workspace.google.com/blog/future-of-work/reimagining-physical-spaces-to-foster-connection.

Kefford, Matt. 2025. 'Top 15 Best Tech Companies To Work For | Glassdoor Ranking 2025'. February 7. https://www.gmac.com/resources/learners/business-careers/employers-salaries/best-tech-companies-work.

Kelly, Richard. 2019. *Constructing Leadership 4.0: Swarm Leadership and the Fourth Industrial Revolution.* 2019th edition. Springer International Publishing: Imprint: Palgrave Macmillan. https://doi.org/10.1007/978-3-319-98062–1.

Kelly, Richard. 2022. *The Nature of Business Transformation: A Swarm Intelligent Approach to Reinventing Organisations.* Routledge.

Klein, G., B. Moon, and R. R. Hoffman. 2006. 'Making Sense of Sensemaking 1: Alternative Perspectives'. *IEEE Intelligent Systems* 21 (4): 70–73. https://doi.org/10.1109/MIS.2006.75.

Leonardi, Paul M., and Tsedal Neeley. 2022. *The Digital Mindset: What It Really Takes to Thrive in the Age of Data, Algorithms, and AI.* Harvard Business Review Press.

Ludema, Jim, and Amber Johnson. 2019. 'How Adobe Enables Creativity Through Diversity, Psychological Safety & Values'. Forbes, May 13. https://www.forbes.com/sites/amberjohnson-jimludema/2019/03/13/how-adobe-enables-creativity-through-diversity-psychological-safety-values/.

Maervoet, Sofie. 2024. *How to Shape a Flexible and Adaptive Workforce.* Company Website. September 2. https://www.randstad.com/workforce-insights/flexible-staffing/how-to-shape-a-flexible-adaptive-workforce/?

Markson, Tevye. 2025. 'All Civil Servants to Get AI Training'. Civil Service World, June 9. https://www.civilserviceworld.com/professions/article/civil-servants-ai-training-one-big-thing-2025.

Maryam, Kooh Givi. 2025. 'The Impact of Coaching Interventions on Employee Performance, Motivation, and Organizational Adaptability: An Experimental Study in the Petrochemical Industry'. *International Journal of Business and Management* 20 (5): 246–257. https://doi.org/10.5539/ijbm.v20n5p246.

McGregor, Lindsay, and Neel Doshi. 2017. 'There Are Two Types of Performance – But Most Organizations Only Focus on One'. *Harvard Business Review*, October 10. https://hbr.org/2017/10/there-are-two-types-of-performance-but-most-organizations-only-focus-on-one, https://hbr.org/2017/10/there-are-two-types-of-performance-but-most-organizations-only-focus-on-one.

Michelman, Paul. 2018. 'Key Words for Digital Transformation'. *MIT Sloan Management Review*, December 4. https://sloanreview.mit.edu/article/key-words-for-digital-transformation/.

Miller, Brian. 2022. 'How We Inspire Great Performance at Adobe'. Company website. *Adobe Blog*, September 5. https://blog.adobe.com/en/publish/2022/05/09/how-we-inspire-great-performance-at-adobe.

Miller, George A. 1956. 'The Magical Number Seven, Plus or Minus Two: Some Limits on Our Capacity for Processing Information.' *Psychological Review* 63 (2): 81–97. https://doi.org/10.1037/h0043158.

Narayen, Shantanu. 2025. 'What We Believe'. https://www.adobe.com/uk/about-adobe/corporate-responsibility/what-we-believe.html.

Newport, Cal. 2016. *Deep Work: Rules for Focused Success in a Distracted World.* Grand Central Publishing.

Nold, Herbert, and Lukas Michel. 2021. 'Organizational Culture: A Systems Approach'. In Accounting and Finance Innovations, edited by Nizar Alsharari. IntechOpen. https://doi.org/10.5772/intechopen.97466.

Park, Sohee, and Sunyoung Park. 2020. 'How Can Employees Adapt to Change? Clarifying the Adaptive Performance Concepts'. *Human Resource Development Quarterly* 32 (1): E1–E15. https://doi.org/10.1002/hrdq.21411.

Peachman, Rachel Rabkin. 2024. 'Forbes World's Best Employers 2024 – Best Companies to Work for Worldwide'. Forbes, October 8. https://www.forbes.com/lists/worlds-best-employers/.

Pidun, Ulrich, Martin Reeves, and Balázs Zoletnik. 2022. 'Are You Ready to Become an Ecosystem Player?' BCG Global, June 23. https://www.bcg.com/publications/2022/major-shifts-to-become-successful-ecosystem-strategy-player.

Pierce, Gloria. 1994. 'Thinking Critically in the Workplace'. In *Basic Skills for the Workplace*, edited by Maurice C. Taylor, Glenda R. Lewe, and James A. Draper. Krieger.

Ployhart, Robert E, and Scott F Turner. 2014. 'Organizational Adaptability'. In *Individual Adaptability to Changes at Work: New Directions in Research*, edited by David Chan. 73–91 Routledge. https://doi.org/10.4324/9780203465721.

Pluck, Graham, and Helen Johnson. 2011. 'Stimulating Curiosity to Enhance Learning'. *GESJ: Education Science and Psychology* 2 (19): 66–78. https://www.researchgate.net/publication/292088477_Stimulating_curiosity_to_enhance_learning.

Prince, Emma-Sue. 2019. *7 Skills for the Future: Adaptability, Critical Thinking, Empathy, Integrity, Optimism, Being Proactive, Resilience*. 2nd edition. Pearson.

Pulakos, E, D Dorsey, and S White. 2006. 'Adaptability in the Workplace: Selecting an Adaptive Workforce'. In *Advances in Human Performance and Cognitive Engineering Research*, vol. 6. Elsevier. 612-624. https://doi.org/10.1016/S1479-3601(05)06002–9.

PWC UK. 2025. *Global Top 100 Public Companies by Market Capitalisation: March 2025*. PwC. https://www.pwc.co.uk/services/audit/insights/global-top-100-companies.html.

Rosenfeldt, Rachel. 2024. 'The Future Is Now: Cultivating an Adaptive Mindset and Skillset for the AI-Powered Workplace'. *Training Journal*, September 12. https://www.trainingjournal.com/2024/content-type/opinion/the-future-is-now-cultivating-an-adaptive-mindset-and-skillset-for-the-ai-powered-workplace/.

Sabet, Nabil and Grant Christofely. 2026. 'Adaptivity Is a Mindset'. *M Moser Associates*. https://www.mmoser.com/ideas/adaptivity-is-a-mindset/.

Saptarini, Nur Ike, and Martina Dwi Mustika. 2023. 'Workforce Agility and Adaptive Performance in Government Institution: The Mediating Role of Work Engagement'. *Jurnal Manajemen Dan Kewirausahaan* 25 (1): 55–62. https://doi.org/10.9744/jmk.25.1.55-62.

Schön, Donald A., and Martin Rein. 1994. *Frame Reflection: Toward the Resolution of Intractable Policy Controversies*. Basic Books.

Schroeck, Michael, Ann Kwan, John Gill, and Divya Sharma. 2020. *Evolving Partner Roles in Industry 4.0: A Partner Ecosystem Can Generate Customer-Ready Solutions and Accelerate Time to Market*. Deloitte Insights. https://www2.deloitte.com/us/en/insights/focus/industry-4-0/partner-ecosystem-industry-4–0.html.

Senge, Peter M. 1990. *The Fifth Discipline: The Art and Practice of the Learning Organization*. 1st edition. Doubleday Currency.

Senge, Peter M., Art Kleiner, Charlotte Roberts, Richard B. Ross, George Roth, and Bryan Smith. 1994. *The Fifth Discipline Fieldbook: Strategies and Tools for Building a Learning Organization*. Currency/Doubleday.

Senge, Peter M., Hal Hamilton, and John Kania. 2015. 'The Dawn of System Leadership'. *Stanford Social Innovation Review* 13: 2733. https://doi.org/10.48558/YTE7-XT62.

Song, Yi, Katrina C. Roohr, and Dessi Kirova. 2024. 'Exploring Approaches for Developing and Evaluating Workplace Critical Thinking Skills'. *Thinking Skills and Creativity* 51 (March): 101460. https://doi.org/10.1016/j.tsc.2023.101460.

Sørensen, Jesper B. 2002. 'The Strength of Corporate Culture and the Reliability of Firm Performance'. *Administrative Science Quarterly* 47 (1): 70–91. https://doi.org/10.2307/3094891.

Spagnoletto, Lyuba, Dianah AlabdulJabbar, Harsha Jalihal, Queenie Chan, and Ravin Jesuthasan. 2019. *HR4.0: Shaping People Strategies in the Fourth Industrial Revolution*. White Paper No. 10122019. World Economic Forum in Collaboration with Saudi Aramco, Unilever, and Willis Towers Watson. https://www3.weforum.org/docs/WEF_NES_Whitepaper_HR4.0.pdf.

StatsPanda. *Terabytes of data created globally (live counter)*. Accessed April 8, 2026. https://www.statspanda.com/live-counters/Terabytes%20of%20data%20created%20globally

Taylor, Bill. 2016. 'How WD-40 Created a Learning-Obsessed Company Culture'. September 16. https://hbr.org/2016/09/how-wd-40-created-a-learning-obsessed-company-culture.

Thoring, Katja, Pieter Desmet, and Petra Badke-Schaub. 2018. 'Creative Environments for Design Education and Practice: A Typology of Creative Spaces'. *Design Studies* 56 (May): 54–83. https://doi.org/10.1016/j.destud.2018.02.001.

Thoring, Katja, Roland M. Mueller, Pieter Desmet, and Petra Badke-Schaub. 2020. 'Spatial Design Factors Associated with Creative Work: A Systematic Literature Review'. *Artificial Intelligence for Engineering Design, Analysis and Manufacturing* 34 (3): 300–14. https://doi.org/10.1017/S0890060420000232.

Thorson, Kristen. 2018. 'Early Learning Strategies for Developing Computational Thinking Skills'. *Getting Smart*, March 18. https://www.gettingsmart.com/2018/03/18/early-learning-strategies-for-developing-computational-thinking-skills/.

Tripathy, Mitashree. 2020. 'Dimensions of Critical Thinking in Workplace Management & Personal Development: A Conceptual Analysis'. *Multidisciplinary Journal for Education, Social and Technological Sciences* 7 (2): 1. https://doi.org/10.4995/muse.2020.12925.

Vaynerman, Michael. 2022. 'Elastic Workforces: The Key to Peak Performance'. April 18. https://www.bluecrewjobs.com/blog/elastic-workforces-the-key-to-peak-performance.

Vijayan, Vineesh. 2019. 'Agility, Adaptability and Organisation Culture'. Medium, September 17. https://medium.com/summit-plus/agility-adaptability-and-organisation-culture-7ebe8a8c5d71.

Weick, Karl E. 1995. *Sensemaking in Organizations*. Foundations for Organizational Science. Sage publications.

Westover, Jonathan H. 2024. 'Building a Resilient and Adaptive Organization Through Mindset Shifts and Continuous Learning'. HCI Consulting, November 9. https://www.innovativehumancapital.com/article/building-a-resilient-and-adaptive-organization-through-mindset-shifts-and-continuous-learning.

Wing, Jeannette M. 2006. 'Computational Thinking'. *Communications of the ACM* 49 (3): 33–35. https://doi.org/10.1145/1118178.1118215.

Yeager, David Scott, and Carol S. Dweck. 2012. 'Mindsets That Promote Resilience: When Students Believe That Personal Characteristics Can Be Developed'. *Educational Psychologist* 47 (4): 302–14. https://doi.org/10.1080/00461520.2012.722805.

Chapter 9

Transformational Change from a Rigid to an Adaptive Organisation

On Friday, 5 January 2024, a closure blew out of an exit doorway on the Alaska Airlines Flight 1282, causing uncontrolled decompression. CNN reported that the detached fuselage plug was found by a Portland schoolteacher, Bob Sauer, in his backyard (Paradis et al. 2024). The aircraft, a Boeing 737 MAX 9, had a history of loose hardware, electrical faults, and quality-control issues. Mark Walker, writing in *The New York Times* (2024), reports that the plane failed over one-third of its safety audits. The incident caused a nationwide grounding. Peter Robison (2021), Clive Irving (2021), and Aram Gesar (2024) all believe that the Boeing 737 MAX 9 technical and safety faults have an organisational culture origin.

This case study is a striking example of a failed organisational transformation. In 1997, the US aerospace giant McDonnell Douglas merged with Boeing, an aviation company with over 100 years of history and a strong reputation for technical and safety excellence. What ensued was a series of ruthless, top-down, formula-driven cultural changes at Boeing, the most significant of which was the adoption of "Neutron Jack" Welch's shareholder value model, originally developed at General Electric. The consequences were disastrous for Boeing. The company, whose renowned technical brilliance supported WW1 and the lunar landings, prioritised revenue and shareholder value over engineering excellence and safety. It went from an engineering-driven, safety-first culture to a finance-first culture that prioritised shareholder value over customer safety.

Rather than undertaking a comprehensive redesign to solve the technical problems,[1] the company tried to save costs by implementing a quick-fix software

 DOI: 10.4324/9781003680345-9

solution. Clive Irving (2021) dubbed it "plane greed". Peter Robison writes, "Like Jack Welch's General Electric before it, Boeing became a collection of assets to be shuffled as managers saw fit to make the most beneficial combination for stockholders, not for customers or employees" (Robison 2021, epilogue). The engineering excellence and innovation which once flowed through Boeing's DNA was now seriously compromised. Clive Irving (2021) observes that this led to an adverse chain reaction at Boeing, including an exodus of highly talented engineers.

This cautionary tale of a sudden and dramatic cultural shift in the organisation where Boeing adopted shareholder value over technical and safety considerations directly led to crises and fatalities that cost billions in compensation payouts, damaged the reputation of a once technically brilliant organisation, led to an irretrievable talent exodus, and cost the CEO his job. It exposes the unintended consequences of a flawed transformational change initiative.

In the post-merger transformation between Boeing and McDonnell Douglas, there was a clear disconnect between strategy, systems, and people, where the implementation was rushed, complexities were underestimated, changes were driven by costs rather than safety, and experienced people were ignored.[2] The disastrous Boeing-McDonnell Douglas merger can be compared with the Disney-Pixar merger presented in Chapter 3, which, according to Gasparini, Vieira, and Dias (2025), was seen as a "strategic triumph" (51) that strengthened both brands and led to renewed profitability.

This final chapter on transformational change weaves together key threads developed throughout the book. It examines how to implement successful transformational change through a fictionalised case study, *Company Hex*, and situates transformational change in relation to adaptive change. The chapter reviews three core approaches to change (programmatic, hybrid, and emergent) emphasising the hybrid approach as the most effective. It also uses the 3D Consulting Model (diagnose, design, deliver) to debrief the change process and concludes with reflections on leading transformational change. Together, these elements provide a practical blueprint and checklist for organisations transitioning to an adaptive model.

Transformational Change: Concept and Context

Transformational change is one of those terms with no clear origin. The term was in circulation by the 1990s, featuring in Burke and Litwin's model of organisational performance and change (1992), in which they identified cultural change as a differentiating factor between transactional and transformational change (Burke and Litwin 1992). Widely used terms for organisational transformation include system transformation, transformational change, and business transformation. Understanding how these terms differ provides some clarity around using transformational change as a preferred term in the context of this book. Business transformation focuses on organisational change in business processes or business operational systems (Kelly 2022). David Cruise (2017), Director of Business Transformation at Change Associates, writes:

> Business Transformation is the process of fundamentally changing the systems, processes, people and technology across a whole business or business unit, to achieve measurable improvements in efficiency, effectiveness and stakeholder satisfaction. As such, a business transformation project is likely to include any number of change management projects, each focused on an individual process, system, technology, team or department.

Transformational change involves systems and culture change within the organisation and its environment or ecosystem. Burke and Litwin remark:

> Transformational change occurs as a response to the external environment and directly affects organizational mission and strategy, the organization 's leadership, and culture.
>
> (Burke and Litwin 1992, 523)

System change is broader in scope, encompassing societal impacts such as health, education, and the environment. Sandra Waddock and Steve Waddell comment:

> System transformation is fundamental, broad, deep, and multiscalar change that involves a paradigm change, i.e., a radical shift, in five key interrelated and interactive dimensions that constitute the whole of a "complexly wicked" socio-ecological system.
>
> (Waddock and Waddell 2021, 31)

Adaptive Change

Building adaptability across systems (including culture, design, technology, people, and the change process) lies at the heart of creating an adaptive organisation. Malcolm McGreevy makes this connection explicit in his discussion of adaptive change and the evolving world of work:

> Adaptive change is systemic, affecting the roots and branches of an organisation, requiring a fundamental reappraisal of beliefs and values in an organisation or a change of organisational culture. In adapting to changes in the external environment, organisations may need to develop new strategies, clarify their values and beliefs and learn new ways of operating.
>
> (McGreevy 2008, 360)

According to Annette Klososky (2024), "Change isn't a one-off pit stop. It's more of an open road trip, constantly evolving and demanding that you map out new routes on the fly".

The Boeing-McDonnell Douglas merger failed because it wasn't a system and culture transformation. The company underwent a technical integration; it merged processes, without integrating the deeper cultural values of the two organisations. This chapter (and the broader book) argues that, to become a truly adaptive enterprise, organisations must pursue an adaptive change approach at the systems and cultural levels. Michael Watkins (2015) refers to this as "rewiring" the organisation. Commentators such as Thomas Brian Whalen argue that the consistently low success rate of change initiatives in organisations[3] is due to a "lack of understanding of how organizational culture forms and then continually adapts to changing circumstances" (Whalen 2014, 1).

Fictionalised Case Study: *Company Hex* and the Road to Becoming an Adaptive Organisation

The following is a fictionalised case study set in the immediate future. The ideas and content are drawn from recent cross-industry examples of prominent large organisations working to become more responsive.

Executive Summary

This fictionalised case study profiles a global energy company that has undergone a major transformational change from a rigid to an adaptive culture. The case study tracks how the company strove to make its organisational design (structures, governance, and workflows) more adaptive by adopting a honeycomb model. It also shows how the company further embedded adaptive change in the organisation by using digital and people strategies to help mobilise the transformational change process. The result was an adaptive organisation that was future-ready to address the challenges of working in an uncertain and complex operating environment.

Background

Company Hex is an invented and fictionalised global energy company with an international workforce. It operates in many countries and jurisdictions and is subject to an increasing degree of environmental and geopolitical conditions. It started as a traditional matrix company with a formal board structure and a rigid chain of command. It was a pyramidal firm where ideas and decisions came from the C-suite and were cascaded down the organisation. The company had experimented with Agile for several years and found it worked effectively in specific contexts, but failed to create an enterprise-wide, adaptive, and sustainable culture. *Company Hex* aspires to become a more culturally adaptive rather than a process-heavy organisation.

The Challenge

A central problem was that its traditional business processes disengaged many of its most capable employees. Its rigid governance and workflow structures failed to attract creative and dynamic digerati, and the company was frequently caught off guard by social media, particularly on issues of decarbonisation and emissions reduction. Furthermore, it maintained a highly insular and secretive culture, avoiding and mistrusting strategic partnerships. The organisation typically reacted to events rather than anticipating them, with change processes that were slow, cumbersome, and constrained by groupthink. Despite its global reach, the company had never fully embraced shared services or integrated operations, limiting its adaptability and responsiveness. This international company faced a complex set of challenges, including technical hurdles related to decarbonisation and emission-reduction targets, localised geopolitical instability, unpredictable markets, restrictive trading conditions, competition for global talent, and adverse attention on social media. These pressures underscored the need for a more responsive and adaptive organisation.

The Solution

The company aimed to achieve cultural adaptability through a three-year transformation plan. This encompassed system-wide cultural change across its structures, governance, and workflows, supported by digital, people, and change strategies designed to drive transformation.

Method

The following describes how *Company Hex* set about achieving this systems and culture transformation from a rigid to an adaptive organisation using the 3D consulting method of diagnose, design, and deliver.

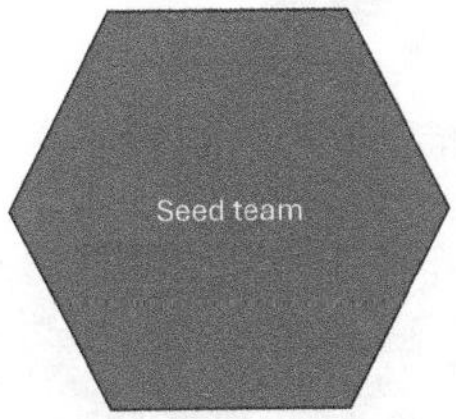

Figure 9.1 A single cell.

Diagnosing the Problem

The diagnosis was undertaken at the C-suite/executive level. Leadership formed a single seed team that functioned as a brain trust (see Figure 9.1). This status-free, non-hierarchical, and informal brainstroming cell engaged in open dialogue, shared thinking, and collective decision-making.

The seed team was acutely aware that their organisation was neither future-ready nor sufficiently responsive to thrive in the volatile conditions already undermining their business and reputation. They favoured small, self-organising cells because Agile Scrum was familiar to them and self-directed teams were already part of the company's DNA. It was clear to the seed team that Agile Scrum created adaptive, self-organising pockets within the organisation but did not contribute strategically to a broader adaptive enterprise or to organisational growth. The company urgently needed to become more connected and aligned, both internally and externally, with an ecosystem mindset. Revisiting digital and people strategy was only part of the solution. It became apparent that the organisation needed a complete rewiring of its business architecture and design (structure, governance, and workflow) to move from a rigid and linear process to a complex adaptive ecosystem. The seed cell set out the goals and vision to become a more adaptive organisation and jointly developed a roadmap.

Designing an Adaptive Business Architecture

The organisational design (presented in Chapters 4–6) consists of structure, governance, and workflow. Creating a more adaptive business architecture requires greater adaptability at the systems level. Here's how *Company Hex* approached it.

i. Structure

The seed team knew they had to involve HR and OD specialists when adapting the business architecture. So, two other cells were formed, which linked to the seed cell to create a cross-functional cluster (see Figure 9.2).

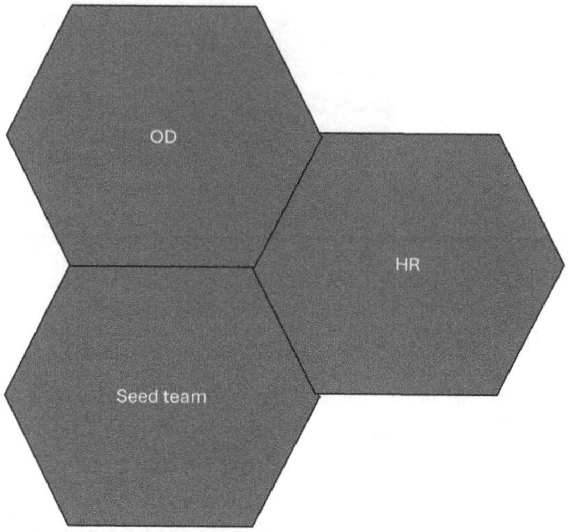

Figure 9.2 Cross-functional cluster.

This cross-functional cluster sought input from teams within the organisation that had experience working in self-organising, modular environments. They involved several project groups familiar with Agile Scrum and drew on organisational culture and IT specialists, as well as the external affairs team. Finally, an external consultant from a business school was brought in to provide an outside perspective on building adaptive organisations. These connecting cells all now formed a cross-functional network (see Figure 9.3).

Using this modular, cell-formation model, the hexagonal structure begins to take shape. This is no longer a simple network, but an emergent, dynamic network that spans internal and external boundaries. This cross-functional network reimagines how business intelligence, ideas, and decisions flow through the enterprise. This goes beyond Agile Scrum. In the words of David Gray and Thomas Vander Wal (2012), it has become a connected company in which different functions and expertise merge. Frans Johansson (2004) refers to this cross-functionality as the Medici Effect. This organisational structure grows and connects like biological cells, creating a strong culture that, over time, becomes the default DNA. The advantage of this model is that it does not require costly and disruptive reorganisations; it grows and emerges alongside the existing culture. It is an evolving ecosystem and not an organising framework.

The honeycomb structure is also an effective model for connecting with external organisations to build ecosystems. *Company Hex* realised that their new recruits benefitted from critical thinking and innovation

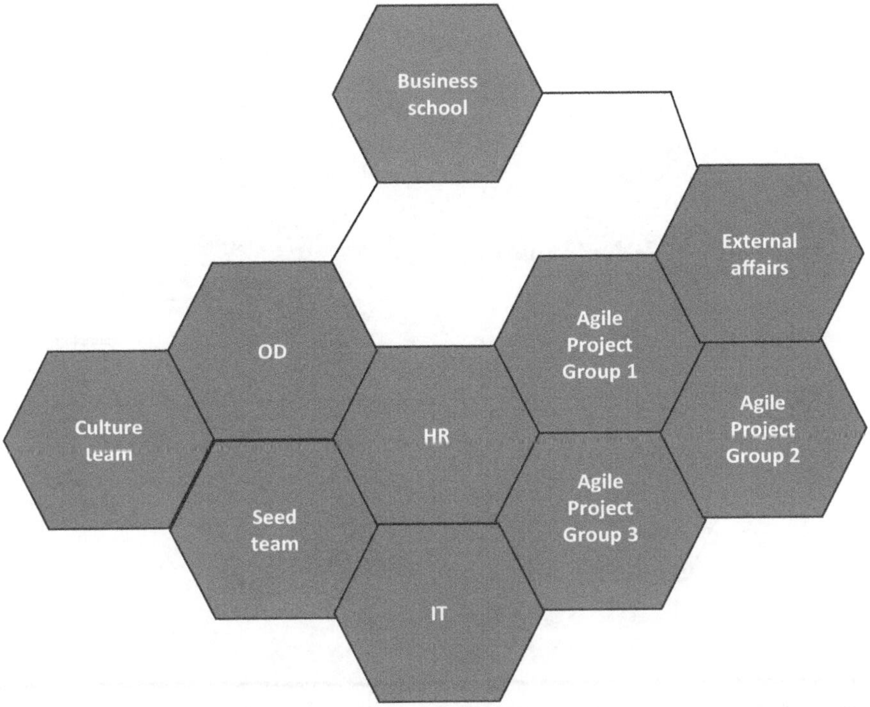

Figure 9.3 Cross-functional network.

skills, so they reached out to local educational centres and offered to help build critical thinking and innovation in schools and colleges. They also connected with the local government to see how they could support innovation in the community. They included in this evolving ecosystem representatives from a supplier and a local competitive business. This is now an ecosystem network (see Figure 9.4).

Company Hex's involvement in the broader community established it as a responsive (STEP-WIDER) organisation. One can see here how structure is an important pillar because it reinforces the governance and workflow.

ii. Governance

One of the advantages of the honeycomb structure is its ability to promote collective, shared governance. At its core, the model relies on self-organisation and self-governance: while individuals may have defined roles, there is no hierarchy or status within a cell. To maximise the impact of the Medici Effect, all participants must be equal, inclusive, and comfortable sharing ideas and making decisions collaboratively. These ideas form the core of system leadership. As cells begin to replicate and connect with other self-organising and emergent cells (such as stakeholders, workstreams, or

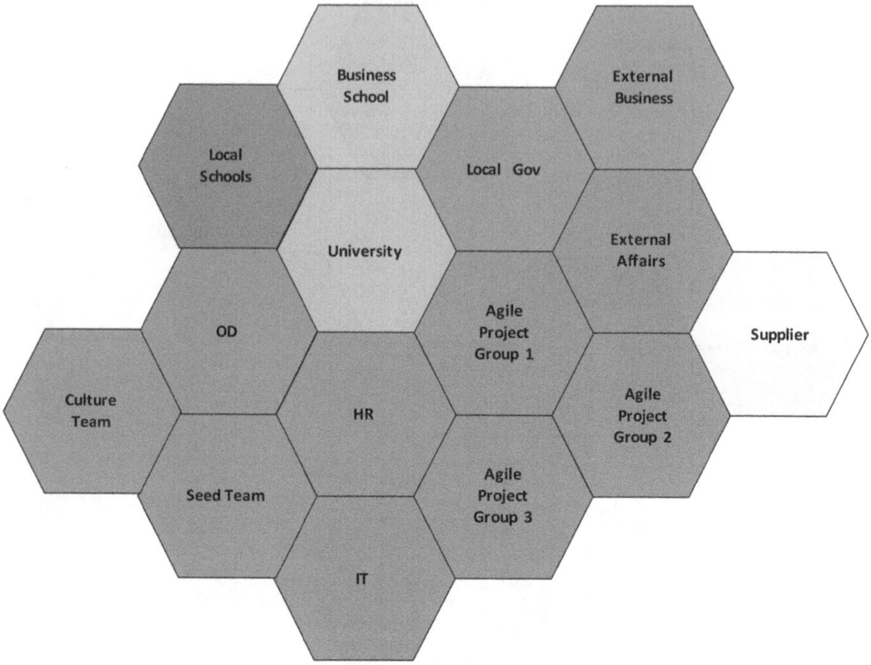

Figure 9.4 *Company Hex* **ecosystem.**

functions), they form the foundations of cross-functional, networked collective intelligence and decision-making. Another advantage of the honeycomb model is its natural alignment with ecosystem governance.

At this stage, the seed team transitions from a purely decision-making strategic cell to a system-mentoring cell, coaching and guiding the organisation in adopting an adaptive culture. They also act as organisational ambassadors, promoting transformational change across the broader ecosystem. It is important to note that this model is based on system leadership, in which everyone is accountable and plays a collective role in driving transformational change.

iii. Workflow

The hexagon structure facilitates cross-collaboration, collective thinking and decision-making. It is a complex adaptive system and not a pyramidal workflow. The structure and governance, combined with the digital ecosystem, enable a better flow of business intelligence and a more collaborative, inclusive, and connected adaptive workforce. The idea of workflow collaboration and connectivity is clearly reflected in the honeycomb model. Business intelligence, diversity, and collaborations flow through the edges, boundaries, and points of connection in the structure. This is represented in Figure 9.5.

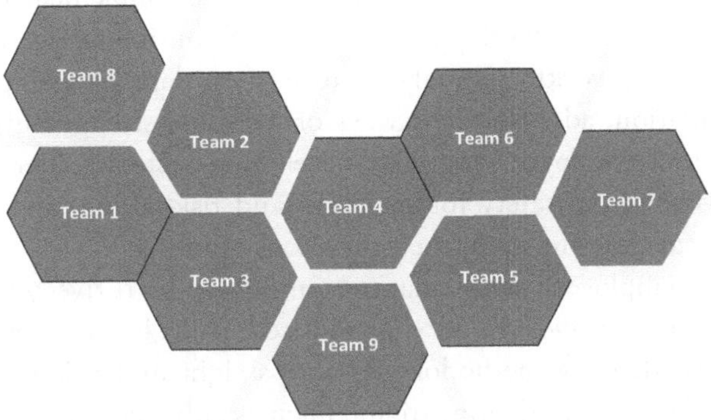

Figure 9.5 Flow through cell boundaries.

In Figure 9.5, the thick lines represent the pivot point between the cell boundaries. This interface, supported by digital transformation connects adaptive governance and workflow. This is also where system leadership naturally occurs and flourishes. It is a dynamic system leadership highway. In Chapters 4 and 8, this connecting line was called wireacracy, a term coined by Jon Husband (2013) to describe "a dynamic two-way flow of power and authority, based on knowledge, trust, credibility and a focus on results, enabled by interconnected people and technology". The workflow naturally blends with the other pillars in the business architecture.

Delivering Strategic Alignment

A final consideration is how *Company Hex* aligns its digital, people, and change strategies to act as transformational levers for delivering an adaptive organisation. Let's briefly review this.

i. Digital transformation

   Technology plays a critical role in supporting and accelerating adaptive organisations. In the honeycomb model presented earlier, the edges of each cell serve as conduits for the flow of data and intelligence. Business intelligence circulates more fluidly in a wirearchical configuration than in traditional hierarchical structures. Technology facilitates this flow: it connects people, supports workflows, and creates new opportunities for collective intelligence to emerge and flourish.

ii. People transformation

   Company Hex developed its adaptive workforce through a dual-people strategy of system and skill-based interventions. Adopting the "people strategy steering wheel" outlined in Chapter 7, they implemented system-led initiatives such as developing a culture of continuous learning and innovation, using workforce analytics to harness data, investing in digital transformation, adopting new ways of working, strengthening talent acquisition and employee retention, developing system leadership, cultivating psychological safety for inclusion and risk-taking, and building strategic partnerships to strengthen their ecosystem.

To equip employees with adaptive mindsets to thrive within this dynamic system, *Company Hex* introduced skills-based interventions using blended delivery methodologies across eight dimensions: building systems thinking, strengthening digital fluency, enhancing situational and sensemaking capabilities, improving feedback and coaching skills, developing an ecosystem mindset, cultivating a growth mindset and resilience, refining critical thinking and decision-making skills, and developing personal focus.

Company Hex used people surveys and structured interviews to assess the effectiveness and impact of its overall people strategy.

Process: Transformational Change Roadmap

Maria Aunsholt Storgaard, Maya Kousholt Schmitt, and Annie Gisslen (2025) argue that "A transformation roadmap is critical to bring the transformation vision and ambition to life". Such roadmaps can clarify direction, align goals and milestones, track progress, act as a transparent communication tool, and help mitigate risk. Figure 9.6 shows *Company Hex's* change transformation roadmap template spanning three years. Specific tasks were added as colour bands to highlight the task and timeline.

Findings and Results

Company Hex achieved measurable improvements in decision-making, responsiveness, and employee engagement after implementing its transformational change initiative. The initiative led to a marked enhancement in decision quality, as employees developed the confidence and capability to make timely, data-informed decisions without reliance on chain-of-command approval. Team organisation and cohesion improved considerably following the dismantling of formal structures, leading to greater collaboration across departments and external ecosystems. Communication channels became more open and transparent, which enabled a faster flow of business intelligence, leading to greater accountability, ownership, shared responsibility, and collective decision-making. Collectively, these outcomes contributed to the development of a more adaptive organisational culture in which employees demonstrated greater independence,

		YEAR 1	YEAR 2	YEAR 3
Culture	Adaptability			
	Responsiveness			
Design	Structure			
	Governance			
	Workflow			
Technology	Diagnose			
	Resource			
	Adopt			
	Weigh-up			
People	System			
	Personal Skills			
	Methodology			
Process	Change model			
	Diagnose			
	Design			
	Delivery			

Figure 9.6 ***Company Hex*** **change transformation roadmap.**

resilience, and a readiness to embrace change. This, in turn, led to increased innovation and growth, as reflected in the organisation's financial performance. The organisation was also recognised as an employer of choice and as an environmentally responsible organisation, helping to improve its social media reputation.

Discussion and Takeaways

Company Hex is an invented and fictionalised company, but the data comes from real case studies. It provides a generic example of an organisation implementing transformational change to become a more adaptive enterprise. It serves as a blueprint for transformational change for any global company that operates across geographies and jurisdictions, that has a highly closed and centralised culture and is looking to become more open and adaptive. Some key takeaways from this case study include:

- Take a temperature check of the organisation and create opportunities for people to dialogue.
- Build momentum for transformational change rather than imposing it (*Company Hex* accomplished this through an emergent modular structure that evolved into a mature cross-functional network). Lasting change occurs when people are active agents of change, rather than passive recipients of

it. This approach also mitigates potential resistance to change and the risk of future sabotage.

- Think and act systemically. Understand that cultural change, such as moving from a rigid to an adaptive culture, can only be self-sustaining and effective by creating adaptability at the organisational design and business architecture levels, through structures, governance, and workflows.
- Align strategy. It is important to have a digital, people, and process strategy that aligns with the cultural and transformational change, so they become levers and mobilisers for change (including a digital infrastructure that genuinely supports the flow of business intelligence and system leadership).
- Communicate the transformational change process transparently to the community, showing a clear beginning, middle, and end. This is vital for any emergent change, so that change doesn't feel arbitrary or chaotic. This helps manage and prevent change fatigue and allows the organisation to track progress.

A Deeper Process Dive: Selecting the Right Transformational Change Model

Two critical decisions in any transformational change process are clarifying what type of transformation is required and choosing a model that aligns with your organisational culture. In LEGO's early-2000s turnaround (profiled in Chapter 2), the company faced significant adaptive challenges and responded by adopting a *hybrid* change model that combined cost-cutting measures, platform-based production development, and open innovation. This approach enabled the organisation to regain financial stability while simultaneously enhancing its capacity for innovation and market responsiveness. Microsoft, under Satya Nadella, also adopted a *hybrid* approach in its mid-2010s cultural transformation, using growth mindset to secure strategic and emergent change. In the mid-2000s, as discussed in Chapter 1, Netflix shifted its business model from DVD rental to streaming services in a largely *emergent* way. It sensed the evolving needs of its customers and understood how emerging technologies could support its business model. Chapter 3 showed how Nokia's leadership launched a *programmatic* initiative in the early 2010s to rescue the company from the "burning platform" caused by its declining mobile phone sales. Each of these companies faced different transformational challenges and required distinct solutions. It supports Esther Cameron and Mike Green's (2010) view that there is no one-size-fits-all model for transformational change.

There are three core approaches to transformational change: programmatic, emergent, and hybrid. Programmatic is a structured top-down approach;

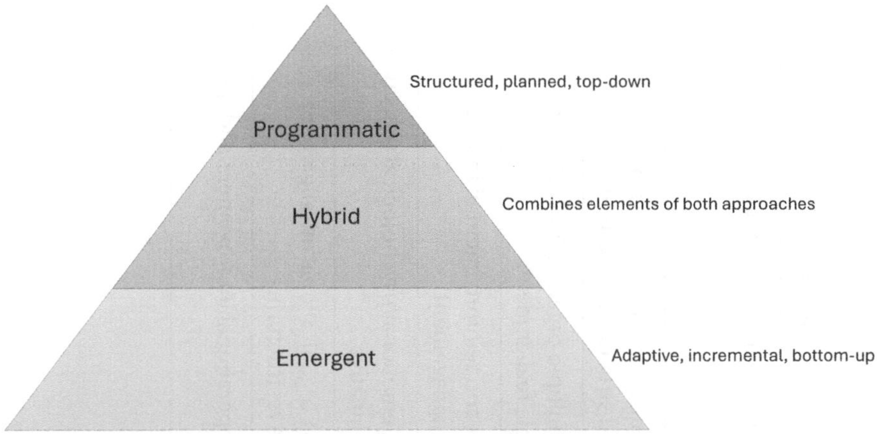

Figure 9.7 Three core approaches to transformational change.

emergent is an adaptive bottom-up (self-organising) change model; hybrid combines elements of both. Figure 9.7 illustrates this.

Programmatic (planned) change, first introduced by Kurt Lewin (1947) and his three-step model, works well for technical change such as rolling out a new system upgrade or a compliance policy. Emergent change, popularised by Weick and Quinn (1999), is effective for deepening an organisation's culture and values. Hybrid change (which includes contingent change) bridges programmatic and emergent models. A hybrid change approach is effective for cultural change because it is less disruptive than a top-down programmatic implementation. It provides a structured model for incremental change alongside business-as-usual.

There is a great deal of research that presents different change models across the planned, hybrid, and emergent domains.[4] Table 9.1 provides an overview and brief assessment of some of the most popular change models.

A cultural transformation from a rigid to an adaptive organisation will require a hybrid change approach: it will need executive leadership, HR, and organisational expertise to lead the initiative, but will also require the entire organisation to support it. An exclusive top-down programmatic change may risk failing to gain buy-in from employees and stakeholders. In contrast, an exclusive bottom-up emergent culture may miss key elements of strategic cultural alignment and transformation momentum.

There is no single suitable off-the-shelf hybrid transformational change model; it benefits from a combination of elements from existing change models. It needs simplicity (Lewin 1947 3-Step Model), alignment with multiple organisational elements (Waterman, Peters, and Phillips 1980 McKinsey's 7-S Framework), an effective diagnostic of the organisational misalignment (Nadler and Tushman 1980 Congruence Model), continuous improvement (Imai 1986

Table 9.1 Overview of Change Models

Type	*Model*	*Source*	*Application*
PROGRAMMATIC (structured, planned, top-down, with clear stages or frameworks)	3-Step Model (Unfreeze–Change–Refreeze)	Lewin (1947)	For simple, clearly defined changes in stable environments.
	8-Step Change Model	Kotter (1996)	For large organisations needing a strong leadership and structured rollout of change.
	McKinsey's 7-S Framework	Waterman et al. (1980)	For aligning multiple organisational elements during strategic realignment.
	ADKAR Model	Hiatt (2006)	For awareness and reinforcement in individual-level change management.
	Transition Model	Bridges (1991)	For managing emotional/psychological transition in an HR-led initiative.
	Congruence Model	Nadler and Tushman 1980	For diagnosing organisational misalignment (useful before restructuring).
	Kaizen (Continuous Improvement)	Imai (1986)	For ongoing operational improvement and quality management.

(Continued)

Table 9.1 (Continued) Overview of Change Models

Type	*Model*	*Source*	*Application*
HYBRID (structured frameworks but flexible/adaptive in execution – combines top-down direction and bottom-up involvement)	Total Quality Management (TQM)	Oakland (1989)	For continuous improvement with both leadership commitment and employee participation.
	Lean Management / Lean Six Sigma	Womack et al. (1990)	For improving efficiency and reducing waste through both structured and local team initiative.
	Balanced Scorecard	Kaplan and Norton (1996)	For strategic management and performance alignment using top-down metrics with bottom-up implementation.
	Accelerate!	Kotter (2014)	For a dual system combining hierarchy and agility to speed up change.
	Agile Change Management	Beck (1999)	For change in dynamic/fast-moving environments using structured sprints but adaptive execution.

(*Continued*)

Table 9.1 (Continued) Overview of Change Models

Type	*Model*	*Source*	*Application*
EMERGENT (organic, adaptive, decentralised change evolves through experimentation, learning, and adaptation)	Complex Adaptive Systems (CAS)	Holland (1975)	For complex, uncertain environments where change evolves through networked, adaptive interactions.
	Learning Organisation	Senge (2014)	For cultivating continuous learning and innovation across an organisation.
	Appreciative Inquiry	Cooperrider and Srivastva (1987)	For emergent culture transformation that focuses on strengths rather than problems.
	Emergent Change Theory	Weick and Quinn (1999)	For organisations to incrementally adapt to external shifts.
	Open Space (OST)	Owen (1997)	For complex stakeholder environments using self-organisation and dialogue.
	Dialogic OD (Organisation Development)	Bushe and Marshak (2015)	For culture and mindset change via conversation, co-creation, and collective sensemaking.

Kaizen approach), modular structures (Beck 1999 Agile approach), and minimum disruption (Kotter 2014 8-step Accelerate! model). It is a complex adaptive system (Holland's 1975 Complex Adaptive Systems Approach) that needs to respond to external shifts (Weick and Quinn 1999 Emergent Change Theory). In short, this unique challenge of transforming an organisation from a rigid to an adaptive culture will require blending existing organisational change models. This reinforces the adaptive nature of this approach, as discussed earlier (McGreevy 2008).

Transformational Change Components Using the 3D Consulting Model

A simple model was introduced in Chapter 1 (see Figure 1.7): the classic 3D consulting model—diagnose, design, and delivery—which provides the organising framework for this book. The 3D consulting model can be used here to reflect on the transformational change approach. Similar to Lewin's 3-step model, it is a simple framework, yet these elements are not steps, but cycles within a complex adaptive system (Waterman, Peters, and Phillips 1980). The 3D consulting model is particularly useful for hybrid transformational change, where programmatic and emergent approaches run in parallel. Let's reflect on transformational change using this model as an organising framework.

Diagnose

Undergoing an organisational diagnostic is a vitally important first phase in a cultural transformation when you are looking to transform from a rigid to an adaptive organisation. A practical diagnostic framework here is Nadler and Tushman's Congruence Model (1980) that takes a systems view and examines the environment, resources, history, and strategy. This model, which examines the organisational operating environment and ecosystem, is excellent for exploring the organisational workflow, people, structure, and culture. The STEP-WIDE tool presented in Chapter 2 is a helpful supplement.

As we explored in Chapter 3, it is essential to assess the organisational culture at the start of a cultural transformation. Assessing how structure, governance, and workflow fit together, alongside evaluating people's mindsets and capacities to transform, is a critical first step in the pre-design phase. Former CEO of GE, Jeffrey R. Immelt (2017) calls this the "soak" period, in which you "have to go through a period of rewiring your brain – getting yourself to the point of profoundly believing that the world is changing and that the survival of your company depends on either anticipating the change or being in the

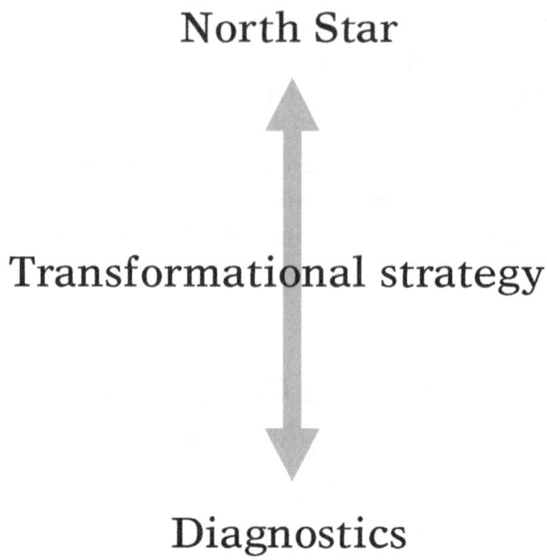

Figure 9.8 Current reality versus envisioning a desired state.

vanguard of those reacting to it". This provides an early indication of the change effort required and the digital and people strategies needed to make the system and culture transformation a success.

These healthy reflections need to be channelled into a strategic focus. A valuable tool for achieving this is the "Creative Tension Model" by Robert Fritz (1986), which contrasts current reality to the desired outcome. Introduced in Chapter 7, it can be recycled here when thinking about transformational change. Figure 9.8 reintroduces the model using 'diagnostics' to determine the current reality and a 'North Star' to envision the desired future state. The pathway from current reality to future state represents the transformational strategy.

The starting point is the vision, or, as Jacqueline Brassey and her colleagues (2024) call it, the North Star. This is a continuation of the diagnostic phase relating to where you are and where you need to be. The stretch in between (or "creative tension") is what needs to be done to accomplish the vision. Different organisations arrive at different solutions and processes based on their unique challenges and long-term vision. Disney wanted to get into the computer animation space to gain a more creative edge; its transformational strategy was to merge with Pixar. Toyota wanted to improve its manufacturing process; its transformational strategy was to embrace lean manufacturing principles. Amazon wanted to strengthen its customer focus; its transformational strategy was a digital solution. Daimler wanted to become a collaborative culture; its transformation strategy was to set a clear target and restructure using swarm-organisation principles (Kelly 2022)

During the diagnostic phase, design choices will need to be made. Clayton M. Christensen advises that "companies must not throw out the capabilities, organizational structures, and decision-making processes that have made them successful in their mainstream markets just because they don't work in the face of disruptive technological change" (Christensen 1997, 207). A major part of the diagnostic phase is establishing a measurement tool to track progress. Lyuba Spagnoletto and coauthors (2019) recommend using standard methodologies, whereas Herbert Nold and Lukas Michel (2021) propose a more holistic approach.

At this stage, organisations need to select their change model. It has been recommended that an off-the-shelf model is unlikely to succeed, and that organisations may need to adapt existing models. It has also been asserted throughout the book that transforming cultures and increasing adaptability in the workplace will not succeed if implemented in a top-down manner; it requires structured emergence at the organisational design level and system leadership. This points to a phased hybrid approach.

Design

Another essential component of transformational change is the organisational design cycle. Chapters 4–6 explored how embedding adaptability into the organisational design supports the transformation towards becoming an adaptive organisation. If the organisation has adaptive structures, governance, and workflows, this creates inherent cultural adaptability that promotes change and supports new cultural norms. The McKinsey 7-S Framework, devised by Waterman, Peters, and Phillips (1980), is a useful programmatic model for transformational change because it supports adaptive change through systems thinking by aligning key organisational elements (such as strategy, structure, and systems) during strategic realignment. It is important to engage with business functions and system architects to create a more adaptive business process across the three cultural pillars. ADKAR by Jeffrey Hiatt (2006) is a useful tool that breaks the change process down, enabling designers to address potential resistance at the design stage.

Below is a brief dive into the three organisational design pillars.

Design an Adaptive Structure

Organisational structures that are cross-functional, support ecosystems, and promote the flow of business intelligence and knowledge sharing are critical. They also facilitate organisational connection and collective decision-making through system leadership, making them essential pillars according to Zjeven Tejano (2024).

Design an Adaptive Governance

Adaptive governance is at the heart of a responsive organisation. It has both internal and external components. Organisations need to design an internal governance strategy that shifts from ego (status-driven) to eco (system-driven) by cultivating system leadership. System leaders are key mobilisers for supporting transformational change and building a self-organising culture. Organisations also need to design an external governance strategy that enables ecosystems and transforms the organisation from reactive to responsive — one that embraces a STEP-WIDE approach and is openly proactive and engaged in local communities and ecosystems. Before commencing a change transformation, it is important to ensure that senior leadership and board members are fully aware of the governance implications of an adaptive organisation (a shift from status to system leadership) and appreciate the intended and unintended consequences of being a self-organising system.

Design an Adaptive Workflow

The third pillar, designing an adaptive workflow, involves improving the flow of business intelligence across the organisation to enable adaptability. It must be strategically aligned with structure and governance. In an adaptive workflow, work is carried out in new ways and through different channels. It is essential to keep the workforce informed about emerging ideas and developments. This not only helps mitigate resistance to change but also supports adaptive workforce planning.

Delivery

A final component of transformational change is delivery. Kotter's Accelerate! model (2014) is a strong example of a hybrid-phased approach that balances business-as-usual with transformational activity. Its modular structure works well because it allows organisations to begin building adaptability locally before scaling up to an organisational-wide level.

Effective delivery in hybrid transformational change relies on strategic leverage. This includes mobilising people and technology to support the roll-out of transformational change and sustain momentum. Reeves, Morieux, and Deimler (2010) highlight the role of strategic alignment in achieving adaptive advantage, underlining the need for a coherent digital and people strategy.

The digital strategy aims to use emerging technologies to create a connected organisation where employees, customers, and stakeholders can collaborate seamlessly. In terms of people strategy, Maor, Reich, and Yocarini (2017) emphasise that people themselves are critical mobilisers of transformational change. A strong people strategy develops the systems and skills needed to build a flexible workforce capable of supporting adaptive change. It also promotes system leadership, a key mobilising force that enhances system awareness and strengthens collective accountability across the organisation.

Reflections

Here are several key insights from this chapter on transformational change that should be considered.

- Don't skip the diagnostic phase. Many change models, such as John Kotter's 8-Step Process for Leading Change (1996), move directly to implementation. In a phased change approach, particularly when transitioning from a closed to an open system, the diagnosis and design phases are essential.
- A transformational change roadmap for phased change is necessary, as it helps keep the transformation on track and serves as an effective communication tool. Storgaard, Schmitt, and Gisslen (2025), you recall, assert that "A transformation roadmap is critical to bring the transformation vision and ambition to life".
- Align with HR and get them on board early in the process. HR knows the organisational pulse, has access to people and business data, and the diagnostic skills to interpret the data and measure progress. They are strategic planners and natural communicators. In recent times, HR has expanded beyond being a mere support function and should be seen as a core system actor that enables the organisation to evolve.
- Manage resistence. McKinsey research indicates that 70 per cent of transformational change initiatives fail because of entrenched mindsets (Ewenstein, Smith, and Sologar 2015). Managing resistance should never be an afterthought; it should be embedded in the design from the outset, across the diagnosis, design, and delivery phases, and supported by meaningful stakeholder involvement at every stage. While many theories address resistance and sabotage, the most effective way to mitigate resistance is to integrate community and stakeholder engagement throughout the transformational change process.
- Don't leave the people strategy component to the end. Organisations should undergo a comprehensive review of human and machine resources and create human employee profiles early in the process so they can begin cultural-fit recruitment and retention and devise a system-and-skills people strategy that reinforces the transformational journey.

- Don't let people discover the changes; *communicate* them. The workplace will begin to look and feel different to stakeholders, board members, employees, contingent workers, partners, and customers. Rather than leaving people to navigate this new culture on their own, actively involve them and clearly explain the changes.

Transformational Change and Leadership

A strong tradition in transformational change holds that only organisational leaders can drive change. This perspective is enthusiastically promoted by John Kotter in *Leading Change* (1996), who believes that leadership is essential to drive transformation, and by Edgar Schein in *Organisational Culture and Leadership* (1985), who views leaders as primary drivers of change. Bernard Bass and Bruce Avolio (1994) present transformational leadership as a catalyst for motivating others. Ronald A. Heifetz and Donald L. Laurie (1997) make the case for change leadership while emphasising the need for adaptive leadership. Another popular stance, from Dave Ulrich, Michael Ulrich, and Wayne Brockbank (2008), is that HR leaders should act as system architects and drivers of change.

As demonstrated in the fictionalised *Company Hex* case study, successful transformational change depends on the endorsement of senior leaders, the board, and HR. That said, the leadership model in *Building Adaptive Organisations* is not formal, status-driven leadership; rather, it is collective leadership, or more specifically, systems leadership. For a company to shift from a closed to an open and adaptive organisation, this book maintains that systems and culture—not status leaders, power-hungry board members, or specialist HR leaders—drive enduring change.

Formal leaders must recognise that their organisation's future depends on becoming more adaptive, and that this can only be achieved through system and cultural change, not via top-down leadership mandates. Practically, this means that formal leaders need to authorise the change transformation and may initially participate in a seed cell that helps shape its direction. However, at some point, they must step back and allow the complex adaptive system to self-organise and self-govern. In this model, everyone assumes shared system leadership, while formal leaders take on more mentoring and ambassadorial roles.

Synthesis: Transformational Change from a Rigid to an Adaptive Organisation

This final chapter presented a transformational change approach designed to help organisations become more open and adaptive. A Boeing case study illustrated how failures in transformational change can have severe consequences. Bringing together themes woven throughout the book, the chapter presented a successful example of transformational change through a fictionalised case study. It compared three change models—programmatic, hybrid, and emergent—arguing that building an adaptive organisation through system and culture change is best supported by a hybrid approach. Altering the business architecture and mobilising both technology and people strategies demands both structure and synergy, which a hybrid approach delivers.

The chapter distilled key concepts of transformational change using the 3D Consulting Model (diagnose, design, deliver). It concluded with some guiding principles and reflections on the role of leadership in driving transformational change.

Coda: Building an Adaptive Organisation

This final chapter on transformational change concludes a book that has explored change throughout. Chapter 1 introduced the five system levers of transforming and building an organisation from a closed company to an open ecosystem. These five system levers are as follows:

Culture

In Chapter 3 we saw how an organisation can transform through cultural normalisation. A culture of adaptability enables transformational change through infusion and exposure to the new adaptive culture. Former GE CEO Jeffrey R. Immelt comments that "You can't have a transformation without revamping the culture and the established ways of doing things" (Immelt 2017). Organisations need to analyse their current culture and create an adaptive North Star.

Design

Chapters 4–6 showed how organisational design or business architecture at the structure, governance, and workflow levels amplifies transformational change by rewiring the organisation from a closed to an open system. Organisations need to reimagine their conditioning structures, governance, and workflows to support self-organising, emergent ecosystems.

Technology

Chapter 7 explored how a digital transformation strategy supports transformational change. Exponential technologies (notably AI, robotics, blockchain, and quantum computing) are key enablers of an open adaptive system. Organisations need to align architectural redesign with their digital transformation strategy to continuously enhance the flow of business intelligence across the enterprise.

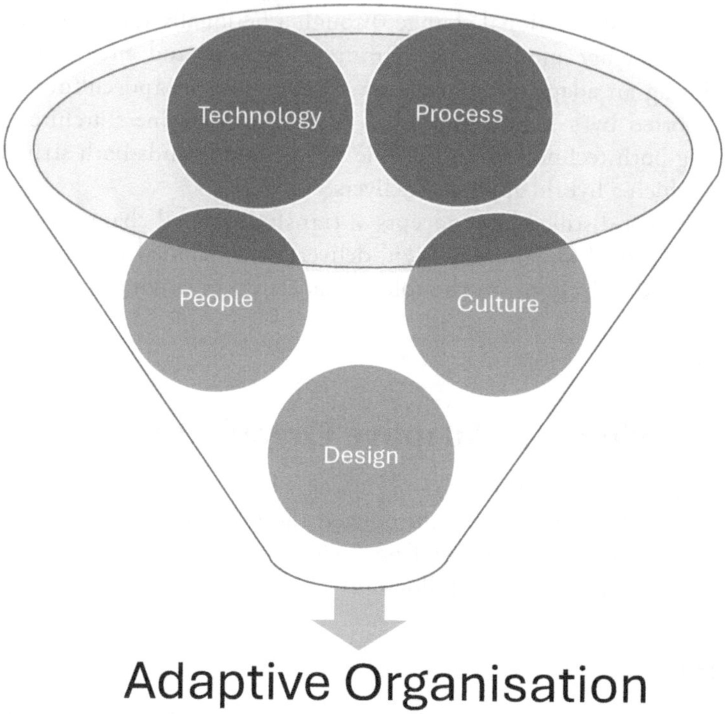

Figure 9.9 The five system levers that drive adaptive organisations in a funnel format.

People

Chapter 8 examined how a people strategy can help mobilise transformational change, recognising that people drive change and are a defining factor in its success. Individuals at every level of the organisation need to be part of the transformational journey. A strategy to mitigate resistance should be embedded in every phase.

Process

This chapter has been exploring the transformational change process. An effective hybrid model, supported by a diagnose-design-deliver approach, enables the smooth implementation of transformational change. Organisations should not rely on off-the-shelf models; instead they should embrace adaptive change and customise a model that works for the enterprise.

Figure 9.9 shows how these five interconnected system levers converge to build the adaptive organisation.

Together, these five system levers form the foundation for building adaptive organisations.

Notes

1. The problem was linked to the Manoeuvring Characteristics Augmentation System (MCAS), the flight control software installed on the Boeing 737 MAX aircraft that controlled the aircraft's nose.
2. It took a Boeing whistleblower, John Barnett, to expose the truth behind the safety concerns at Boeing.
3. This perspective is consistently argued by such commentators as Strebel (1996), Beer and Nohria (2000) and Cameron and Quinn (2011).
4. Good resources include Kazmi and Naarananoja (2014); Cameron and Green (2010); Kotter and Schlesinger (2008).

Bibliography

Bass, Bernard M., and Bruce J. Avolio. 1994. *Improving Organizational Effectiveness Through Transformational Leadership*. Sage.

Beck, Kent. 1999. *Extreme Programming Explained: Embrace Change*. Addison-Wesley.

Beer, Michael, and Nitin Nohria, eds. 2000. *Breaking the Code of Change*. 1st edition. Harvard Business School Press.

Brassey, Jacqueline, Aaron De Smet, Dana Maor, and Sheida Rabipour. 2024. 'Developing a Resilient, Adaptable Workforce for an Uncertain Future'. *McKinsey Quarterly*, December 6. https://www.mckinsey.com/capabilities/people-and-organizational-performance/our-insights/developing-a-resilient-adaptable-workforce-for-an-uncertain-future.

Bridges, William. 1991. *Managing Transitions: Making the Most of Change*. 1st edition. Addison-Wesley.

Burke, W. Warner, and George H. Litwin. 1992. 'A Causal Model of Organizational Performance and Change'. *Journal of Management* 18 (3): 523–45. https://doi.org/10.1177/014920639201800306.

Bushe, Gervase R., and Robert J. Marshak. 2015. *Dialogic Organization Development: The Theory and Practice of Transformational Change*. Berrett-Koehler Publishers.

Cameron, Esther, and Mike Green. 2010. *Making Sense of Change Management: A Complete Guide to the Models, Tools & Techniques of Organizational Change*. 2nd edition, Repr. Kogan Page.

Cameron, Kim S., and Robert E. Quinn. 2011. *Diagnosing and Changing Organizational Culture: Based on the Competing Values Framework*. 3rd edition. The Jossey-Bass Business & Management Series. Jossey-Bass.

Christensen, Clayton M. 1997. *The Innovator's Dilemma : When New Technologies Cause Great Firms to Fail*. With Internet Archive. Harvard Business School Press. http://archive.org/details/innovatorsdilem000chri.

Cooperrider, David L., and Suresh Srivastva. 1987. 'Appreciative Inquiry into Organizational Life'. In *Research in Organizational Change and Development*, edited by William A. Pasmore and Richard W. Woodman. JAI Press.

Cruise, David. 2017. 'What Is Business Transformation? | Definition'. Company Website. *Change Associates*, July 10. https://changeassociates.com/what-is-business-transformation/.

Ewenstein, Boris, Wesley Smith, and Ashvin Sologar. 2015. 'Changing Change Management'. *McKinsey & Company Featured Insights – Leadership*, July 1. https://www.mckinsey.com/featured-insights/leadership/changing-change-management.
Fritz, Robert. 1986. *The Path of Least Resistance: Designing Your Life for Success*. Ballantine Books.
Gasparini, Pedro Paulo Rigoni, Keitiane Barros Vieira, and Murillo de Oliveira Dias. 2025. 'Disney's Pixar Animation Studios Acquisition Case: Revitalization or Trouble?' *GPH-International Journal of Social Science & Humanities Research* 8 (4): 46–57. https://doi.org/10.5281/zenodo.15365962.
Gesar, Aram. 2024. *Boeing's Shift from Engineering Excellence to Profit-Driven Culture: Tracing the Impact of the Mcdonnell Douglas Merger on the 737 Max Crisis*. Air Guide. January 13. https://airguide.info/boeings-shift-from-engineering-excellence-to-profit-driven-culture-tracing-the-impact-of-the-mcdonnell-douglas-merger-on-the-737-max-crisis/.
Gray, David. 2012. *The Connected Company*. With Thomas Vander Wal. O'Reilly.
Heifetz, Ronald A., and Donald L. Laurie. 1997. 'The Work of Leadership'. *Harvard Business Review* 75 (1): 124–34.
Hiatt, Jeffrey M. 2006. *ADKAR: A Model for Change in Business, Goverment and Our Community*. 1st edition. Prosci Learning Center Publications.
Holland, John H. 1975. *Adaptation in Natural and Artificial Systems*. Reissued by MIT Press, 1992. University of Michigan Press.
Husband, Jon. 2013. 'What Is Wirearchy ?' Wirearchy, February 16. https://wirearchy.com/what-is-wirearchy/.
Imai, Masaaki. 1986. *Kaizen (Ky'zen): The Key to Japan's Competitive Success*. 1st ed., Print. McGraw-Hill.
Immelt, Jeffrey R. 2017. 'How I Remade GE'. *Harvard Business Magazine*. https://hbr.org/2017/09/how-i-remade-ge.
Irving, Clive. 2021. 'How Boeing Was Set on the Path to Disaster by the Cult of Jack Welch'. *Daily Beast*, November 29. https://www.thedailybeast.com/how-boeing-was-set-on-the-path-to-disaster-by-the-cult-of-jack-welch.
Johansson, Frans. 2004. *The Medici Effect: Breakthrough Insights at the Intersection of Ideas, Concepts, and Cultures*. Harvard Business School Press.
Kaplan, Robert S., and David P. Norton. 1996. *The Balanced Scorecard: Translating Strategy into Action*. Harvard Business School Press.
Kazmi, Syeda Asiya Zenab, and Marja Naaranoja. 2014. 'Collection of Change Management Models – An Opportunity to Make the Best Choice from the Various Organizational Transformational Techniques'. *GSTF Journal on Business Review (GBR)* 3 (3): 1. https://doi.org/10.7603/s40706-014-0023-9.
Kelly, Richard. 2022. *The Nature of Business Transformation: A Swarm Intelligent Approach to Reinventing Organisations*. Routledge.
Klososky, Annette. 2024. 'Forget Change Management: Building An Adaptive Culture That Inspires'. Forbes, May 13. https://www.forbes.com/councils/forbestechcouncil/2024/05/13/forget-change-management-building-an-adaptive-culture-that-inspires/.
Kotter, John P. 1996. *Leading Change*. Harvard Business School Press.
Kotter, John P. 2014. *Accelerate: Building Strategic Agility for a Faster Moving World*. Harvard Business Review Press.

Kotter, John P., and Leonard A. Schlesinger. 2008. 'Choosing Strategies for Change'. Harvard Business Review, August. https://hbr.org/2008/07/choosing-strategies-for-change.

Lewin, Kurt. 1947. 'Frontiers in Group Dynamics: Concept, Method and Reality in Social Science; Social Equilibria and Social Change'. *Human Relations* 1 (1): 5–41. https://doi.org/10.1177/001872674700100103.

Maor, Dana, Angelika Reich, and Lara Yocarini. 2017. *The People Power of Transformations*. McKinsey & Company. https://www.mckinsey.com/~/media/mckinsey/business%20functions/people%20and%20organizational%20performance/our%20insights/the%20people%20power%20of%20transformations/the-people-power-of-transformations.pdf.

McGreevy, Malcolm. 2008. 'Adaptive Change in an Evolving World of Work'. *Industrial and Commercial Training* 40 (7): 355–63. https://doi.org/10.1108/00197850810912225.

Nadler, David A., and Michael L. Tushman. 1980. 'A Model for Diagnosing Organizational Behavior'. *Organizational Dynamics* 9 (2): 35–51. https://doi.org/10.1016/0090-2616(80)90039-X.

Nold, Herbert, and Lukas Michel. 2021. 'Organizational Culture: A Systems Approach'. In *Accounting and Finance Innovations*, edited by Nizar Alsharari. IntechOpen. https://doi.org/10.5772/intechopen.97466.

Oakland, John S. 1989. *Total Quality Management*. Butterworth-Heinemann.

Owen, Harrison. 1997. *Open Space Technology: A User's Guide*. Berrett-Koehler Publishers.

Paradis, Afshar, Elizabeth Wolfe, Gregory Wallace, and Pete Muntean. 2024. 'New Details Emerge on Piece of Alaska Airlines Plane That Blew Off Midflight as Investigators Probe "Explosive Decompression"'. CNN, January 8. https://www.cnn.com/2024/01/08/us/alaska-airlines-plug-door-found-investigation-monday/index.html.

Reeves, Martin, Yves Morieux, and Michael Deimler. 2010. 'People Advantage'. BCG Global, March 25. https://www.bcg.com/publications/2010/strategy-behavior-culture-people-advantage.

Robison, Peter. 2021. *Flying Blind: The 737 Max Tragedy and the Fall of Boeing*. Doubleday.

Schein, Edgar H. 1985. *Organizational Culture and Leadership*. Jossey-Bass.

Senge, Peter M. 2014. *The Fifth Discipline Fieldbook: Strategies and Tools for Building a Learning Organization*. With Art Kleiner, Charlotte Roberts, Richard B. Ross, and Bryan J. Smith. Crown/Archetype.

Spagnoletto, Lyuba, Dianah AlabdulJabbar, Harsha Jalihal, Queenie Chan, and Ravin Jesuthasan. 2019. HR4.0: Shaping People Strategies in the Fourth Industrial Revolution.White Paper No. 10122019. World Economic Forum in collaboration with Saudi Aramco,Unilever, and Willis Towers Watson.https://www3.weforum.org/docs/WEF_NES_Whitepaper_HR4.0.pdf.

Strebel, Paul. 1996. 'Why Do Employees Resist Change?' Organisational Behavior. Harvard Business Review, May 1. https://www.hbsp.harvard.edu/product/96310-PDF-ENG.

Strebel, Paul. 1996. 'Why Do Employees Resist Change?' Organisational Behavior. Harvard Business Review, May 1. https://www.hbsp.harvard.edu/product/96310-PDF-ENG.

Storgaard, Aunsholt Maria, Maya Kousholt Schmitt, and Annie Gisslen. 2025. Configuring the Transformation Roadmap Using the Capability Model. Deloitte. https://www.deloitte.com/dk/en/services/consulting/perspectives/configuring-the-transformation-roadmap-using-the-capability-model.html.

Tejano, Zjeven. 2024. 'Adapting to Change: Exploring Organizational Structures and Their Impact on Transformation'. *SSRN Electronic Journal*, ahead of print. https://doi.org/10.2139/ssrn.4652219.

Ulrich, Dave, Michael Ulrich, and Wayne Brockbank. 2008. *HR Transformation: Building Human Resources from the Outside In*. McGraw-Hill.

Waddock, Sandra, and Steve Waddell. 2021. 'Five Core Dimensions of Purposeful System Transformation'. *Journal of Management for Global Sustainability* 9 (2): 45–62. https://doi.org/10.13185/2244-6893.1141.

Walker, Mark. 2024. 'FAA Audit of Boeing's 737 Max Production Found Dozens of Issues'. *The New York Times* (Manhatten, NYC), March 11. https://www.nytimes.com/2024/03/11/us/politics/faa-audit-boeing-737-max.html?searchResultPosition=1.

Waterman, Robert H., Thomas J. Peters, and Julien R. Phillips. 1980. 'Structure Is Not Organization'. *Business Horizons* 23 (3): 14–26. https://doi.org/10.1016/0007-6813(80)90027-0.

Watkins, Michael D. 2015. *To Implement Change You Must Rewire Your Organization*. IMD. https://www.imd.org/research-knowledge/organizational-design/articles/to-implement-change-you-must-rewire-your-organization/.

Weick, Karl E., and Robert E. Quinn. 1999. 'Organizational Change and Development'. *Annual Review of Psychology* 50 (1): 361–86. https://doi.org/10.1146/annurev.psych.50.1.361.

Whalen, Thomas Brian. 2014. 'Utilizing The Social Transaction Theory Of Social Ontology To Understand Organizational Culture Change'. *Journal of Business & Economics Research* 12 (1): 6. https://www.researchgate.net/publication/315559769_Utilizing_The_Social_Transaction_Theory_Of_Social_Ontology_To_Understand_Organizational_Culture_Change.

Womack, James P., Daniel T. Jones, and Daniel Roos. 1990. *The Machine That Changed the World: Based on the Massachusetts Institute of Technology 5-Million Dollar 5-Year Study on the Future of the Automobile*. Rawson Associates Maxwell Macmillan international Collier Macmillan Canada.

Afterword

As I write this afterword in 2026, I am mindful that you may be reading it several years from now. From your future vantage point, some of what I describe in the book may already have unfolded; what is, for me today, emerging scenarios, may be your lived reality.

Three recurring questions dominate the business press in 2026: Will working models return to pre-pandemic norms? Is AI a bubble about to burst? And what, ultimately, will become of human work? Naturally, in a book about systems, these questions are deeply interconnected and closely tied to the book's underlying assumptions and scenarios:

- The pandemic does not just disrupt work; it permanently expands our imagination of what it can be, shifting the future workplace from a physical space to a virtual hub.
- The current protectionist and multipolar climate eases, and economies return to connected ecosystems that ecosystems that partner to solve global challenges.
- Human-machine collaboration intensifies, boosting productivity and reshaping organisational governance, with AI remaining a transformative force despite uncertainty about its future form.

Even if a small part of these assumptions and scenarios holds true, the workplace of the future will be profoundly disrupted. In the face of such extraordinary uncertainty, one conclusion feels increasingly clear: adaptability is our most sensible strategy at both individual and organisational levels.

Yet there seems to be a troubling complacency among political and business leaders regarding these shifts. Research suggests a surprising number of CEOs seem nostalgic for the pre-pandemic order and are not thinking outside the pyramid. Politicians with rigid mindsets seem intent on restoring borders and control, viewing ecosystems as a threat. Meanwhile, only moral philosophers appear to be seriously contemplating a machine-intelligent future that challenges our deepest assumptions about human value and contribution.

This book has presented the case for an adaptive organisation, along with a systems and culture blueprint to build it. What is now needed, however, is for business and political leaders to shift their closed mindsets, embrace adaptive thinking, and act.

Index

For Product Safety Concerns and Information please contact our EU representative GPSR@taylorandfrancis.com Taylor & Francis Verlag GmbH, Kaufingerstraße 24, 80331 München, Germany